Deviant Logic

Some philosophical issues

Deviant Logic

Some philosophical issues

Susan Haack

Lecturer in Philosophy, University of Warwick

Cambridge University Press

Published by the Syndics of the Cambridge University Press
Bentley House, 200 Euston Road, London NW1 2DB
American Branch: 32 East 57th Street, New York, N.Y. 10022

© Cambridge University Press 1974

Library of Congress Catalogue Card Number : 74–76949

ISBN 0 521 20500 X

First published 1974

Printed in Great Britain
by Cox & Wyman Ltd
London, Fakenham and Reading

for
J O S
S P S

If sheer logic is not conclusive, what is?
(Quine [1970], p. 81)

Contents

Preface   xi
Acknowledgements   xiii
Note on notation   xiv

Part One

Chapter 1. 'Alternative' in 'Alternative Logic'   *page* 1
 1. Rival versus supplementary logics   1
 2. Deviant versus extended logics   4
 3. The argument against genuine rivalry   8
    (i) The argument from the theory-dependence of the meanings   11
        of connectives
    (ii) The argument from translation   14
 4. Varieties of Deviance   21

Chapter 2. Reasons for Deviance   25
 1. The problem: could there be good reason for a change of logic?   25
 2. A radical view of the status of logical laws   25
 3. Two absolutist views   26
    (i) Logic as a completed science: Kant   26
    (ii) The alleged self-evidence of logical laws: Frege   29
 4. In favour of the pragmatist view   30
 5. Objections to the pragmatist conception of logic   35
    Objection (i): this view is incoherent   35
    Objection (ii): this view is methodologically vicious   37
 6. A weakness in the pragmatist conception   39
 7. Reasons offered in favour of Deviant systems   40
 8. Global or local reform?   42

Chapter 3. Deviance and the theory of truth   47
 1. The third truth-value, and some alternatives   47
    (i) The no-item thesis   48
    (ii) The misleading-form thesis   53

(iii) and (iv) Truth-value gaps and new truth-values: (*a*) What kind of system is appropriate to the truth-value gap thesis? (*b*) Does the use of a many-valued system commit one to the new truth-value(s) thesis?   55

2. Consequences for the theory of truth   64
   (i) The principle of bivalence   65
   (ii) The law of excluded middle   66
   (iii) The (*T*) schema   68

Part Two

Chapter 4. Future contingents   73
   1. Aristotle's argument: exposition   74
      Comments   77
   2. The issue about truth-bearers   82
   3. An inadequacy in Aristotle's 'solution'?   83
   4. The inadequacy of Łukasiewicz's 'solution'   84
      An alternative proposal   85
   5. Modal interpretations of Łukasiewicz's system   87
   6. Conclusions   90

Chapter 5. Intuitionism   91
   1. The Intuitionist view of mathematics and logic   91
   2. The Intuitionist critique of classical logic   93
   3. Intuitionist logic: rival or supplement?   95
   4. Assessment of the Intuitionist criticism   97
   5. An 'Intuitionist' theory of meaning   103
   6. Conclusions   108

Chapter 6. Vagueness   109
   1. Location of the problem   109
   2. The consequences of vagueness: arguments for the failure of classical logic   112
   3. Are the arguments against classical logic sound?   115
   4. Are vague sentences within the scope of logic?   116
   5. Can vagueness be eliminated?   118
   6. Conclusions   124

Chapter 7. Singular terms and existence   126
   1. The problem   126
   2. Some possible reactions   126
      (i) It could be admitted that classical logic embodies some existential assumptions, but denied, nevertheless, that any modification is called for   127

Contents ix

(ii) Accommodation of non-denoting terms could be achieved by changes in the manner of translation into logical formalism   131

(iii) Modification of deductive apparatus could be allowed, but confined to the predicate calculus level   135

(iv) The most radical reaction requires modification at the propositional calculus level   137

3. Some comments on these alternatives   141

4. A rather conservative proposal   142

5. Conclusions   147

Chapter 8. Quantum mechanics   148

1. The problem   148

2. The arguments for a change of logic   149
   Reichenbach's argument   149

3. Objections to Reichenbach's argument   153

   (i) It is methodologically improper to modify logic in response to physical difficulties   153

   (ii) Modification of logic to avoid difficulties in quantum theory involves too great a sacrifice of simplicity   155

   (iii) Reichenbach is wrong to think causal anomalies are derivable in quantum mechanics   157

   (iv) Reichenbach's logic does not avoid the causal anomalies   159

4. Will a different change of logic avoid the anomalies?   161

5. Objection (v): quantum logics are not really 'logics'   164

6. Conclusions   167

Appendix   168

Bibliography   178

Index   187

Preface

Since the work of Peirce [1902], MacColl (e.g. [1906]), and Vasiliev (e.g. [1910], [1911]), and particularly since the pioneering papers of Łukasiewicz [1920] and Post [1921], a considerable range of non-standard systems of logic has been devised. The formal properties of these systems have been fairly extensively studied.

However, although there have long been critics of 'classical' logic (Aristotle himself raised some problems), and although there has been much discussion of the possible interpretations of non-standard logics, there has been relatively little sustained discussion of the philosophical issues raised by proposals for a change of logic. What discussion there has been (e.g. in Zinoviev [1963], and Rescher [1969]), has suffered from too exclusive preoccupation with many-valued logics. The philosophical issues raised by many-valued logics, and those raised by intuitionist logic, minimal logic, 'quantum' logic, etc., are, I shall argue, comparable, and should be investigated together. It is the purpose of this essay to try to get some of these issues clearer.

I shall address myself, in particular, to the questions:

1. Is it possible for there to be systems which are genuinely rivals of classical logic? What, indeed, might it mean to say that one system rivals another?
2. If there could be systems rivalling classical logic, is it possible that there should be reason to prefer such a rival system? And what kind of reason would be a good one?
3. What would be the consequences for the theory of truth, and of truth bearers, of the adoption of a non-standard system?

These will be the concern of Part One.

When I turn, in Part Two, to close study of a number of disputes in which change of logic has been proposed, I shall try to show how these same general issues recur, despite the variety of subject matter, and how the conclusions of Part One may be applied.

I shall, inevitably, raise as many questions as I shall answer. My answers to these questions will, no doubt, be in various ways unsatisfactory, but I hope, at least, to convince the reader that these are interesting and important questions. It should become increasingly apparent that the issues raised by the possibility of 'alternative' logics are absolutely central to the philosophy of logic. This is not just because a whole range of issues in the philosophy of logic (the meaning of the connectives, the nature of truth bearers, the definition of truth, etc.) will be raised in the course of the discussion; but also, and more fundamentally, because one cannot hope to understand what an 'alternative' logic might be, or what kind of reason one might have for adopting one, without getting clear some basic questions about the nature and status of logic.

Rosser and Turquette suggested ([1952], p. 2) that discussion of the motivation and interpretation of non-standard systems was premature; it should have waited upon comprehensive examination of the formal characteristics of these systems. But, as I shall argue, it is still unclear, for instance, what formal distinction there might be between non-standard systems which are rivals, and those which are merely supplements, of classical logic; or between systems embodying the assumption that there are truth-value gaps, and systems embodying the assumption that there are intermediate truth-values. And so, in advance of some philosophical work, it is sometimes uncertain what formal investigations are likely to be fruitful. This is why – although I do not deny the interest of formal work in non-standard logic, on which indeed I shall frequently have occasion to draw – I think that serious examination of the philosophical, rather than the purely formal, consequences of adoption of non-standard systems, is now overdue.

Acknowledgements

This book is based on work supervised by Dr T. J. Smiley and Dr I. M. Hacking, leading to the degree of Ph.D. in the University of Cambridge. Thanks are due to all the friends and colleagues, in Cambridge and at Warwick, with whom I have discussed the problems raised here; especially to Robin Haack, who read the whole of the manuscript as well as providing moral support.

Note on Notation

'Russellian' notation is used throughout, even in discussion of writers, such as Łukasiewicz, who used Polish notation. I use

$A, B \ldots$	meta-variables
$p, q \ldots$	sentence letters
$\sim$	negation
v	disjunction
&	conjunction
$\supset$	material implication
$\equiv$	material equivalence
$x, y \ldots$	individual variables
$(\exists \ldots)$	existential quantifier
$(\ )$	universal quantifier
$F, G \ldots$	predicate letters
L	necessity
M	possibility
*	beside an entry in a truth table indicates that that value is designated

Distinct symbols ('⌐', '∧', '→', '↔') are sometimes used when it is important to distinguish the connectives of a Deviant system.

Formal features of the systems referred to are described, in such detail as is necessary for my purposes, in the Appendix.

PART ONE

I

'Alternative' in *'Alternative logic'*

There are many systems of logic – many-valued systems and modal systems for instance – which are non-standard; that is, which differ in one way or another from classical logic. Because of this plurality of logics, the question whether, or in what way, non-standard systems are *'alternatives'* to classical logic, naturally arises. I shall try, in this chapter, to throw some light on this question. The procedure adopted will be as follows. I begin by distinguishing (§1) a weaker and a stronger sense in which non-standard systems may be 'alternatives' to classical logic. I then investigate (§2) whether there is any formal criterion by which to judge in which category a system falls. It is found that any formal test needs to be supplemented by considerations of meaning, and that there are arguments which, if sound, would show that there can be *no* system which is an alternative to classical logic in the stronger sense. In (§3) these arguments are shown to be inadequate. And so, in (§4), I proceed to investigate some of the possible varieties of change of logic.

1. Rival versus supplementary logics

Sometimes non-standard systems have been devised and investigated out of purely formal interest. Often, however, the construction of non-standard systems is motivated by the belief that classical logic is in some way mistaken or inadequate. And when one investigates the motivation for non-standard systems more closely, one notices a difference between the kind of change of logic which a proponent of e.g. Intuitionist or many-valued logic takes himself to be advocating, and the kind of change which e.g. the modal logician advocates. To speak roughly at first: an important difference between the claims made by an Intuitionist or a many-valued logician, on the one hand,

1

and the modal logician, on the other, seems to be that the former takes
his system to be an alternative to classical logic in the strong sense that
his system should be employed *instead* of the classical, whereas the
latter takes his system to be an alternative to classical logic only in the
weaker sense that it should be employed *as well* as the classical. A
symptom of this difference – which is noticed by Ackermann ([1967],
p. 15) – is that the former tends to regard classical logic as *mistaken*,
as including assertions which are not true, whereas the latter tends to
regard classical logic as *inadequate*, as not including assertions which
are true. I shall say that the Intuitionist or many-valued logician takes
himself to be proposing a *rival*, whereas the modal logician takes
himself to be proposing a *supplement*, to classical logic. A rival system
is, then, one the use of which is incompatible, and a supplementary
system one the use of which is compatible, with the use of the standard
system.

I can now readily enough distinguish the systems which are proposed
as rivals from those proposed as supplements:

Systems proposed as rivals	*Systems proposed as supplements*
Intuitionist logic	Modal logics (e.g. T, the Lewis systems; not Łukasiewicz's 4-valued 'modal' logic)
Minimal logic	Epistemic logics
Łukasiewicz's, Bochvar's many-valued logics	Deontic logics
van Fraassen's presuppositional languages	Tense logics
Reichenbach's, Destouches-Février's, Birkhoff and von Neumann's logics for quantum mechanics	

The question, whether a system is proposed as a rival or as a supplement to classical logic, should not be confused with either of two other
kinds of question which also arise in the philosophy of non-standard
logics: questions concerning the kind of *ground* which might be
given for the choice of logic, and questions concerning the view
which should be taken of the *scope of application* of an alternative
system.

Some of those who propose systems which they take to be rivals to
classical logic think that logic may be in some absolute sense verified

or falsified; I shall call these *realists*. Others think that the choice of logic is to be made on grounds of convenience, simplicity, economy; I shall call these *pragmatists*. Brouwer, for example, is in my sense a realist; he thinks that classical logic can be shown to be mistaken. (See Brouwer [1952].) Putnam, on the other hand, is in my sense a pragmatist; he thinks that a relatively simple physics and Birkhoff and von Neumann's logic should be preferred, on grounds of simplicity and economy, to a more complex physics and the standard logic. (See Putnam [1969].) The distinction between proponents of rival, and proponents of supplementary, systems should not be confused with the distinction between realists and pragmatists. (Rescher in [1969], ch. 3, is in some danger of making this confusion.) Among proponents of allegedly rival systems there are *both* realists and pragmatists.

Again, some of those who propose systems which they take to be rivals to classical logic think that their system should replace classical logic in *all* applications; I shall call these *global* reformers. Others think that their system should replace classical logic only in *some* applications; I shall call these *local* reformers. Dummett, for instance, is a global reformer; he wants to replace classical by Intuitionist logic in all applications (see Dummett [1959]); whereas the traditional Intuitionists are local reformers; they take classical logic to fail only in mathematical reasoning. The distinction between proponents of rival, and proponents of supplementary, systems should not be confused with the distinction between global and local reformers. (Farber [1942], is in some danger of making this confusion.) Among proponents of allegedly rival systems there are *both* global and local reformers. It is, indeed, arguable that a proponent of a rival system *ought* to be a global reformer; but this is a separate issue.

It is tempting to take the claims made by proponents of non-standard logics at their face value; to assume, that is, that Intuitionist or many-valued logics really are, as their proponents say they are, rivals to classical logic, whereas modal logics really are, as their proponents say they are, supplements to classical logic; and to leave the question, in what sense non-standard logics are alternatives to classical logic, there. But this would obviously be unsatisfactory. One must, at least, raise the question, whether Intuitionist or many-valued logics really are, as is claimed, alternatives to classical logic in the strong sense that they are in conflict with it. A natural way to tackle this question is to ask whether there is any *formal* feature of these systems by which one can recognise their rivalry to classical logic?

2. Deviant versus extended logics

Systems may differ from each other *syntactically* (i.e. with respect to the set of theorems) or *semantically* (i.e. with respect to interpretation) or, of course, both. I begin by investigating the possible syntactic differences between systems.

Differences between the theorem sets of two systems L_1 and L_2 may or may not be associated with differences in vocabulary. I distinguish three relevant possibilities:

(1) the class of wffs of L_1 properly includes the class of wffs of L_2 and the class of theorems/valid inferences of L_1 properly includes the class of theorems/valid inferences of L_2, the additional theorems/ valid inferences of L_1 all containing essentially occurrences of L_1's additional[1] vocabulary.

In this case I call L_1 an extension of L_2. For the case where L_2 is classical logic, I call L_1 an *extended logic*.

Examples: Classical propositional calculus is an extension of the implicational fragment; modal logics such as *T*, or the Lewis systems, are extensions of classical propositional calculus.

(2) the class of wffs of L_1 and the class of wffs of L_2 coincide, but the class of theorems/valid inferences of L_1 differs from the class of theorems/valid inferences of L_2.

In this case I call L_1 and L_2 *deviations* of each other. For the case where L_2 is classical logic, I call L_1 a *deviant logic*.

Examples: Łukasiewicz's 3-valued logic (without the addition of the Słupecki '*t*' operator) is a deviation of classical 2-valued logic, its theorems being a proper subset of the theorems of classical logic.

(3) the class of wffs of L_1 properly includes the class of wffs of L_2, and the class of theorems/valid inferences of L_1 differs from the class of theorems/valid inferences of L_2 not only in that L_1 includes additional theorems involving essentially the additional vocabulary, but also in that the sets of theorems involving only the common vocabulary differ.

In this case I call L_1 and L_2 *quasi-deviations* of each other. For the case where L_2 is classical logic, I call L_1 a *quasi-deviant logic*.

---

[1] The question, *which* vocabulary is 'additional' is easy to answer for e.g. modal systems, but may be tricky for e.g. many-valued logics with, say, more than one 'implication'.

Example: Reichenbach's 3-valued logic is a *quasi-deviation* of classical 2-valued logic.

If L_1 is a quasi-deviation from L_2, there is a sub-system of L_1, obtained by excising from L_1 all additional vocabulary over and above that of L_2, which is a deviation from L_2. So in what follows I shall refer to both deviant and quasi-deviant systems as Deviant logics.

Now, the systems proposed as supplements to classical logic typically differ from it in the first way, and the systems proposed as rivals typically differ from it in the second or third ways. It is therefore tempting to conclude that extended logics are supplements to, and deviant and quasi-deviant logics rivals of, classical logic. This conclusion seems plausible, especially in view of the following consideration: the proponent of a deviant or quasi-deviant logic would take this system to be a rival to classical logic precisely because it lacks certain theorems which classical logic has, or, more rarely, but e.g. in the case of Post's many-valued systems, vice versa. There are, that is to say, principles to which the classical logician assents but to which the Deviant logician does not, or, rarely, vice versa, and this is why a Deviant system rivals the classical. (It may be worth observing that the rule of thumb used by Hackstaff in [1966], p. 207, to discriminate 'non-standard' systems is that if a system lacks certain 'characteristic' theorems of classical logic, it is to count as non-standard.)

One should, perhaps, distinguish two possibilities: that a Deviant system should have as a theorem the contradictory of a wff which classical logic has as a theorem; and that a Deviant system should merely lack as a theorem a wff which classical logic has as a theorem. It is the second possibility which is realised in the case of the systems under consideration. However, in accepting, say, '*p* or not *p*' as a theorem the classical logician is asserting something implicitly general (that, whatever *p* may be, '*p* or not *p*' is true) and when e.g. the Intuitionist refuses to accept '*p* or not *p*' as a theorem he does so because he thinks that in certain instances '*p* or not *p*' is not true. So although the conflict is not as sharp as it would be in the case of a logic with 'not (*p* or not *p*)' as a theorem, still, there is, apparently, conflict – something, that is, which the classical logician asserts and the Deviant logician denies.

Similarly, it seems plausible to expect extended systems to be supplements to classical logic – one would expect the proponent of an extended logic to take his system to be a supplement, precisely because it takes nothing away, but adds new vocabulary in terms of which new theorems are expressible.

Nevertheless, it would be a mistake too hastily to take Deviance as the test of rivalry. The difficulties come from two directions. First, there is a question whether Deviance is a necessary condition for rivalry, for there are some logics in the list of 'systems proposed as rivals' which may fail to satisfy the criteria of Deviance.

Van Fraassen's 'presuppositional languages' are in this category; see van Fraassen [1966], [1968], and especially [1969]. Such languages have exactly the theorems of classical logic; but they are interpreted in such a way as to allow truth-value gaps. For a 'supervaluation' assigns to a molecular wff, components of which lack truth-value, that value which any classical valuation would assign it, if there is a unique such value, and otherwise no value. Thus a supervaluation would assign 'true' to '$p \vee \sim p$', since both the classical valuation in which 'p' is assigned 'true' and the classical valuation in which 'p' is assigned 'false', give it 'true'; but it would assign no value to '$p \vee q$' since some classical valuations (e.g. $|p| = |q| = t$) give it 'true' and others (e.g. $|p| = |q| = f$) give it 'false'. In consequence all and only the classical tautologies are designated. This suggests that one should regard such language as semantically non-standard although syntactically conventional. Van Fraassen claims, however ([1969], pp. 79–86) that the change he proposes has consequences for deducibility, though not for theoremhood. So it is possible that his presuppositional languages *are* within the scope of the definition of deviance.

There is also some difficulty with Bochvar's 3-valued logic. For the truth tables for the 'internal' connectives are such that whenever there is intermediate input, there is also intermediate output, so that there are no uniformly t-taking wffs containing only internal connectives. The 'external' connectives are defined in terms of the internal connectives and an 'assertion' operator, which takes 'true' if its argument takes 'true', but otherwise 'false', so that their truth-tables are such that whatever the input, the output is always classical. This suggests that it would be natural to think of the external connectives as corresponding to their classical counterparts, and the internal connectives as the new vocabulary. On this interpretation Bochvar's appears as an extended rather than a Deviant logic. (cf. Rescher [1969], pp. 30–2.) But, of course, this might lead to the conclusion that Bochvar's logic is a supplement rather than a rival, instead of the conclusion that Deviance is not, after all, a necessary condition of rivalry.

The second, and more serious, difficulty is that it is not certain whether Deviance is *sufficient* for rivalry. For suppose one were to ask how 'classical logic' is to be demarcated. This is to be done, I have supposed, by reference to its set of theorems and valid inferences. Any system with the same theorems/inferences as, say, *Principia Mathematica*, counts as a formulation, a version, of 'classical logic'. In particular, a system which differs from that of PM only in employing a distinct, but intertranslatable, notation – say '&' in place of '.' for conjunction – is only a *notational variant* of classical logic.

And now I am faced with the following problem: a system, L_1, which has as theorems a typographically distinct set of wffs from the set of wffs of PM is only a notational variant of that system, if uniformly replacing certain symbols of L_1 by symbols of PM renders the set of theorems identical. Someone who thought that L_1 was a rival to PM just because such wffs as '$p \cdot q \supset p$' were lacking from its set of theorems would have mistaken a purely typographical difference for a substantial disagreement. But now the question arises, whether the apparent disagreement between Deviant and classical logicians may not similarly be mere appearance? I supposed Łukasiewicz's 3-valued logic, for instance, to be a rival to classical logic, because classical logic has as theorems certain wffs, such as '$p \vee \sim p$', which are not theorems of Łukasiewicz's logic. But the mere absence from the set of theorems of L_3 of wffs of a certain typographical form is not sufficient, as is now clear, to show that there is real conflict between L_3 and classical logic. There remains the question, whether those wffs, so to speak, mean the same in both systems. If, for example, one came to believe that Łukasiewicz was employing '$\vee$' as a (perverse) notation for the operation usually written '&', one would certainly not suppose that the absence from its set of theorems of the wff '$p \vee \sim p$' showed L_3 to be a rival to classical logic.

So I am faced with another problem. I have found formal features – deviance and quasi-deviance – which it seemed plausible to take as sufficient conditions of rivalry. And so it looked as though there were systems, the deviant and the quasi-deviant logics, which could properly be described as *rivals* of classical logic, *alternatives* to it in a strong sense of 'alternative'. But now it has become apparent that it could be argued that this appearance of rivalry is misleading. This line of argument must be investigated.

3. The argument against genuine rivalry

While there is no doubt that deviant and quasi-deviant systems have been *proposed as* rivals to classical logic, some writers have argued that the systems so proposed turn out not really to be rivals at all, because their apparent incompatability with classical logic is explicable as resulting from *change of meaning* of the logical constants. Quine, for example, writes:

> departure from the law of excluded middle would count as evidence of revised usage of 'or' or 'not'.... For the deviating logician the words 'or' and 'not' are unfamiliar or defamiliarised
>
> ([1960a], p. 396.)

and

> Alternative logics are inseparable practically from *mere change in usage of logical words.*
>
> ([1960a], p. 389, my italics.)

The train of thought which leads to this position seems to be somewhat as follows:

(a) if there is change of meaning of the logical constants, there is no real conflict between Deviant and classical logic,

(b) if there is Deviance, there is change of meaning of the logical constants,

so

(c) there is no real conflict between Deviant and classical logic

Putnam, whose attitude to Deviant logic is more sympathetic than Quine's, writes:

> the logical words 'or' and 'not' have a certain core meaning which is ... *independent* of the principle of the excluded middle. Thus in a certain sense the meaning does not change if we go over to a three-valued logic or to Intuitionist logic. Of course, if by saying that a change in the accepted logical principles is tantamount to a change in the meaning of the logical connectives, what one has in mind is the fact that changing the accepted logical principles will affect the global use of the logical connectives, then the thesis is tautological and hardly arguable. But if the claim is that a change in the accepted

logical principles would amount *merely* to redefining the logical connectives, then, in the case of Intuitionist logic, this is demonstrably false.

([1962], p. 377.)

As this passage suggests, discussion of this kind of attempt to trivialise Deviance in logic has concentrated on premiss (b); (a) has been conceded or ignored.

However, it is not hard to see that premiss (a) is, as it stands, false. (a) says that if it can be shown that the Deviant logician means by his logical constants something different from what is meant by the classical logical constants, it follows that there is no real conflict between the Deviant and the classical systems. Now it is true that if the Deviant logician means by a certain connective, *c*, something different from what is meant by the typographically identical connective of classical logic, then, if the Deviant logic lacks as a theorem a wff, *w*, which contains *c* as sole connective, and which is a theorem of classical logic, then, in an important sense, what the Deviant logician denies is not what the classical logician asserts. However, it does not follow from the fact that what the Deviant logician denies, when he denies that *w* is logically true, is not what the classical logician asserts, when he asserts that *w* is logically true, that *nothing* the Deviant logician says is inconsistent with *anything* the classical logician says; there may nonetheless be conflict.

For consider the following case: a Deviant logician, *D*, denies that the wff '$(p \vee q) \supset (\sim p \supset q)$' is logically true. The classical logician, *C*, takes this wff to be a theorem. However, it is discovered that *D* means by '$\vee$' what *C* means by '&'. It follows that when *D* denies that '$(p \vee q) \supset (\sim p \supset q)$' is logically true, what he denies is not what *C* asserts when *C* asserts that '$(p \vee q) \supset (\sim p \supset q)$' is logically true. But it does not follow that there is no real disagreement between *C* and *D*, for *C* also thinks that '$(p \mathbin{\&} q) \supset (\sim p \supset q)$' is logically true, so when *D* denies that '$(p \vee q) \supset (\sim p \supset q)$' is logically true, what he denies is after all something which *C* accepts. This shows that difference of meaning of the connectives between classical and Deviant systems is *not sufficient* to establish lack of rivalry between them.

Another consideration supports the same conclusion. For there are some cases at least of difference between logics which, prima facie, resist explanation of apparent conflict in terms of difference of meaning of connectives. If L_D (the Deviant system) lacks certain principles which L_C (the classical system) accepts, *and these principles contain no occurrences of any connectives*, then the apparent difference between L_D and L_C cannot straightforwardly be explained away as due to an idiosyncrasy in the meanings of the connectives of L_D. Since, in a consistent system, atomic formulae are not provable, the possibility of explanation in terms of changed meaning of connectives is always available when the difference between L_D and L_C lies in the set of theorems. But now consider Gentzen's formulation of minimal logic (L_J): it differs from classical logic, not in respect of the introduction and elimination rules for the connectives, but in respect of the structural rules for deducibility; namely, it results from restricting the rules for classical logic (L_K) by disallowing multiple consequents. Since this restriction involves no essential reference to any connectives, it is hard to see how it could be explicable as arising from divergence of meaning of connectives. The same argument applies to the Heyting calculus, which results, in Gentzen's formulation, from adding to L_J the rule 'from A and $\neg A$ to infer B', while retaining the restriction on multiple consequents. The argument is not wholly conclusive, since it could be suggested that the reason for the restriction on deducibility lies in a desire to avoid certain theorems, e.g. '$p \vee \neg p$', and that the desire to avoid these theorems may spring from idiosyncrasy of connectives. But the argument is at least suggestive. And it cannot be dismissed by suggesting that the difference between classical and minimal logic be attributed to idiosyncrasy in the meaning of '⊢'. The advocate of minimal or Intuitionist logic is not comparable to those philosophers who have been sufficiently impressed by the 'paradoxes' of strict implication to deny that strict implication can be identified with entailment or logical consequence. Such writers might (as suggested in Smiley [1959]) propose alternative principles for '⊢', and if they did so it would be precisely because of their special interpretation of '⊢'. The Intuitionist, by contrast, means the same by '⊢' as the classical logician, but nevertheless believes that a principle for '⊢', which the classical logician accepts, does not hold.

So change of meaning is not sufficient for absence of conflict. Whether difference of meaning is sufficient to account for apparent conflict depends upon the exact nature of the meaning change. However, there are arguments which, if sound, would show that adoption of a Deviant system must involve a wholesale change in the meanings of the logical connectives which would be sufficient to account for the appearance of incompatability with classical logic.

(i) *The argument from the theory-dependence of the meanings of connectives*

The most obvious argument for a strong version of premiss (b) would appeal to the thesis that the meaning of the logical connectives is wholly given by the axioms and/or rules of inference of the system in which they occur. (See Carnap [1937], and cf. Fremlin [1938], Campbell [1958].) It presumably follows immediately from this thesis that adoption of a Deviant axiom set entails wholesale change in the meaning of the connectives. For consider the question, how sets of axioms or rules are to be individuated. A proponent of the thesis that the meanings of the connectives are given by the axioms or rules of the systems in which they occur would presumably wish to count two axiomisations as, from this point of view, the same, if, although there were not the same wffs in each set, the sets were equivalent, i.e. yielded the same set of theorems; since otherwise he would be forced to say that the connectives differed in meaning in alternative axiomatisations of the classical propositional calculus. So he would count two axiom sets involving the same connectives as different only if they yield different sets of theorems, i.e. are Deviations of each other.

There is an interesting analogy between this view and Feyerabend's thesis, that differences between two ostensibly rival scientific theories involve differences of meaning of terms occurring in the theories (analogue: differences between two ostensibly rival logics involve differences of meaning of logical constants); and between premiss (a) and the criticism made of Feyerabend, e.g. by Shapere, that his meaning-variance thesis would entail that scientific theories which are proposed as rivals to each other are not really incompatible after all (analogue: what the deviant logician denies is not, appearances to the contrary, anything the classical logician asserts). cf. Feyerabend [1962], [1963], Shapere [1966].

Indeed, prima facie, at least, the meaning-variance thesis sounds more plausible when applied to logics than when applied to scientific theories, for in the latter case there seem to be certain restraints upon the meanings of the theoretical terms, to the extent that they have some connection with observables, whereas in the former case there are no such apparent restraints upon the meanings of the connectives.

The possibility of this kind of argument is recognised both by Quine, in [1960a], and by Putnam, in [1969]. However, neither Quine nor Putnam thinks that the concept of meaning is sufficiently clear for the thesis that the meaning of the constants of a system is given by the axioms/rules of the system to amount to anything upon which such weight could be placed. Putnam, indeed, offers against this argument the following considerations, which are especially interesting in view of the analogy noted above between meaning-variance theses for scientific theories and for logics. He suggests that for logical as for scientific terms there are operational constraints, which provide a degree of community of meaning between theories sufficient to allow genuine incompatibility. He argues, further, that just as, with relativity theory, the cluster of laws, geometrical and physical, involved in the Euclidian concept of *straight line* 'fell apart', so, with quantum mechanics, the cluster of laws, logical and physical, involved in the classical concepts of *conjunction* and *disjunction* have 'fallen apart'. The solution he proposes is:

> to *deny* that there are *any* precise and meaningful operations or propositions which have the properties classically attributed to 'and' and 'or'.
>
> ([1969], p. 232.)

So, he argues, we must replace the old logic by a new one, and the old concepts of conjunction and disjunction by new ones, but ones which share a 'core' of meaning with the old. (cf. Putnam [1957] for the notion of 'core' meaning, and [1962] for the notion of 'law cluster concept'.)

However, it may not be necessary, in order to avoid the meaning change argument, to agree with Putnam that there are operational constraints upon even logical terms. For the premiss upon which the argument rests – that the meanings of the logical connectives are given by the axioms and/or rules of inference of the system in which they occur – has been challenged.

Prior tries, in [1960] and [1964], to show that the meanings of the connectives *cannot* be given by the axioms/rules of a system, by considering a system which includes the connective 'tonk', governed by the rules:

From *A* to infer *A* tonk *B*

and

From *A* tonk *B* to infer *B*

However, the conclusion which Prior apparently favours, that the connectives must have independently specified meaning before it can be discovered what logical principles hold for them, rather than specification of those principles *constituting* giving their meaning, hardly follows. For it is clear that there are independent arguments against the 'tonk' rules, which are neither syntactically adequate, since they would allow $A \vdash B$, nor semantically adequate, since no unique truth table could be given for 'tonk' consistent with them. (cf. Belnap [1961] and Stevenson [1961], respectively, on these points.) Since the 'tonk' rules are unacceptable, it is not surprising if they cannot give the meaning of 'tonk'. It does not follow that *no* rules could give the meanings of the connectives occurring in them.

Even so, however, it is doubtful whether the thesis that meaning is given by axioms and/or rules of inference can be made to support a strong version of the meaning variance thesis for Deviant logics. For the typical situation with Deviant systems is that their axioms/rules of inference are very similar to but not quite the same as those of classical logic. For instance, as Putnam points out in [1969], in Birkhoff and von Neumann's as in classical logic all the following rules for '&' and 'v' are valid:

$A, B \vdash A \& B$
$A \& B \vdash A$
$A \& B \vdash B$
$A \vdash A \vee B$
if $A \vdash C$ and $B \vdash C$, then $A \vee B \vdash C$,

but nevertheless this system deviates from the classical, notably in lacking the distributive laws for '&' and 'v'. Because there is such a degree of overlap, even if one was convinced of the thesis that the meanings of the connectives are given by the axioms/rules of the system, the conclusion, that Deviant logics must involve a degree of meaning-variance sufficient to dispose of all apparent rivalry with classical logic, would hardly be unambiguously forthcoming. For the thesis that the meaning is given by the axioms/rules yields, in the case of axioms/rules partly but not wholly differing from the classical, only the conclusion that the meanings of the connectives in such systems are partly but not wholly different from their meanings in the classical; and this gives no clear answer to the question, whether there is real rivalry.

Some similar difficulties would arise if it were suggested, as by Stevenson, that the meaning of the connectives is given, at least in part, by their truth-tables. (cf. Lewis [1932].) Suppose it were asked whether on this view, the connectives of, say, $Ł_3$ differ in meaning from their typographical analogues in classical logic. One might say that they *do*, since the truth-tables of Ł₃ are different, being 3-valued, from those of Łc. On the other hand, one might say that they *do not*, since the truth-tables of Ł₃ are normal, i.e. they have classical, true or false, output wherever they have classical input. (cf. here the 'conditional' account of the meaning of the connectives in Strawson [1952], p. 19.) And there are further difficulties. What is one to say of the meanings of the connectives in systems such as Intuitionist logic which have no finite characteristic matrix? And of the meanings of the connectives in a system like van Fraassen's which is conventional so far as its theorems are concerned, but semantically deviant?

Prior seems to think that since, as he supposes, he has shown that the thesis that meaning is given by the axioms/rules of a system is untenable, the meanings of the connectives can only be fully specified with reference to their ordinary language readings. If this view were adopted, it would presumably follow that the meaning of the connectives does *not* change in the move to Deviant logics, since Deviant logicians employ the usual ordinary language readings for their connectives. (The Intuitionists, who sometimes employ idiosyncratic readings, are an exception.) However, since so many writers have found difficulty with the usual ordinary language readings of the connectives (consider, e.g. the literature which exists on the question, how proper a reading of ' ⊃ ' is 'if . . . then . . . '?) Prior's thesis, that the meaning is finally and fully given by the ordinary language reading, is not obviously any more acceptable than the alternatives already considered.

So no conclusive argument has yet been given, from an acceptable premiss concerning the meanings of the connectives, to the conclusion that in Deviant logics meaning-variance accounts for apparent rivalry.

Quine has, however, a different argument for the same conclusion.

(ii) *The argument from translation*

Quine's argument purports to show that *apparent conflict in logic should always be accounted the result of mistranslation.*

In 'Carnap and Logical Truth' the argument appears in a form which appeals directly to standards of translation between one language and another:

> Oversimplifying, no doubt, let us suppose it claimed that . . . natives accept as true certain sentences of the form '*p* and not *p*'. Or – not

to oversimplify too much – that they accept as true a certain heathen sentence of the form '*q* ka bu *q*', the English translation of which has the form '*p* and not *p*'. But now just how good a translation is this, and what may the lexicographer's method have been? If any evidence can count against a lexicographer's adoption of 'and' and 'not' as translation of 'ka' and 'bu', certainly the natives' acceptance of '*q* ka bu *q*' counts overwhelmingly . . . prelogicality is a myth invented by bad translators.

([1960a], p. 387.)

In [1960] also, this argument is deployed against the possibility of prelogical peoples. In [1970] the argument is applied to 'translation' of the deviant logician's 'dialect' into our own:

> We impute our orthodox logic to [the deviant logician], or impose it upon him, by translating his deviant dialect.

([1970], p. 81.)

It is worth observing at the outset that this argument of Quine's, which, if it were sound, would show that there can be no genuine rivals to classical logic, is incompatible with another thesis, propounded in e.g. the last section of 'Two Dogmas of Empiricism' (Quine [1951]), to the effect that none of our beliefs, beliefs about the laws of logic included, is immune from revision in the light of experience. According to this view it is at least theoretically possible that we should revise our logic. In practice, as Quine observes in 'Two Dogmas', he is inclined to be conservative about his logic, for the ramifying adjustments necessitated by a change of logic are liable to be excessively widespread. But, in principle at least, the possibility of revising logic is left open. However, the *Philosophy of Logic* thesis is that there can be no such thing as a real, but only an apparent, change of logic. It is worth stressing, also, how important a change is made in Quine's philosophy by his acceptance of this thesis. For it commits him to admitting a distinction between linguistic change and factual change which it was one of the crucial points of [1951] to deny. Indeed Grice and Strawson, in [1956], take it that the concession of this distinction would be a major advance against Quine.

The *Philosophy of Logic* thesis derives from Quine's theory of translation (Quine [1959], [1960a], [1968] and, especially [1960], ch. 2.) In [1960], ch. 2 Quine is arguing for the thesis of the *indeterminacy of translation*, which may be summarised as follows:

QIT   Alternative, and mutually incompatible, translations may con-
       form to all data concerning speakers' dispositions to verbal
       behaviour.

The primary interest here is in the reasons for an exception which
Quine makes to QIT: translation of the truth-functional connectives
is, he claims, immune from indeterminacy.

   In order to understand the reasons for excepting the truth-functions,
and the relevance of this exception to Deviant logics, it will be necessary
to look more closely at QIT. In Quine's work on translation three
theses are to be found:

   (1) There is *inductive uncertainty* in the translation even of *observation sentences*.
   (2) There is *radical indeterminacy* in the translation of *words and
phrases*.
   (3) There is *radical indeterminacy* in the translation of *theoretical
sentences*.

Theses (2) and (3) together constitute QIT: although Quine accepts
thesis (1) he takes pains to emphasise that it is distinct from, and less
important than, his indeterminacy theses.

   Quine begins from the premiss that the evidence for a linguistic
theory consists of information concerning the verbal behaviour and
dispositions to verbal behaviour of the speakers of the language being
translated. He takes assent and dissent as basic behavioural co-
ordinates, and defines the affirmative/negative stimulus meaning of a
sentence for a speaker as the class of all stimulations which would
prompt his assent/dissent, and the stimulus meaning of the sentence
for the speaker as the ordered pair of its affirmative and negative stimulus meanings. He then points out that there are certain difficulties
even in discovering the stimulus meaning of observation sentences.
These difficulties arise from the underdetermination of a linguistic
theory by its data, from the availability of alternative ways of account-
ing for given evidence. This is thesis (1). But Quine takes this 'merely
inductive' uncertainty relatively lightly. (See [1960], p. 68.)

   Radical indeterminacy is a much more serious matter; where it
arises, the problem is not that there is difficulty in finding a translation,
but rather, that there is no uniquely correct translation to be found.
Radical indeterminacy arises at the level of analytical hypotheses –
hypotheses, that is, concerning the segmentation of heard utterances

into meaningful units, and the parsing and translation of these units. For alternative analytical hypotheses, incompatible with each other, but yielding the same net output at the observation sentence level, will always be available, since compensating adjustments, either in the choice of meaningful unit, e.g. construing some segment as pleonastic, or in the form of the hypothesis that the meaning of certain segment(s) is context dependent, are always possible. (See [1968].) This is thesis (2).

Radical indeterminacy also arises at the level of translation of certain sentences, those, namely, which are theoretical rather than observational. For consider the problem of how to translate theoretical sentences, given only evidence concerning speakers' dispositions to verbal behaviour. Assent to/dissent from a theoretical sentence does not depend in any direct way upon stimulation; indeed, in [1970b] this is treated as a defining characteristic of theoreticity of sentences. Now suppose that all the observation sentences which constitute the data for a native theory T, the sentences of which are to be translated, have been translated. By the 'Duhem theses', the theses, that is, that no hypothesis can be conclusively verified or falsified by any amount of data, these observation sentences are compatible with rival theories, say T and T'. And so T and T', though *ex hypothesi* incompatible, are indistinguishable in point of stimulus meaning. To put the argument in another way; if meaning is given by assent/dissent conditions (the 'Dewey principle') and if the assent/dissent conditions of theoretical sentences are indeterminate (the 'Duhem theses') then the meanings of theoretical sentences are indeterminate. (See [1970a].) This is thesis (3).

Now on this interpretation there is some explanation of why Quine should make the exception to QIT – the alleged determinacy of translation of the truth-functional connectives. In §12–13 of *Word and Object* Quine argues that whereas the quantifiers are vulnerable to the radical indeterminacy, the truth-functions are not. The discrimination here between quantifiers and truth-functions is comprehensible, now, if one remembers that the truth-functions *link whole sentences*, whereas the quantifiers occur *within whole sentences*. More precisely, the truth functional operators are sentence-forming operators on sentences, while the quantifiers are sentence-forming operators on open, i.e. incomplete, sentences. Therefore the quantifiers, but not the truth-functions, are vulnerable to that form of radical indeterminacy which strikes below the sentence level; semantic criteria, in terms of assent and dissent, can be given for the truth-functions, but not for the quantifiers.

It has been shown why Quine should except the truth-functions from QIT, why he should take them to be determinately translatable. It has yet to be shown how their translatability is supposed to yield a meaning-variance thesis for Deviant logics. The argument seems to run as follows: semantic criteria, in terms of assent and dissent, can be given for the truth-functional connectives; when a construction fulfils these criteria, this is sufficient reason to translate it by the appropriate truth-function. And this rules out the possibility of a correct translation in accordance with which the natives dissent from (classical) tauto-logies or assent to (classical) contradictions. Thus, Quine is main-taining both:

(1) It is possible to tell that a certain expression of (the language being translated), L, should be translated by a certain connective, e.g. 'and',

and

(2) It is not possible that a correct translation of expressions of L by sentential connectives should be such that sentences translated by (classical) contradictions are assented to by speakers of L, nor that sentences translated by (classical) tautologies are dissented from by speakers of L.

I shall argue that even if (1) is true, (2) follows only given some further assumptions which are themselves doubtful, so that Quine's argument against rivalry between logics fails.

The assumptions which support Quine's claim that correct transla-tion of a native's or a Deviant logician's utterances must be such as to make them conform with classical propositional calculus are:

(a) the principle of maximising agreement (hereafter, M),
(b) the adoption of classical criteria for the truth-functions and,
(c) the adoption of assent and dissent as behavioural co-ordinates.

Quine recognises that he is taking for granted the principle so to translate another's utterances as to maximise agreement. He writes:

the maxim of translation underlying all this is that assertions startl-ingly false on the face of them are likely to turn on hidden differences of language.

([1960], p. 59.)

and

> It behooves us, in construing a strange language, to make the obvious
> sentences go over into English sentences which are true and, prefer-
> ably, also obvious.
>
> ([1970], p. 82.)

To put the matter another way: faced with a choice of attributing to
the native, or to the Deviant logician, a disagreement in belief or a
divergence in meaning, one should choose the latter rather than the
former. Now (M) yields (2) in conjunction with the assumption that
the person doing the translating accepts classical logic. And just this
assumption is embodied in (b) – Quine's adoption of criteria for the
truth-functional connectives which (with 'assent' replacing 'true' and
'dissent' replacing 'false') simply follow the 2-valued matrices.

This choice of criteria is, in turn, made plausible by Quine's adoption of assent and dissent as co-ordinates. For suppose one took three
co-ordinates, assent, dissent, and puzzlement, as basic. Then one could
state alternative criteria, e.g. as follows:

> The *disjunction* of two sentences is that sentence to which one would
> assent if one assents to either component, from one which one would
> dissent if one dissents from both components, and to which one
> would react with puzzlement if one reacts with puzzlement to both
> components, or reacts with puzzlement to one component and
> dissents from the other.
>
> The *negation* of a sentence is that sentence to which one would
> assent if one dissents from the sentence, from which one would
> dissent if one assents to the sentence, and to which one would react
> with puzzlement if one reacts with puzzlement to the sentence.

On *these* criteria the possibility that natives might fail to assent to
some sentence translatable as 'p or not p' is not at all absurd, and might
be evidence that they employ a 3-valued logic. And if these criteria
were used Quine's (1) could be true but (2) false.

That in order to yield the conservative conclusion that everybody
really accepts classical logic, (M) must be supplemented by the further
assumption that classical logic is correct, can be seen clearly, if it is
not already sufficiently apparent, by the following consideration.
Suppose that the linguist were an Intuitionist. If he accepts (M), he
will so translate the natives' utterances as to attribute to them an
Intuitionist logic. To an Intuitionist linguist it would be absurd to

suppose that a sentence which commands invariable assent could correctly be translated '*p* or not *p*'. Quine might object that although an Intuitionist would indeed so translate native sentences that they do not invariably assent to the sentence he translates as '*p* or not *p*', the Intuitionist does not mean by that sentence what the classical logician means. But this form of argument simply is not legitimately available to Quine at this stage; for he has yet to establish that an Intuitionist cannot mean the same as a classical logician by '*p* or not *p*'.

The principle of maximising agreement entails that correct translation invariably preserves classical logic in a privileged position, only if one assumes that classical logic is the right one. When Quine asks 'Not to be dogmatic about it, what criteria for the connectives might one prefer?', his rhetorical question only thinly masks the *petitio principii*. His maxim, 'Save the obvious', preserves classical logic only granted that classical logic *is* obvious.

A further difficulty with Quine's argument is that it seems most doubtful whether, even supposing (b) granted for the sake of argument, (*M*) would take the weight Quine places on it. (*M*) may, quite properly, be thought of as a pragmatic principle applying to the choice of linguistic theory: the principle that, if it is reasonably obvious to the translator that *p*, and the translator has no special reason to suppose that this is not obvious to his respondent, then a translation which preserves the translator's and the respondent's agreement that *p* is preferable to one that does not. This pragmatic principle may be given a certain amount of support by the consideration that without assumption of *some* agreement in beliefs between translator and respondent, translation could hardly begin.

Still, if (*M*) is sensible pragmatic principle, still it *is* only a pragmatic principle; it may be overridden. Sometimes translations violating it might be simpler than translations in conformity to it. (*M*) surely has greatest weight in cases like that of the fictional logician of *Philosophy of Logic*, who takes all classical laws governing conjunction to govern disjunction, and vice versa, where the beliefs that would have to be attributed to the respondent in order to preserve homophonic translation are very extraordinary. It has less weight in cases, like that, say, of Birkhoff and von Neumann's logic, where there would be a large though incomplete measure of agreement in belief even under homophonic translation. Worse, its verdict is quite ambiguous where the Deviant logician holds, besides his (apparently) idiosyncratic logical beliefs, the further belief, that he disagrees with the classical logician.

One may also observe that, if (M) were as unreservedly acceptable as Quine supposes, it would yield not only the conclusion that Deviance in propositional calculus is attributable to idiosyncracy of meaning of the truth-functional connectives, but also the conclusion that Deviance in predicate calculus is attributable to idiosyncracy of meaning of the quantifiers. This is, indeed, a view to which Quine seems sympathetic in *Philosophy of Logic*, e.g. when he discusses what the Intuitionist means by '$(\exists x)\ldots x$'. But once one has noticed this, one cannot avoid the conclusion that Quine must have overestimated the importance of the exceptions to the indeterminacy of translation in the case of the truth-functions. That is, if the predicate calculus analogue of (2) follows from (M), even without the predicate calculus analogue of (1), the connection between (1) and (2) themselves must be less close than, in *Word and Object*, Quine seems to suppose.

So, I conclude, Quine's argument from translation is no more successful than the argument from the theory dependence of the meanings of logical terms in establishing that there can be no real rivals to classical logic.

I have found no general argument adequate to show that Deviance must involve wholesale meaning-change, or, therefore, adequate to show that genuinely rival logics are impossible. It does not, however, follow from this failure – and neither do I assert – that Deviant logics never involve any meaning-change, or that all Deviant logics necessarily stand in real conflict with classical logic. I shall suggest, in what follows, that the extent to which a Deviant system involves change of meaning may depend upon the particular system in question.

4. Varieties of Deviance

It is unsurprising, in view of their contrasting attitudes to Deviant logics, to find Quine concentrating on the fictional logician of *Philosophy of Logic*, when the plausibility of the thesis that the change is only one of notation is maximal, and Putnam concentrating on the kind of Deviance typified by the Intuitionist or by Birkhoff and von Neumann, when the plausibility of the thesis that the change is only one of notation is minimal.

Short of the possibility of straightforward rivalry, when there is Deviance unaccompanied by any meaning variance, one might distinguish three kinds of possible case. Quine more or less explicitly acknowledges their possibility, but concentrates almost wholly on the first, which is the most favourable to a conservative position.

(A) One possibility is that all theorems of the Deviant logic, L_D, can be translated into theorems of classical logic, L_C, and vice versa. This is the situation with Quine's fictional example; if each wff A of L_C is translated by the wff A' of L_D which results from replacing all occurrences of '&' in A by 'v' and all occurrences of 'v' in A by '&', then ⊢ $_{LC}$ A iff ⊢ $_{LD}$ A'. Quine concludes, very plausibly, that L_D should be regarded as only a notational variant of L_C.

But there is a second possibility, viz:

(B) that it should be impossible to translate everything which the Deviant logician asserts into something to which the classical logician would assent and everything from which the Deviant logician dissents into something from which the classical logician would also dissent. Suppose e.g. that for every wff A of L_C there is a translation of A' of L_D such that if ⊢$_{LC}$ A then ⊢$_{LD}$ A', but there are some theorems of L_D which have no translations in L_C. Then L_D is, if not a rival, at least a supplement, and not merely an uninteresting notational variant, of L_C.

A quasi-deviant system which might not implausibly be thought of as falling into this category is that of 'Sense Without Denotation' (Smiley [1960]), which is formally similar to Bochvar's. Here there is some reason to say that the secondary connectives do not differ in meaning from the classical connectives, since exactly the same logical principles hold for these as for those. The primary connectives now appear as new connectives, bearing some, but only an imperfect, analogy to the old, and the system appears as an extension of the classical.

Another possibility is:

(C) that a system should employ a set of connectives differing in meaning from those of classical logic, while lacking the means to express classical connectives. Such a system would be neither straightforwardly a rival, nor straightforwardly a supplement, of classical logic.

An example might be the 3-valued system considered in Lewis [1932]. Let 1 = certainly true, 2 = certainly false, 3 = doubtful. In terms of these categories, Lewis argues, the meaning of the classical 'or' is simply inexpressible. For consider what value is to be given to 'p or q'

when $|p| = |q| = 3$. If 'p' and 'q' are doubtful, is 'p or q' also doubtful? Well, generally, yes; but not if 'p' and 'q' are so related (as when 'p' = ' $\sim q$') that when 'p' is true, 'q' must be false, and vice versa. The moral to be drawn is, presumably, that the question, whether at least one of 'p', 'q' is true, cannot be answered given only information, concerning 'p' and 'q', whether they are certainly true, certainly false, or not certainly either. Quine comes close to explicit recognition of the possibility of cases of types (B) and (C) when he writes:

> There may, of course, still be an important failure of intertranslatability, in that the behaviour of certain of our logical particles is incapable of being duplicated by paraphrases in the native's or deviant logician's system or vice-versa. If translation in this sense is possible . . . then we are pretty sure to protest that he was wantonly using the familiar particles 'and' and 'all' (say) when he might unmisleadingly have used such and such other familiar phrasing.
>
> ([1960a], p. 386.)

The important conclusion which, returning to his conservative mood, Quine leaves undrawn, is this: that if straightforward and wholesale intertranslation is *not* possible, the Deviant logician will have to be taken seriously after all.

I have up to now been considering the question, whether Deviant logics really are, as their proponents claim, rivals of classical logic, or whether considerations of meaning inevitably show that the rivalry is only apparent, and I have concluded that genuine rivalry *is* possible. But there is another point, so far neglected, that deserves mention. It is this: even if the edge of the disagreement between the classical and a Deviant system were blunted by some degree of meaning change, this meaning change might be neither unmotivated nor unimportant, Quine is half aware of this:

> in repudiating 'p or $\sim p$' the deviant logician is . . . giving up classical negation, or perhaps alternation, or both; and *he may have his reasons*.
>
> ([1970], p. 87, my italics.)

Lewis recognised this. And Putnam is acutely aware of it, when he stresses ([1969]) that a change of logic, even if less than a genuine repudiation of the classical system, might constitute an important 'conceptual revision'.

And so I make, against those who would trivialise 'alternative logics', two claims: that it is not true that there can be no such thing as a genuine rival to classical logic; and that it is not true, either, that adoption even of a Deviant system which involves some degree of meaning-variance may not constitute a real and interesting change of logic. Of course, the question, whether there could be *good reasons* for adopting an alternative logic, remains.

2

Reasons for Deviance

dictators may be powerful today, but they cannot alter the laws of logic, nor indeed can even God do so.

(Ewing [1940], p. 217.)

1. The problem: could there be good reason for a change of logic?

There is no question that there have been devised numerous deviant and quasi-deviant logical systems, nor that such systems have sometimes been proposed as rivals to classical logic. And I have argued, in ch. 1, that it is possible for these systems to be genuinely rivals of the classical. A real change of logic, that is, is possible.

However, it remains to be shown that it is possible, even in principle, that there should ever be good reason to make a change of logic. The question is crucial: for if it were *not* possible, there would be little point in examining, in detail, the reasons offered by the proponents of rival systems, since it would be certain in advance that their reasons must be inadequate. And the question is serious: for the view that logic is absolutely certain, and so completely unalterable, has had some powerful adherents.

2. A radical view of the status of logical laws

But I shall argue that logic is *not* unalterable, that there *could* be reasons for changing it. Fortunately, although I have some powerful opponents, I am not without allies. Quine writes:

no statement is immune to revision. Revision even of the logical law of the excluded middle has been proposed as a means of simplifying quantum mechanics; and what difference is there in principle between such a shift and the shift whereby Kepler superseded Ptolemy, or Einstein Newton, or Darwin Aristotle?

([1951], p. 43.)

And Putnam:

> could some of the 'necessary truths' of logic ever turn out to be false *for empirical reasons*? I shall argue that the answer to this question is in the affirmative
>
> ([1969], p. 216.)

The view I shall support is the one I called, in ch. 1, a 'pragmatist'[1] conception of logic; according to which logic is a theory, a theory on a par, except for its extreme generality, with other, 'scientific' theories; and according to which choice of logic, as of other theories, is to be made on the basis of an assessment of the economy, coherence and simplicity of the overall belief set. The very existence of arguments in favour of Deviant logics lends some prima facie plausibility to this view. But, of course, the proponents of such logics could be mistaken about the nature of their own enterprise. (The inventors of non-Euclidean geometries, after all, intended to prove the dependence of the parallel postulate.) More argument is necessary.

The pragmatist conception is radically opposed to 'absolutist' views of logic, according to which logical laws are unalterable, because they have a special status which guarantees their certainty. A proponent of a deviant logic *could* take the view that the principles of *his* logic are certain and unalterable, but it is, significantly, much commoner for absolutists to maintain the unalterable certainty of *classical* logical laws. (cf. Rescher [1969], ch. 3.)

I shall begin my case in favour of the radical conception by arguing *against* some influential absolutist views. I shall then offer some arguments which directly favour the pragmatist view, and, to close the case, some arguments against influential objections made to it.

3. Two absolutist views

(i) *Logic as a completed science*: *Kant*

According to Kant:

> There are but few sciences that can come into a permanent state, which admits of no further alteration. To these belong Logic and

---

[1] I do not intend to place much weight on this label. I use it because my view has similarities with those of Dewey, White and Quine.

Metaphysics. Aristotle has omitted no essential point of the understanding.

In our own times there has been no famous logician, and indeed
we do not require any new discoveries in Logic, since it contains
merely the form of thought.

([1800], pp. 10–11.)

Logic, he thought, was a completed science, admitting no change.

Now one might, with some plausibility, offer an historical argument
against this view. Kant attributed *a priori* truth to Newtonian physics
and to Aristotelian logic, because they were, when he wrote, without
serious rivals; but the development of Einsteinian physics, of non-
Euclidean geometries, and non-Aristotelian logics showed him to have
been mistaken. Kant's position illustrates Peirce's shrewd comment on
the *a priori* method:

one may be sure that whatever scientific investigation shall have put
out of doubt will presently receive *a priori* demonstration on the
part of the metaphysians.

([1877], p. 68.)

This counter-argument *is* plausible. An absolutist view of the status of
logic is, to some extent, threatened by the very existence of alternative
logics. Kant could plausibly hold that Aristotle's logic is absolute and
unalterable, just because Aristotelian logic was then so firmly
entrenched.

Nevertheless, it is possible to maintain that the historical argument
is not conclusive. There are two points which could be made, in spite
of this argument, in Kant's favour. Few, if any, writers would nowa-
days agree with Kant that *Aristotelian* logic is complete, perfect and
unalterable. But many would hold that '*classical*' (i.e. *Principia*) logic
is beyond revision. That is, it could be said that Kant was essentially
right about the status of logical truths, although the logic he favoured
was inadequate. And, second, it could be maintained that the present
existence of rivals to classical logic does not show a Kantian view of
the status of classical logic to be mistaken. Kant was wrong about
physics; but he might yet have been right about logic. For it was not
the mere existence of a non-Newtonian physics which showed Kant
wrong; it was the discovery that Einstein's was the better theory. And
it could still be held that although alternative logics exist, nevertheless

no possible experience could show one of these to be preferable to classical logic, for logic makes no assertions about the world, it is true independently of experience. Kant maintained the *a priori* status of Euclidean geometry, after all, even though he was aware of the possibility of non-Euclidean geometry.

That Kant would have held an absolutist view of logic, even if he had taken the possibility of alternative logics seriously, is pretty clear from the last sentence of the above quotation. Logic is unalterable because 'it contains merely the form of thought'. Kant's absolutism springs not just from a myopic view of the possible variety of logics, but also, and perhaps more importantly, from a view about the nature and status of logical laws. According to him, the laws of logic are 'the conditions of the use of the understanding in general', and hence are 'discernable *a priori*' (p. 2).

Is this view of the status of logical laws tenable? Logic, Kant says, consists of the necessary rules for the exercise of the understanding, those, that is, without which 'no exercise of the understanding would be possible at all' (p. 2). There is an obvious difficulty in this view: if the understanding could not operate at all except in accordance with the laws of logic, it would be inexplicable how people can, as they certainly do, argue invalidly, contrary to these laws. Kant seems to be aware of this difficulty:

> But *how error is possible in the formal sense of the word, that is, how a form of thought inconsistent with the understanding* is possible; this is hard to comprehend; as indeed in general we cannot comprehend how any faculty can deviate from its own essential laws.
>
> ([1800], p. 44.)

But his solution to it falls far short of adequacy. Formal error cannot, on his theory, arise from within the understanding itself; nor can it arise from sense, since sense does not judge. So it must arise from the unnoticed influence of sensibility on judgement. The trouble with this suggestion is that it does not seem to offer any real explanation of the kind of mistake which needs explaining. It is comprehensible how the unnoticed influence of sensibility on judgement might explain, e.g. the error of attributing external reality to time; but not how it might explain e.g. the error of affirming the consequent. How *could* sensibility cause a *formal* error? This form of absolutism is untenable.

(ii) *The alleged self-evidence of logical laws: Frege*

It is sometimes said that the laws of logic are certain, and so, unalterable, because they are *self-evident*. A view of this kind apparently underlay Frege's logicism;[2] for the logicist programme, to express the axioms of arithmetic in purely logical terms, and to derive them from purely logical truths, draws its epistemological importance from the idea that, in this way, the certainty of logic will be transmitted to arithmetic. But there are two things wrong with self-evidence as a sign of certainty: that principles accepted as self-evident turn out false, and that people disagree about what principles are self-evident. The first problem arose in dramatic form in Frege's programme. One of his axioms turned out to be inconsistent. Russell's paradox is a theorem of Frege's system. Frege's comment on this disaster is very revealing:

I have never disguised from myself its [i.e. the axiom of abstraction's] lack of the self-evidence that belongs to the other axioms and that must properly be demanded of a logical law.

([1884], p. 234.)

If a statement can be self-evident, and yet turn out to be false, self-evidence cannot be a guarantee of certainty. So Frege confesses that the axiom of abstraction had never really seemed sufficiently self-evident to count as a purely logical truth. But once it is admitted that there can be serious doubt which statements are, and which are not, *really* self-evident, the second problem arises: because people disagree about what is self-evident, self-evidence is, again, useless as a sign of certainty.

The force of this point can be better seen if one asks whether something of Frege's position could not be saved by pointing out that the axiom which failed was a *set-theoretical* one. Could it not be argued that its failure simply shows that set theory is not part of logic? This manoeuvre would, of course, still leave Frege's programme in considerable disarray, since he could not claim to have reduced arithmetic to logic alone. But it might promise to salvage the laws of logic from the wreck. And after all, that set theory is *not* part of logic is something that has been argued on other grounds. Here, however, it becomes relevant that the Intuitionists think arithmetical truths more basic, more certain, than logical ones; and that one of the reasons Quine gives ([1970], ch. 5) for the exclusion of set theory from logic is the

[2] This is puzzling, in a way: for self-evidence is presumably a psychological property, and elsewhere Frege enthusiastically combats psychologism.

existence of alternative set theories, which is very far from convincing
in view of the fact that there are alternative logics too.

The supposed self-evidence of logical truths is no reliable guarantee
of immunity from revision:

> many time-honoured and highly credited self-evident principles
> have been found to be in conflict either with one another or with
> empirically established principles, and have accordingly been dis-
> credited as false or later recredited as only probable or postulable.
> When there are so many instances of error in the products of a
> criterion of knowledge which purports to be free from error, there
> would seem to be adequate grounds for discrediting the criterion
> itself.
>
> (Pepper [1961], p. 24.)

4. In favour of the pragmatist view

Arguments against rival views need to be supplemented by some
positive reasons in favour of the pragmatist conception. The difficulty,
in arguing for a thesis of such generality, is to find premises from
which to begin, upon which one can hope for any degree of agreement.
In 'Two Dogmas' this conception appears as one strand of a radical
epistemological position, which may be summarised as follows:

(1) No statement is *conclusively verifiable* by experience.
(2) No statement is *conclusively falsifiable* by experience.
(3) No statement is *immune from revision* in the light of experience.
(4) The criteria for deciding which statements to retain, and which
to abandon, in the face of recalcitrance, are *pragmatic* ones, notably
simplicity and economy.

Thesis (1) amounts to a repudiation of 'justificationist' epistemology
– the view that it is possible to provide certain foundations for knowledge. Thesis (2) amounts to a repudiation of 'falsificationist' epistemology – according to which, although one cannot conclusively
verify one's beliefs, one can falsify some of them, so that the rational
procedure is to retain those beliefs which are in principle vulnerable
to, but have in practice resisted, falsification. Thesis (4) provides the
criteria which are now needed – given that, by (1) and (2), one's
beliefs are underdetermined by the data – to choose between alternative
belief sets.

The crucial thesis for my present concern is thesis (3), the claim that all our beliefs, *beliefs about logic included*, are vulnerable to revision. Quine, in 'Two Dogmas' at least, subscribes to this thesis: no statement whatever is absolutely immune to revision. Other writers, however, have thought that a line can be drawn between those beliefs which are, and those which are not, vulnerable to revision; and though they differ about exactly where the line should come, they tend to *exclude* logical beliefs from the domain of revisability.

Interestingly enough, Duhem, who in *The Aim and Structure of Physical Theory* ([1904]) argues for a position which so much resembles that of 'Two Dogmas' that the latter is often referred to as 'Duhemian', excludes the principles of logic and mathematics from vulnerability to revision. Duhem propounds principles analogous to each of (1)–(4), except that the application of each is restricted to statements of *physics*. He allows that there are in physics some statements so basic as to be true 'by definition', and argues that these might even so be revised, that if certain experimental results obtained, the simplest and most economical adjustment might be a change in definitions such that even those very basic statements ceased to hold. (cf. Putnam on 'law cluster concepts' in [1962].) But he explicitly denies that *mathematical* statements could be given up:

> in this confidence accorded the law of fall of weights, we see nothing analogous to the certainty that a mathematical definition draws from its very essence, that is, to the kind of certainty we have when it would be foolish to doubt that the various points on a circumference are all equidistant from the center.
>
> ([1904], p. 211.)

And Duhem does not trouble even to discuss the question, whether *logical* principles might not also be modified. He seems to think of logic as a tool for deriving the consequences of one's beliefs, and takes it for granted that such a device is presupposed by experimental procedure, and so cannot itself be liable to test.

So the question is, how might one motivate the extension of revisability to include even the statements of logic? It might look promising to appeal to those considerations to which Duhem himself alludes when he argues, against Le Roy, that even statements which are, in a given theory, analytic, may be changed if need be. Duhem admits that there are statements of physics which are true by definition, but he denies that this makes them unalterable; for if the world were sufficiently recalcitrant the simplest solution might be to alter the relevant definition. The analogous position with respect to logic would be, that the laws of logic are true 'by definition of the logical constants', or 'in virtue of their meaning' (or, etc.), but that nevertheless they are alterable. The resulting position would be something like this: the logical/factual distinction is maintained, but logical as well as factual statements are admitted to be revisable. This has an unsatisfactory consequence: that revision of logic must involve change of meaning, so that the altered logic cannot be properly speaking a rival of the original. I argued in the previous chapter that there can be logics which are rivals of the classical, and so I shall not use *this* strategy to establish the revisability of logic.

But there is another way. This is to deny that it is possible adequately to demarcate a class of statements true in virtue of their meaning. Instead of admitting the distinction between logical and factual truth, but extending revisability to include the former as well as the latter – which was the strategy I just rejected – one could deny that there *is* any clear distinction between them, and deny, in consequence, that there is any justification for discriminating between 'logical' and 'factual' beliefs in respect of revisability.

Some passages suggest that this is the structure of the argument in 'Two Dogmas'; for instance:

> My present suggestion is that it is nonsense, and the root of much nonsense, to speak of a linguistic component and a factual component in the truth of any individual statement.
>
> (Quine [1951], p. 42.)

But in places Quine seems to use the premiss that no statement is immune from revision in an argument against the analytic/synthetic distinction (to show that 'analytic' cannot be defined as 'true come what may'), rather than using his rejection of the analytic/synthetic distinction to support the revisability of logic. It is the latter strategy I am recommending.

White's attack on the analytic/synthetic distinction in [1956], and Quine's in [1951], rest on the dependence of the distinction upon meaning notions, and the hopeless unclarity of the latter. In each case, appeal is made to the difficulty encountered, in practice, in making, and obtaining agreement upon, judgements of synonymy, etc. And, indeed, it is hard to read these papers without being convinced – if one needed convincing – that meaning notions are indeed very far from satisfactory. The argument could rest here, with, I think, considerable plausibility.

But Quine's later work goes further than this. For according to the indeterminacy of translation thesis, meaning notions are worse than unsatisfactory: they are indeterminate. And, of course, if this were correct, it would amply justify the scepticism which in [1951] Quine manifests towards the prospect of an adequate explication of meaning concepts.

It is worth pursuing this line of argument a little further. For QIT, as I argued in ch. 1, is supported by two arguments, one relevant to the translation of words and phrases, the other to the translation of (some) sentences. Since 'analytic' and 'logically true' apply to sentences, it is the latter argument, the argument 'from above', which is relevant here. The argument in question is a 'second order Duhemian' argument; it appeals, that is, to the underdetermination of theories by observational data, to show that the translation of theoretical sentences is underdetermined by the translation of observation sentences. This means that the support for (3) derives ultimately from theses (1) and (2). So it is worth sketching briefly some of the arguments in favour of (1) and (2).

One line of argument in favour of (1) points to the failure of 'justificationist' programmes – e.g. Descartes', Frege's or Carnap's attempt to provide certain of our beliefs with respectively, an indubitable, or self-evident, or epistemologically prior, foundation. (See Descartes [1641], Frege [1884], Carnap [1928], and cf. Quine [1969].) A second line of argument supplements the first by indicating how these programmes, although in detail very different from each other, fail for rather similar reasons: the use of implicit assumptions outside the explicitly acknowledged foundation; failure to derive from the foundation the whole body of beliefs that was to have been justified; and vulnerability to the objection that the foundation, in its turn, needs to be justified. A third line of argument suggests that these kinds of difficulty are inevitable, by appealing to the notorious difficulties in the justification of induction (see Popper [1959] and Quine [1969]), and perhaps, also, to the less notorious difficulties in the justification of deduction (see Quine [1936], Black [1965], and Haack [1972]).

Some arguments in favour of thesis (2) are to be found in *The Aim and Structure of Physical Theory*. Duhem claims that no hypothesis of physics is conclusively falsifiable, because there are always auxiliary assumptions involved in the derivation of observational consequences from a physical hypothesis, so that if these consequences fail to obtain the most one is entitled to conclude is that *either* the hypothesis *or* the auxiliary assumption is mistaken. The thesis that from '$((H \& A) \supset O)$' and '$\sim O$' one can derive only '$\sim (H \& A)$', and not '$\sim H$', is a simple logical point. The claim that one always has '$((H \& A) \supset O)$' rather than '$(H \supset O)$', however, is more substantial. In support of this claim, that auxiliary assumptions will always be involved, Duhem argues that such assumptions will be needed for the interpretation of reports of experimental results, which are to some degree theory-laden, as observational consequences, and, furthermore, that they will be needed to establish the reliability of instruments employed. Duhem thinks that this latter consideration applies primarily to physics, because he thinks of physics as peculiarly dependent upon the use of instruments; but he does consider the possibility that the auxiliary assumptions may be drawn from outside physics. And this suggests Duhem's defence of (2) might be extended from physics to the whole of the belief set, thus making the general version of (2) plausible. Given any hypothesis, H, and any observational consequence of that hypothesis, O, failure of O to obtain given the relevant initial conditions need not be taken to falsify H since there are likely to be at least these kinds of auxiliary assumptions: that any instruments employed are reliable; that the apparent failure of O is not merely hallucination; that the relevant initial conditions did in fact obtain; that any mathematical and/or logical principles employed in deriving O from H are valid . . . etc. There is, however, a difficulty with appeal to the last kind of auxiliary assumption in the present argument. If it is supposed that a certain class of beliefs, e.g. logical beliefs, is absolutely immune from revision, then the fact that these beliefs function as auxiliary assumptions will not establish the no-conclusive-falsification thesis. And I cannot assume here that logical beliefs are *not* immune from revision, for that they are not is precisely what I am hoping to use thesis (2) to establish. So at this stage my attempt to make thesis (2) plausible must rest upon the possibility of the other sources of auxiliary assumptions.

If thesis (2) is accepted another line of argument, due again to Duhem, is now available for thesis (1). That is, that no hypothesis can be conclusively verified by a 'crucial experiment' which falsifies its only rival; for, by (2), there can be no such unambiguously falsifying experiments.

I hope, then, that my radical conception of logic has been given some plausibility. The following diagram represents in outline the structure of the arguments offered in its favour.

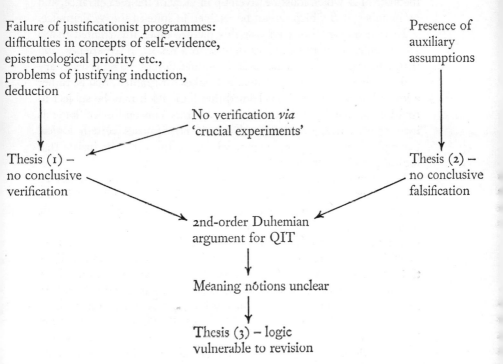

Failure of justificationist programmes: difficulties in concepts of self-evidence, epistemological priority etc., problems of justifying induction, deduction

Presence of auxiliary assumptions

No verification *via* 'crucial experiments'

Thesis (1) – no conclusive verification

Thesis (2) – no conclusive falsification

2nd-order Duhemian argument for QIT

Meaning notions unclear

Thesis (3) – logic vulnerable to revision

5. Objections to the pragmatist conception of logic

I have presented, above, at least an outline of arguments in favour of a radical conception of the status of logic. But before I am entitled to proceed on the basis of this conception I must look at certain objections which are rather commonly made to it. These objections are of two kinds: that the conception in question is *incoherent*: and that it is *methodologically vicious*.

Objection (i): *this view is incoherent*

The favoured epistemological picture is somewhat as follows. An individual or community S holds a set B of beliefs $\{b_1 \ldots b_m\}$: if S

is faced with a 'recalcitrant experience', i.e. an experience describable by a statement, b_n, the negation of which is implied by the set B, then some modification of this set is required. But there is no particular member of B which must be given up in view of the recalcitrance, and no member of B which cannot be retained in spite of the recalcitrance.

Now it may be objected that this picture takes for granted that a set of sentences may be inconsistent with a report of experience, and that, when such inconsistency arises, modification of the set is necessary and sufficient to restore consistency. It takes for granted, that is, rather a lot of logic. And yet it is claimed that logic itself may be subject to revision in the light of experience. So this conception of logic is incoherent, since, on the one hand, it presupposes certain logical principles for its very statement, while, on the other, it insists that logical principles are revisable.

It is true that, unless it is assumed that a contradiction cannot be true, the concept of *recalcitrance* cannot play its crucial role in the pragmatist picture. For if one were to contemplate employing a logic in which both, a contradiction was possible, and, in which from a contradiction anything could be derived, then one would no longer be entitled to the presumption that recalcitrance necessitates modification of the belief set. Now, this kind of Deviant system has not been seriously proposed as an alternative to classical logic, and it is easy to see why not; from a contradiction anything is derivable, so that such a logic would be useless for the purpose of discriminating valid from invalid inferences. Indeed, some writers have suggested that there is reason to deny that such a system should be counted as a 'logic' at all. (See Hacking [1971], and cf. Quine [1970], p. 81.)

But even if I avoid part of the difficulty by excluding contradictory systems from the domain of logic, my critic may persist in his objection. What determines *which* modifications in the belief set will restore consistency, he may argue, is the logical connections which hold between members of the set, so how could these connections be coherently supposed to be vulnerable to doubt? (This question is suggested, at least, by remarks of Bennett's in [1959].) The reply is, surely, that if no acceptable way can be found of modifying the set within the limits imposed by the classical logical relations holding between the members it may be necessary to consider adopting a new logic which is such that some of these relations no longer obtain. This is, for instance, exactly what Reichenbach suggests, in [1944], for quantum mechanics.

So the general reply to this objection should be as follows. Certainly some logic is taken for granted in the presentation of the pragmatist picture. But to suppose that this shows that picture to be incoherent is to forget, what is quite crucial, that we are, to use Neurath's figure, *rebuilding our raft while afloat on it.*

Objection (ii): this view is methodologically vicious

Popper argues as follows:

> If we want to use logic in a critical context, then we should use a very strong logic, the strongest logic, so to speak, which is at our disposal; for we want our criticism to be *severe* . . . Thus we should (in the empirical sciences) use the full or classical or two-valued logic.
>
> ([1970], p. 18.)

Popper's position seems to be like this: logic is a tool employed in the programme of attempted falsification. Since it is methodologically desirable that a test of an hypothesis should be as stringent as possible, the strongest possible logic should be used in deriving consequences from the hypothesis, so that its class of potential falsifiers may be as inclusive as possible. This viewpoint is particularly forcibly expressed when Popper discusses the proposal that logic be modified in order to avoid certain 'anomalies' allegedly arising in quantum physics; if there are anomalies, Popper argues, they show that there is something wrong with quantum theory, and modifying logic to avoid them is a dangerous evasion. Feyerabend [1958] shares this opinion.

Now, if Popper's point amounted only to the warning that change of logic is not to be frivolously undertaken – if there is room for modification elsewhere in the belief set, this possibility should be investigated before one tampers irresponsibly with logic – it would be quite proper; and also, quite consistent with my position. It is no part of my view that the principles of logic are, or ought to be, as vulnerable as any other beliefs to revision in the light of experience. Indeed, since logical principles are of extreme generality, so that modification of them will necessitate widespread further adjustments, the criteria of simplicity and economy tend to militate against logical adjustments when less far-reaching alternatives are available.

But Popper's thesis is stronger than this. He wants to rule out altogether the possibility of *ever* resorting to change of logic rather than of some other beliefs. Against him, I urge the following considerations. First, I question the assumption that use of the strongest possible logic necessarily constitutes the severest possible test. A criticism of a theory which needed to use only, say, Intuitionist logic, could be thought more severe than one which needed the full classical logic. And it seems doubtful whether Popper would accept, what seems to follow from his thesis, that in a critical context one ought to employ, say, a modal logic rather than the plain propositional calculus, yet the usual modal calculi contain, and so are stronger than, propositional logic. Second, while Popper continually stresses the importance of submitting our theories to the severest possible tests, his proposal would leave *logic* totally immune from criticism.

The reasons for Popper's criticism lie, however, deeper than my comments have so far revealed. They become apparent when one asks the following question: *why* does Popper think that revision of logic would be contrary to the progress of science? One could argue: if logic were revised in response to the anomalies of quantum theory, this would avoid the need for a development of a new microphysics, but, equally, if microphysics·were revised this would avoid the need for the development of a new logic. Why doesn't the latter impede scientific progress? But this misses an important point; that Popper would not count logic as part of science. This is why changing logic *must* impede scientific progress, if 'scientific' is understood as Popper understands it.

According to Popper's criterion of demarcation, a statement is scientific to the extent that it is falsifiable by basic statements. Now tautologies, like existential statements, according to [1959], §23, are inconsistent with *no* basic statements whatsoever, and so, are not scientific at all. But this means that Popper's argument against the revisibility of logic has the following form. Logic must not be revised, because to do so would be to impede the progress of science. It would impede the progress of science because it involves revising something (logic) which doesn't count as part of science, rather than something (e.g. physics) which does. But logic is excluded from science precisely on the grounds that it is not falsifiable (i.e. revisable) in the light of experience. The argument has come full circle. So I reject it.

6. A weakness in the pragmatist conception

The radical view of logic which I have been advocating has, I think, both initial plausibility in view of the existence of rival logics, and positive support from the epistemological considerations I have mentioned. The major objections which have been made to it, furthermore, fail.

But it has a weakness which ought not to be disguised. It is this: it is recommended that choice of logic be made on such grounds as simplicity and economy. But the criteria of simplicity and economy are, though intuitively plausible, far from adequately clear. And there is a further difficulty, in that it threatens to be hard to show *why* simplicity and economy are desirable.

The first of these difficulties carries a serious danger that the apparent radicalness of the pragmatist conception will be sacrificed once the criteria of choice have been specified. Quine succumbs to this danger. For he is disposed *either* to count familiarity as in itself a criterion, or, worse, to identify simplicity with conservatism. (See Quine [1970], ch. 6 and Quine and Ullian [1970], ch. 5.) The apparently radical recommendation to choose the simplest theory then lapses into the most stringent conservatism.

There is also the danger that classical logic will be given a privileged position, not directly on account of its entrenchment, but indirectly, on account of its intuitively greater simplicity than many-valued or non-truth-functional logics. It would not be easy to *prove* that a 2-valued logic is simpler than a 3-valued one; but it is not unplausible intuitively. This danger can however be avoided by pointing out that it involves what one might call, after a famous culprit, the Poincaré fallacy. Poincaré argued that, since Euclidean geometry is simpler than any of its rivals, then, although the choice of geometry is a matter of convention, Euclidean geometry will always be the best choice. (Poincaré [1952].) He was, notoriously, badly caught out by history. The mistake in his reasoning is this: that even if it be granted that Euclidean geometry is simpler than any other, it does not follow that the conjunction of Euclidean geometry and Newtonian physics with Lorentz modifications is simpler than the conjunction of non-Euclidean geometry and Einsteinian physics. Similarly, even if it were granted that classical logic is simpler than any of its rivals, it by no means follows that it must be the best choice when the simplicity of the overall belief set is considered.

Here another issue arises: maybe conservatism is not guaranteed by the criterion of simplicity, but is it not the inevitable consequence of another criterion, equally acceptable intuitively, that changes should not be more far-reaching than necessary – Quine's maxim of minimum mutilation? For changes of logic are bound to be *more general* than changes in any other theories. There is something in this: it explains why a change of logic is something of a last resort, to be undertaken only when other modifications fail. But it is not quite right; for *scale* of modification and *simplicity* of modification may compete, and, a large scale but simple change might prove preferable to a small scale but complex one.

So I by no means claim that the view I favour is without difficulties. I claim only that it seems to me the most acceptable of the alternatives available.

7. Reasons offered in favour of Deviant systems

The reasons which have been offered, why one or another of the Deviant systems should be adopted, are very various; but they are quite often of just the kind which the pragmatist view of logic suggests as appropriate. That is, it is claimed that the conjunction of certain accepted beliefs with classical logical principles yields unacceptable consequences, and that the simplest means of avoiding this recalcitrance is to modify the logical principles.

For example: Aristotle, and following him, Łukasiewicz, argue that if classical logic is allowed to govern future tense sentences, an unacceptable consequence, in the form of fatalism, follows; to avoid this consequence, they propose that logic be modified. Again, Reichenbach, and, following him, Putnam, argue that if classical logic is employed to draw consequences from current quantum mechanical theory, results inconsistent with the rest of physics follow; to avoid these consequences, they propose that logic be modified.

In another dispute, that concerning the most appropriate formalisation of sentences containing denotationless singular terms, a crucial issue is the comparative overall simplicity (on the one hand) and fruitfulness in yielding desired inferences (on the other) of the rival proposals.

This was very much what was to have been expected. However, not all proponents of rival systems share my view of logic; and those who do not, naturally enough, offer reasons of different kinds in favour of their systems.

The Intuitionists Brouwer and Heyting provide a striking example. They conceive of logic as a highly general description of the forms of inference which are truth-preserving, which is to be devised and tested by an *a posteriori* investigation of which forms of reasoning turn out universally successful. They take mathematical thought to be primary, and thus think of logic as – so to speak – an inductively constructed description of the successful forms of inference. They then support their proposal to modify classical logic by arguing that this system does not embody only successful principles; it includes some, e.g. the 'principle of excluded third', which sometimes fail.

I shall, naturally, look with most favour upon those reasons for Deviance which are of the kinds which my conception of logic suggests are appropriate. However, even where the reasons offered are of the appropriate kind, it does not follow that they are *good* reasons. And even where the reasons offered are of a kind which I consider inappropriate, because based upon a conception of logic which I reject, it does not follow that there *are no* good reasons in favour of the system in question. The reasons offered must be looked at in detail.

Criteria for assessing the reasons offered

An appropriate argument for a change of logic, then, will presumably take the form of an appeal to the unacceptable consequences of the conjunction of classical logic with other well-entrenched beliefs, and to the advantages, in terms of simplicity and economy, of modification of the logical rather than some other beliefs. So when I come to examine in detail the arguments for Deviant logics, I shall have to ask:

(1) whether the alleged consequences really follow;
(2) whether these consequences are really unacceptable;
(3) whether there is no less radical modification than revision of logic sufficient to avoid them;

and

(4) whether the particular Deviant system proposed is such as to avoid the unwanted consequences, and if not, what kind of system would be. (Even if affirmative answers to (1)–(3) were established, this would show at most that there is a need for *some* change of

logic; the question, exactly *what* change of logic is the appropriate one, then needs to be investigated separately.)

Interestingly enough, objections have been made to arguments for Deviant systems on *all* these points; in the dispute about quantum mechanics, for instance, where Reichenbach had argued in [1944] that unacceptable consequences followed from the conjunction of classical logic and quantum physics, and that the best way to avoid these anomalies was to use a 3-valued logic, this position has been attacked on the grounds that the anomalies don't really follow; that although they *do* follow, they aren't really unacceptable; that although they *do* follow and they *are* unacceptable, there are better ways than a change of logic to avoid them; and that although they do follow and they *are* unacceptable and we *do* therefore need a change of logic, the change Reichenbach proposes is not the right one.

8. Global or local reform?

I have argued that there *could* be good reasons for a change of logic, and offered criteria for assessing the kind of reason which might be given. So far, however, I have avoided a number of rather difficult questions; questions which I can no longer avoid once the existence is recognised of a considerable variety of arguments for change of logic, some favouring one and some another Deviant system. Among the most serious of the questions raised by this variety are the following:

(1) Is it possible that there should be more than one good argument, each appealing to unacceptable consequences of classical logic in a different area of discourse, and each favouring adoption of the same Deviant system?

(2) Is it possible that there should be more than one good argument, each appealing to unacceptable consequences of classical logic in a different area of discourse, and each favouring adoption of a different Deviant system?

(3) Is it possible that we should have good reason to use a Deviant logic in one area of discourse, while continuing to use classical logic in other areas?

The first of these questions is the easiest to answer. Suppose there are two arguments, A_1 and A_2, from different domains of discourse, both favouring adoption of a Deviant logic L_{D_1}. A_1, perhaps, appeals to difficulties arising if classical logic is applied to future-tense sentences: and A_2 to difficulties arising if it is applied to quantum-mechanical sentences. In such circumstances, if both arguments are good ones, there would simply be an especially strong case in favour of L_{D_1}. For if classical logic gives unacceptable consequences not just in one but in two areas of discourse, and if furthermore the same adjustment will cope with both kinds of difficulty, then that adjustment has obvious advantages in terms of economy and simplicity. Something like this situation arises when van Fraassen proposes his 'presuppositional' logic to deal both with future contingents and with denotationless terms ([1966]), and Lambert suggests ([1969]) that the same modification might also be appropriate to deal with difficulties in quantum theory.

However, this is not a situation which often arises. It is more usual for one Deviant system to be proposed as the solution of one kind of difficulty (e.g. Łukasiewicz's 3-valued logic to avoid fatalism) and another as the solution of another kind (e.g. Reichenbach's 3-valued logic to avoid 'causal anomalies' in physics). This brings me to my second question.

The second and third questions are rather closely connected, since the following consideration bears on them both. Since I characterised systems as *rivals* of each other if they are incompatible, I can presumably conclude that if two Deviant systems L_{D_1} and L_{D_2} are rivals of each other, or if a Deviant system L_{D_1} is a rival of classical logic, it is not possible that there should be good reason to use L_{D_1} *and* good reason to use L_{D_2}, or good reason to use L_{D_1} *and* good reason to use classical logic. That is: one couldn't have good reasons for adopting both of two incompatible theories. Perhaps I should emphasise that by 'adopting' a theory I mean something like accepting it, at least provisionally, as true. It would clearly be improper to accept, as true, even provisionally, two incompatible theories. But it would nevertheless be possible, and indeed, might be desirable, for several rival theories to be developed, even though it was certain that only one of them could be acceptable. I agree with Feyerabend that lack of adequately developed alternatives is liable to hinder progress.

The situation would however be quite different if the systems concerned were not rivals but supplements of each other. In this case there would be no impossibility about the use of the more extensive system in one area and the less extensive system elsewhere. For it could be the case, since an extended system contains new vocabulary over and above classical logic, that the extra expressive power was required in one area of discourse to yield desired inferences, but unnecessary elsewhere. In such a case, local reform might be appropriate. For example: (classical) predicate logic is an extension of (classical) propositional logic; there is no incompatibility between them, so that there would be nothing improper about using sometimes the one and sometimes the other system; and furthermore there is no point in using predicate logic to formalise arguments which are in any case valid in virtue of their propositional structure. The situation is rather similar in the case of modal versus non-modal propositional logics – since the modal systems contain propositional calculus there is nothing improper in using a modal calculus only when its extra power is needed, and otherwise a non-modal system. (But naturally when it comes to deciding between alternative modal systems, at least if one thinks that they are rivals of each other, one can no longer be so tolerant. Interestingly, however, it has been suggested by Lemmon, in [1959], that considerations of meaning show that the various modal systems are not genuinely rivals of each other.)

These arguments suggest the following rather clear-cut answer. If the two systems between which one has to choose are rivals, then one must reform globally if at all; whereas if one of the systems is a supplement of the other, one may reform locally if this is convenient. Except in so far as considerations of meaning suggest otherwise, Deviant systems may be expected to be rivals, and extended systems supplements, of classical logic, so that adoption of a Deviant system may be expected to be global, while adoption of an extended system could be local. So one would expect this kind of set up:

extended systems – supplements to classical logic
          – local reform permissible
Deviant systems – rivals to classical logic
          – global reform required

However, as I observed in ch. 1, there are local as well as global reformers among the proponents of Deviant logics. Putnam, for instance, seems not unwilling to envisage that classical logic be reformed only in its application to microphysics. This suggests the possibility that a Deviant system should be thought of as a rival to classical logic in the sense that its use *in any particular area of discourse* is incompatible with the use of classical logic *in that area*, without there being any incoherence in supposing that classical logic was the appropriate system for one area, and the Deviant system for another. There is, after all, nothing incoherent in the supposition that two, say, physical theories, which would be incompatible if they were applied to the same phenomena, may not both be used, each for a different domain of application.

Against this suggestion, the following consideration might be urged. The principles of logic are characterised by an extreme generality – what makes them *logical* principles, as opposed to e.g. high-level *physical* principles, is precisely their neutrality as regards subject-matter. (Ryle, in [1954], proposes 'topic-neutrality' as a criterion for picking out the logical constants.) If this is right, there is certainly something odd about supposing that one set of logical principles might apply to one subject matter, and a rival set to another. For *logical* principles would be precisely those which apply to *any* subject matter.

This argument is not without merits. It does, however, have one drawback; it relies rather heavily on the possibility of distinguishing the *form* from the *content* of an argument. But this distinction is one which proves difficult to draw precisely. Most seriously, the question, what the (or, better, the most appropriate) logical form of an argument is, is not to be settled independently of the question, whether the argument is judged to be valid. For the clearest sense which can be given to the notion 'logical form of an argument' is 'correct translation of the argument into a formal language' – and clearly one would not count as correct a translation of what one judged to be a valid argument into an invalid form, or vice versa.

There is a different version of the 'limited applicability' view which is also of some interest. This is the view that one logical system may be applicable to sentences of certain forms, and another to sentences of certain other forms. For example, it has been suggested that whereas classical logic applies to sentences from which tense indicators are absent, a different system may be appropriate to the formalisation of tensed sentences. The special interest of this kind of suggestion is this: that when one system L_1 applies to sentences of one form, and a rival system L_2 to sentences of another form, there seems little reason to take L_1 and L_2 to be rivals. Suppose for instance that L_1 has and L_2 lacks the theorem '$p \vee \sim p$'; if the sentence letters of L_1 stand for tenseless sentences, whereas those of L_2 stand for tensed sentences, there seems to be no incompatibility between them.

Thus, when two allegedly rival logical systems are said one to apply in one domain and the other in another, if the grounds for distinguishing the domains refers to content, one will be disposed to say that the systems are not really logical, and if the ground for distinguishing the domain refers to form, one will be disposed to say that the systems are not really rival. In spite, then, of reservations about the form/content distinction, I conclude that adoption of a rival logic, if justified at all, should normally be global.

The qualifications made earlier about 'adoption' of course apply here too. It could be thought for instance that although quantum mechanical considerations show that a non-classical logic should be adopted, nevertheless the inadequacy of classical logic for most purposes is negligible; and I have no objection to the use of a not strictly correct system within the range for which it *is* all right. Similarly, there is no objection to using Euclidean geometry for, e.g. surveying purposes. This concession may, I hope, be sufficient to appease the 'local' reformers.

3

Deviance and the theory of truth

I begin by investigating some alternative reactions to the kind of difficulty which, as I argued in the last chapter, is likely to motivate adoption of a non-standard logic. Having distinguished and discussed these alternative reactions, I proceed to investigate some of their consequences for the theory of truth. These consequences bear on the right of non-standard systems to be called 'logics', just as my conclusions concerning the degree of change of meaning involved in the move to Deviant logics bore on the right of non-standard systems to be called 'rivals'.

1. The third truth-value, and some alternatives

Although the reasons offered for the adoption of non-standard logics are very various, they frequently take – as in view of the arguments of ch. 2 one would expect – the form of an appeal to the unacceptable consequences of assigning either 'true' or 'false' to sentences of certain sorts, e.g. future-tense sentences or quantum-mechanical sentences. Now, one possible reaction to such a difficulty is to conclude that, since the sentences concerned can't have one of the *ordinary* truth-values, they must have some *extraordinary* truth-value. But this is – though perhaps the most obvious – not the only possible reaction. There are at least these four possibilities:

(1) Despite appearances, the items in question are not of the kind with which logic is, or should be, concerned. (The 'no-item' thesis.)

(2) The items in question, though within the scope of logic, do not really have the form they appear to have. (The 'misleading form' thesis.)

(3) The items in question, though within the scope of logic, are neither true nor false, but truth-valueless. (The 'truth-value gap' thesis.)

(4) The items in question, though within the scope of logic, are neither true nor false, but have some other truth-value(s). (The 'new truth-value' thesis.)

Some examples:

(a) Future-contingent sentences: the Kneales [1962], among others, favour the first alternative, Prior, at least in [1957], the second, Aristotle [DI] and van Fraassen [1968] the third, and Łukasiewicz [1930] the fourth.

(b) Sentences containing non-denoting singular terms: an argument in favour of the first alternative is to be found in Strawson [1950], though he also, especially in [1964], uses an argument which favours the third alternative, which is the conclusion also of an argument given by Frege [1892] and the position which van Fraassen [1969] intends his formal work to embody; the second alternative is favoured by Russell [1905], and the third by Keenan [1971].

The alternatives are arranged in order of *increasing radicalness*. Adoption of (1) can be thought of as a means of avoiding the need for the adoption of a non-standard system, by banning the offending items from logic altogether. Adoption of (2) also avoids the need for a Deviant logic, this time by presenting the offending items in a new and inoffensive form, in which standard logical apparatus can be applied to them. (3) and (4) are more radical, however, since both apparently require modification of the classical theory of truth. But (3) apparently calls for the less radical modification since it does not, like (4) require the admission of (a) non-classical truth-value(s).

I examine these alternatives in turn.

(i) *The no-item thesis*

The form which this thesis usually takes is as follows: the item in question is not of a certain kind, e.g. does not make a statement, or, does not express a proposition; but only items of that kind are within the scope of logic; so the item in question is outside the scope of logic. Thus, that it should prove recalcitrant to the application of the usual logical principles is no cause for surprise, and, furthermore, gives rise to no need for revision of those principles.

Consider, for example, the following argument, something very like which, at least, is to be found in 'On Referring' (Strawson [1950]).

It is sentences which have meaning, but statements (uses of sentences) which have truth-values and between which logical relations hold. A sentence whose subject term fails to denote is meaningful; but, because the utterance of such a sentence necessarily involves failure to refer, such an utterance cannot be a genuine, but only a 'spurious' use of the sentence, and hence does not constitute a statement. So uses of sentences with non-denoting subject terms are not statements, and are, therefore, not within the scope of logic at all, and, *a fortiori*, not counter-examples to classical logical principles. Other, not wholly dissimilar, arguments for the 'no-item' thesis are to be found in Jeffrey [1967] (*à propos* of vague sentences) and in Cohen and Nagel [1934], especially pp. 183–5.

An interesting variant on this strategy is employed by Lewy in [1946]. Lewy argues that certain sentences which have been thought by some to constitute counter-examples to classical logic, namely, sentences which are too vague to be assigned a classical truth-value, are not in fact counter-examples, because they do not express propositions, and it is with propositions only that logic concerns itself. But it turns out that what Lewy means by 'proposition' is, precisely, 'item of which classical logic is true'. And because of this his argument has no force against the proponent of a non-standard logic, who could simply retort that he sees no reason for restricting logic to 'propositions' in Lewy's sense of the word. Lewy is, indeed, quite candid about this:

if we are to continue to mean by 'proposition' what we now mean by the word, we cannot suppose that in certain circumstances an inference made in accordance with [the principle of double negation] may be invalid. But there is no reason why *we should not change our concept of proposition*. And one of the ways of doing so is to construct a logical calculus in which the principle [of double negation] does not hold. Such a logic cannot be said to be inconsistent with ours: for it is not a logic of propositions in *our* sense of 'proposition'.

([1946], p. 38.)

The introduction into a dispute about change of logic of the no-item thesis has a tendency to trivialise the dispute, even when the argument given for the no-item thesis is not as candidly trivial as Lewy's.

This is because there are at least two versions of the argument; a version which, like Lewy's, is hardly deniable, but also powerless to counter proposals for a change of logic, and another version which appears to be more substantial, but which, if so interpreted, turns out also to have a conclusion which is not really conservative after all. It is because these two versions of the argument are not distinguished that it may look as if there is a substantial argument for a no-item thesis which will avoid the need for any change of logic. And I shall argue that there is a temptation to confuse the two arguments, on account of unclarities in the notions of 'statement' and 'proposition'.

Arguments for the no-item thesis have, in outline, the following form:

(1) Logic only applies to items of a certain kind (statements, propositions).

(2) The recalcitrant sentences, those the assignment of 'true' or 'false' to which is thought to give rise to difficulty, do not make statements, or, do not express propositions.

∴ (3) The recalcitrant sentences are not items of the kind to which logic applies, and so are not counter-examples to logical principles.

This kind of argument is susceptible of two interpretations, according as one understands by (1):

(1a) *Classical* logic *is only true of* items of a certain kind (statements, propositions);

(1b) *Logical principles* (classical or otherwise) only apply to items of a certain kind (statements, propositions), that is, only items of that kind are 'potential falsifiers' of logic, items of which it *should be true.*

It seems clear, on reflection, that no version of the argument which uses (1a) can carry any weight in the context of discussion of proposals for a change of logic. For someone who argues that certain sentences, because the assignment to them either of 'true' or of 'false' gives rise to anomalies, constitute 'counter-examples' to classical logic, so far from asserting that the sentences in question *are* 'of the kind to which logic applies', in the sense of 'of the kind of which classical logic is true', is, precisely, denying this. His problem arises because, as he thinks, the recalcitrant sentences are in the scope of logic, in the sense of 'of the kind of which logic should be true', but that as it turns out classical logical principles are *false* of them. In other words: someone who thinks he has a 'counter-example' to classical logic, thinks he has an item which is of a kind to which logical principles should apply, but of which classical logical principles are apparently false. And such a person will not be moved by the reply that his 'counter-example' is an item of which classical logic is false – *that* is just what *he* said. He will be impressed only if it can be shown that his 'counter-example' is not an item to which logical principles ought to apply, is an item to which logical principles are somehow irrelevant.

If the argument is to carry weight against a proponent of a Deviant logic, then, it should proceed rather via (1b). It looks as if it is this version of the argument which Strawson favours. For Strawson argues in *Introduction to Logical Theory* ([1952], specially pp. 3–4) that it is between statements, rather than sentences, that logical relations hold, and this apparently on the grounds that it is statements, rather than sentences, which are the truth-bearers. His argument, though it is not fully explicit, would presumably be: the predicates 'true' and 'false' are only applicable to statements, not sentences, and logic is concerned with relations such as consequence and inconsistency which can hold only between truth-bearing items, so it is between statements, not sentences, that logical relations hold.

It can, I believe, be shown that the arguments, used by Strawson and others, why it is improper to call sentences 'true' or 'false', and why it is therefore necessary to introduce statements or propositions as truth-bearers, are wholly inadequate. (See e.g. Haack R. J. and S. [1970] or Gochet [1972] for substantiation of this claim.) But I shall try to show that the no-item argument which Strawson bases on this thesis about the truth-bearers would be unsuccessful even if his views about truth-bearers were acceptable.

Consider the principle, which underlies the Strawsonian version of the no-item argument, that only truth-bearing items are within the scope of logic. It is surely plain that if this means that only items which actually have a truth-value, 'true' or 'false', are within the scope of logic, it assumes too much. For to suppose that logical principles are relevant only to true or false items, is to guarantee, in advance, a privileged position for classical logic, which is true of all and only such items.

If, on the other hand, what is assumed is that only items which, whether or not they actually *are* true or false, at least *could be* true or false, are within the scope of logic, Deviant logics are not after all ruled out. (One objection which could be made to this principle, but which I shall not follow up here, is that it would exclude imperative, and possibly deontic, 'logic', as not really logical at all. This is rather a hard consequence. But my major objection bears rather more closely on the present issue.) The proponent of a non-standard logic – a logic, say, admitting truth-value gaps, or admitting intermediate truth-values, could *agree* that logical relations hold only between items capable of bearing a truth-value, *but*: whether or not they actually have one, or, whether the value taken is classical or non-classical.

The importance of this point emerges when we notice that Strawson is unable to confine himself comfortably to the no-item thesis, but also, and inconsistently, argues for the truth-value gap thesis. For Strawson (rather obscurely in [1950] but more patently in [1952] and [1964]) is attracted to the view that sentences containing non-denoting subject terms stand in the relation of *presupposing* to the corresponding existential statements. And he insists, in [1952] and [1954], that presupposing is a logical, not a pragmatic, relation. But if he is to maintain this position Strawson must allow that some statements lack truth-value, and that logical relations can hold between these truth-valueless items, or between them and truth-valued items. Such logical relations cannot be those canonised by classical logic, and so some non-standard logic must be allowed.

To put the matter another way: in the form, that logic ought to apply only to items which actually are either true or false, (1b) only questionbeggingly rules out Deviant logics; and in the form that logic ought to apply only to items which could be, though they may not in fact be, true or false, (1b) doesn't rule out Deviant logics at all. Very often, indeed, the interest of the kind of recalcitrant sentence with which the deviant logician is concerned is precisely that it seems, on the one hand, to resist assignment of a classical truth-value, but, on the other, to stand in logical relations to other sentences.

I have argued for the trivialising tendency of no-item arguments, without needing to specify the definition of 'statement' or 'proposition' (or whatever privileged item is chosen) which may be employed. That is to say, my arguments against this kind of view in no way depend upon the adoption of any particular definition of 'statement' or 'proposition'. But it is not hard to see that the variety of accounts of 'statement' and 'proposition' current in the literature contributes to the false allure of no-item arguments. On the one hand, 'statement' or 'proposition' may be defined (as by Lewy) as 'item of which classical logic is true', in which case (1a) is forthcoming immediately, but the question, whether interesting, although non-classical, logical relations hold between sentences which do not, in this sense, make statements or express propositions, is left untouched. On the other hand, 'statement' or 'proposition' may be independently defined, as 'genuine use of meaningful declarative sentence' or as 'meaning of declarative sentence', in which case neither (1a) nor (1b) is automatically forthcoming.

The danger of triviality is splendidly illustrated by the following dialogue:

Mr. Rossette: It is raining.

Mr. Turquer: You mean it is raining in Ithaca, New York, at 2 p.m. July 14th, 1950, for you do not know whether or not it is now raining at El Paso, Texas.

Mr. Rossette: Would you agree, then, that my statement is neither true nor false?

Mr. Turquer: No, that is not my opinion, since every statement is either true or false. Hence, our only conclusion is that what you called a 'statement' is not really a 'statement' at all . . .

Mr. Rossette: But is this not a bit arbitrary? It seems to me that you assume that every statement is either true or false and then distinguish between statements and statement forms to avoid being refuted . . .

(Rosser and Turquette [1952] p. 3.)

(ii) *The misleading-form thesis*

The form which this thesis usually takes is as follows: if the 'grammatical' form of the recalcitrant sentence is taken as indicative of its 'logical' form then, indeed, assignment either of 'true' or 'false' to it gives rise to difficulty. Once, however, it is recognised that the grammatical form of the sentence is misleading as to its logical form, the difficulty vanishes; either because the assignment of a classical truth-value now appears satisfactory after all, or because an explanation of the difficulty of assigning a classical truth-value is now forthcoming.

Consider, for example, the following argument, used by Russell in [1905]. The sentence 'The King of France is bald' is *grammatically* of the subject–predicate form. But if it is construed as *logically* of the subject–predicate form, a difficulty arises, since 'The King of France', which denotes nothing, cannot be a logical subject. Russell's solution is to construe the sentence as of existential form, that is, not as

(i) Fa

('F' a predicate, and 'a' a logical subject) but as

(ii) $(\exists x)\,(Gx\ \&\ (y)\,(Gy \equiv x = y)\ \&\ Fx)$

And the puzzle about what truth-value to assign to the sentence is now solved, since the existential sentence, having a false conjunct, is false. Furthermore, the problems concerning the truth-value to be assigned to the denial of the sentence ('The King of France is not bald') can now be solved by pointing out that the denial is ambiguous, between:

(iii) $\sim (\exists x) (Gx \,\&\, (y) (Gy \equiv x = y) \,\&\, Fx)$

and

(iv) $(\exists x) (Gx \,\&\, (y) (Gy \equiv x = y) \,\&\, \sim Fx)$

of which (iii) which is the contradictory of (ii), is true, and (iv), which is only the contrary of (ii), is false.

A similar argument is used by Prior, in [1957], to solve the difficulties which, according at least to Aristotle and Łukasiewicz, arise from the assignment of 'true' or 'false' to future-contingent sentences. Prior writes 'p' for present-tensed sentences, 'F' for 'it will be the case that', so that 'There will be a sea-battle tomorrow' would be written:

(v) Fp

He then argues that such a sentence as 'There will not be a sea-battle tomorrow' is ambiguous, between

(vi) $\sim Fp$

and

(vii) $F \sim p$

He then proposes to solve the problem of future contingents by arguing that *both* (v) and (vii) are false. Whether this really solves the problem about future-contingents is very doubtful. But my present concern is simply to note the use of the 'misleading-form' strategy.

Sometimes this strategy is used, not to justify the assignment of a classical truth-value, but to explain why the sentence should resist such assignment. For instance, in [1906] Russell proposes that tensed sentences (which are, of course, grammatically complete) be construed as, not propositions, i.e. closed sentences, but propositional functions, i.e. open sentences, with a free variable for time. 'Mrs Brown is [present tense] at home' is thus to be construed as 'Mrs Brown *is* [tenseless] at home at t'. The point of this manoeuvre is that, whereas a closed sentence which lacks truth-value is an anomaly, an open sentence is not expected to be true or false. So an explanation of any recalcitrance of tensed sentences to the assignment of classical truth-values is forthcoming. The context of this proposal of Russell's is a suggestion of MacColl's, that certain sentences are neither true nor false but 'variable'. The effect of Russell's proposal is to replace the suggestion that tensed sentences have a non-classical truth-value, 'variable', by the less radical thesis, that tensed sentences are open sentences whose classical truth-value varies according to the time argument substituted. This suggestion of Russell's has, indeed, certain affinities with the no-item strategy, since it represents a recalcitrant item as not of the kind to which, in classical logic, a truth-value is assigned; not, however, as an item altogether outside the scope of logic.

One can see the value of this strategy without having to suppose – as Russell's way of putting these arguments might suggest – that a sentence has a unique 'logical form' which may or may not be mirrored in its grammatical form. If one thinks instead of (a) logical form of a sentence as (a) correct translation of that sentence into a formal language, the misleading-form strategy can be represented as follows: certain sentences resist the assignment of classical truth-values if they are translated into formal language in a way which closely parallels their grammatical structure; but this recalcitrance can either be avoided, or at least be explained, by an alternative translation.

The conservatism promised by this strategy – unlike that offered by no-item arguments – may be genuine. If the recalcitrant items can be given an acceptable new translation, they can be accommodated within classical logic. This accommodation may, of course, not be achieved without cost; the cost, for instance, of a translation which may be thought unnatural. (Strawson, for instance, finds Russell's translation of non-denoting sentences discordant with his intuitions about 'ordinary language'.) And the possible gain in simplicity achieved by the retention of classical logic will, of course, have to be balanced against a possible loss of simplicity in translation into the formal language.

(iii) and (iv) *Truth-value gaps and new truth-values*

It seems, on the face of it, that the view that there are truth-value gaps (3) is quite distinct from the view (4) that there is(are) intermediate truth-value(s). So it is quite surprising to find that some writers deliberately assimilate the two views. For example, Goddard [1966] and Halldén [1949] both employ '3-valued logics' in which the '3rd truth-value' is defined as 'neither true nor false'. (They also go on to identify this value with meaninglessness. But the propriety of this identification is a separate question, into which I cannot enter here.) So these writers seem to think that to say that there are some sentences which are neither true nor false is just the same as to say that there are some sentences which have the truth-value 'neither-true-nor-false'. McCall remarks, pertinently, that one is not tempted to suppose that 'either-true-or-false' is an extra truth-value over and above 'true' and 'false' ([1970]).

The arguments for thesis (3) look rather different from those for (4). Consider, for instance, Frege's argument [1892] about sentences containing non-denoting terms. According to Frege's theory of sense and reference, the reference of a compound expression depends upon the references of its parts; in particular, the truth-value of a sentence (which is its reference) depends upon the references of the component expressions of the sentence. So, if one of the components lacks reference, so, too, will the sentence itself. And so a sentence like 'The King of France is wise' must be truth-valueless. Frege's argument leads directly to the conclusion that non-denoting sentences have *no* truth-value.

The Intuitionists' arguments why certain mathematical sentences are neither true nor false also seem to support a truth-value gap thesis, not so directly, but because they would be equally good as arguments against the assignment of an intermediate truth-value. Thus, Heyting in [1966] considers the number, L, defined as follows:

L is the greatest prime such that $L - 2$ is also prime,
or $L = 1$ if no such number exists.

Though it has been neither proved nor disproved that there are infinitely many twin primes, the classical mathematician would nevertheless maintain that '$L = 1$' *is* either true or false. The Intuitionist, however, denies this: he thinks that to suppose that '$L = 1$' *has* a truth-value, though one can't tell *which*, requires appeal to unacceptable metaphysics. And presumably an Intuitionist would, or should, find the claim that '$L = 1$' has some non-classical truth-value as unintelligible as the claim that it is true or the claim that it is false.

By contrast, those who are impressed by such locutions as 'half true', 'partly true', 'approximately true' (e.g. Austin in [1950]) or by the apparent analogy between truth and high probability (e.g. Reichenbach in [1935]) are liable to favour thesis (4) rather than thesis (3); for this kind of consideration suggests that there are degrees of truth, a kind of continuum of intermediate truth-values between the limit cases, 'true' and 'false'.

Some formal considerations. I suggested above that whereas theses (1) and (2) would apparently allow accommodation of recalcitrant items without change of logic, adoption either of (3) or (4) would require some modification of classical calculi. An interesting – and curiously difficult – question which now arises is: given that an advocate either of (3) or of (4) would need a non-bivalent logic, in what way might, or should, the system adopted by an advocate of (3) differ from that favoured by an advocate of (4)? What, that is, might be the formal mark of the distinction between truth-value gaps and intermediate truth-values?

It might well be thought that the clue to the relevant formal distinction is to be found in consideration of the semantics of the rival systems. That is to say: alternative systems (differentiated in terms of their theorem sets) are satisfied by different interpretations – $Ł_3$, for instance, has a 3-valued characteristic matrix, Intuitionist logic an infinite-valued one. And is it not natural to suppose that the thesis, that there is a third truth-value, is appropriately represented by a formal system with a 3-valued characteristic matrix?

This suggestion needs to be made more precise. To say that a matrix M is characteristic for a system S, is to say that all and only the theorems of S take, uniformly, a designated value in M. So a system S, may have more than one characteristic matrix; classical, 'two-valued' logic, for instance, has the 3-valued characteristic matrix:

$\sim$	A		A	v	B	(usual definitions
						of '$\supset$', '&')
			t	i	f	
f	t^*	t	t	t	t	
f	i	i	t	t	t	
t	f	f	t	t	f	

So I shall call a system '*n*-valued' if the *n* is the smallest number of truth-values which any characteristic matrix for that system has. It is in this sense that classical logic is '2-valued'. I call a system many-valued if it is *n*-valued for $n \neq 2$ and $n \neq \infty$.

This enables me to reformulate the suggestion I was considering: a system appropriate to the thesis that there are $n - 2$ intermediate truth-value(s) should be, in the sense defined, *n*-valued. Thus, to formalise the view that there is *one* intermediate truth-value, one would expect to need a 3-valued logic.

But this suggestion is still inadequate. For it fails to answer two crucial questions: (i) if a 3-valued system is appropriate to the third truth-value thesis, what kind of system is appropriate to the truth-value gap thesis? and (ii) does the use of a 3-valued system necessarily commit one to the third truth-value thesis? I take these questions in turn.

(a) *What kind of system is appropriate to the truth-value gap thesis?* One answer to the first question is given by van Fraassen in [1966], [1968], and [1969] and, more explicitly, by Lambert in [1969]. They suggest that whereas thesis (4) would lead to a many-valued logical system, (3) allows one to retain the classical set of logical truths, via adoption of a non-truth-functional semantics. Van Fraassen proposes a semantics the principle of which is as follows: a *supervaluation* assigns to a compound sentence some component(s) of which lack truth-value, that value which all classical valuations would assign it, if there is a unique such value, and otherwise no value. These semantics are not truth-functional, since when in each case both disjuncts lack truth-value, they would assign 'true' to '$p \vee \sim p$' but no truth-value to '$p \vee q$'. The treatment in terms of supervaluations is, as van Fraassen points out in [1970], formally equivalent to treatment in terms of an infinite matrix. The resulting set of designated formulae is the usual, classical one.

The formal ingenuity of this treatment is evident. But I have some difficulty with the suggestion that whereas truth-functional, many-valued systems are appropriate to represent thesis (4), a non-truth-functional semantics like van Fraassen's is appropriate to thesis (3). For the attractiveness of van Fraassen's system seems to depend upon the plausibility of the principle that a *wff should be assigned a value,* '*v*', *if it would be assigned that value by a classical valuation whether its components were true or false.* This principle is indeed plausible if it is supposed that the wff in question must *be* either true or false, though, perhaps, one doesn't, or can't, know which. But if it is supposed that some wffs have *no* truth-value, why should the fact that certain compounds of such wffs would have a given truth-value whichever truth-value the components had, be any reason for giving the compounds that value anyway? The principle upon which van Fraassen's semantics rests, so far from being specially appropriate to the accommodation of items which lack truth-value altogether, is plausible precisely on the assumption that the items in question have truth-values, though perhaps unknown truth-values.

There is, indeed, one position to the representation of which van Fraassen's semantics are particularly appropriate, viz., the Aristotelian position on future contingents. According to Aristotle, future-contingent sentences, though they are now neither true nor false, will eventually turn out true or false, so that one can assign 'true' now to 'Either there will be a sea-battle tomorrow or there will not be a sea-battle tomorrow' since one or the other disjunct will turn out true, and, whichever does, the whole disjunction is true. This Aristotelian theory is indeed a truth-value gap theory, but of a special kind, since what is claimed is that the sentences in question do not have a truth-value *yet*. And even here the fit of van Fraassen's system is not quite perfect; for 'There will be a sea-battle tomorrow' might – if Aristotle is right – never get to have a truth-value, for if the matter is not causally fixed until, say, 10 a.m. tomorrow, it is 'There will be a sea-battle today' and not 'There will be a sea-battle tomorrow' which becomes true or false. (cf. ch. 4.)

An argument which might be offered here – though neither van Fraassen nor Lambert gives it – is this: that if some component of a compound wff lacks truth-value, the truth-value of the whole compound cannot, *a fortiori*, depend on the truth-values of the components, and so, the compound cannot be a truth-function of its components. And thus a truth-value gap theory calls for non-truth-functional, and a third truth-value theory for a truth-functional, semantics. But this argument is not very conclusive. For it could be the case that the truth-value of a compound depended solely on (a) whether its components had truth-values, and (b) if they had truth-values, *which* truth-value they had. In an extended, but not unnatural, sense, such a compound would be truth-functional.

If, then, it is not clear that a system suitable to thesis (4) should be truth-functional, but a system suitable to thesis (3) non-truth-functional, perhaps it is possible to discriminate somehow within truth-functional systems. An elementary consideration to take into account is this. The kinds of argument (from partial truth, approximate truth etc.) which support thesis (4) might favour the introduction of any number, finite or perhaps even infinite, of intermediate truth-values. But if thesis (3), the truth-value gap thesis, is to be represented by a many-valued system, any appropriate system would presumably have to be 3-valued – since thesis (3) apparently only allows three possibilities, 'true', 'false' and 'truth-valueless'. Thus what I have to ask is whether any particular 3-valued system is specially appropriate to truth-value gaps rather than a third truth-value.

Kleene claims ([1952] §16) that his matrices are especially appropriate to his purpose (which is, to provide a logic suitable for handling undecidable mathematical statements) because they embody the assumption that the third truth-value has a status different from that of 'true' and 'false', that it is, as he puts it, 'not independent' of them. Might his matrices not, therefore, be appropriate to thesis (3), since, as I commented earlier, *lack* of truth-value is not a truth-value of equal status with 'true' and 'false'? In what way, then, is the status of Kleene's 'third truth-value' different? Apparently in this: that information that a wff has value u is merely lack of information either that it is true or that it is false. And how is this difference reflected in his matrices? They differ from Łukasiewicz's only in setting $|u \to u| = u$ rather than $|u \to u| = t$. The justification Kleene offers for adopting these matrices is that a function, F, of sentences A, B, should be decidable if its arguments are. Thus, Kleene argues that $|A \lor B|$ for $|A| = t$, $|B| = u$, should be t, for, since $|A| = t$, '$A \lor B$' would be true whether B were true or false. So the principle underlying this argument is, that if $F(A, B \ldots)$ would be t (f) whether A, $B \ldots$ were true or false, then it is to be t (f) if A, $B \ldots$ are u. But then, by an extension of the same argument, $|A \lor \sim A|$ for $|A| = |\sim A| = u$, should be t, since '$A \lor \sim A$' would be true whether A were true or false. However, this argument would not justify the assignment of 'true' to '$A \lor B$' for $|A| = |B| = u$; so that it would yield, not Kleene's matrices, but a non-truth-functional semantics. The principle Kleene is using is, in fact, precisely the one which justifies van Fraassen's semantics. So, in the first place, this principle doesn't justify Kleene's matrices; and, second, this principle is not appropriate, as I have already argued, to the truth-value gap thesis.

Frege's argument for thesis (3) suggests a different answer to our question, whether any particular kind of 3-valued matrix is especially suitable to thesis (3). Frege's principle is that the reference of a compound expression (and thus, the truth-value of a sentence) depends upon the reference of its parts. This suggests (though it does not entail) that matrices appropriate to the truth-value gap thesis should be such that if a component of a compound wff lacks truth-value, the whole wff should lack truth-value. The matrices of Bochvar's 'internal' connectives and Smiley's 'primary' connectives have this property. But it is none too clear why the truth-valueless input – truth-valueless output principle should be accepted (especially if Frege's theory of sense and reference, which, as we saw, gives this principle some support, is rejected); it is, after all, arguable that the presence of a false conjunct should be sufficient to give a truth-value to a conjunction, even if the other conjunct lacks truth-value. (cf. ch. 7.)

(b) *Does the use of a many-valued system commit one to the new truth-value(s) thesis?* It is not, when one looks closely, so clear as many writers (e.g. van Fraassen, Lambert) suppose, that employment of one of the many-valued systems (e.g. Kleene's or Bochvar's, Łukasiewicz's or Post's) need commit one to thesis (4). For one could use a many-valued system and yet hold both:

(1) There are just two truth-values, 'true' and 'false'.

and

(2) Every wff of the system has just one of these values.

For some of the more plausible interpretations of the intermediate values of many-valued systems are such that 'true' and 'false' remain (mutually exclusive and) jointly exhaustive. Consider, for example, the following interpretation offered by Prior for a 4-valued system:

1 = true and purely mathematical
2 = true but not purely mathematical
3 = false but not purely mathematical
4 = false and purely mathematical.

On this interpretation, any wff is either true or false; those with values 1 or 2 are true, those with values 3 or 4 are false. The division into four values is effected by an epistemological subdivision of the two garden-variety truth-values 'true' and 'false'. Granted only that *truth*-values are not evidence-relative or epistemological, it follows that use of a 4-valued system, on *this* interpretation, really commits one to no more than two *truth*-values after all. Similar remarks would apply to another proposed interpretation of the values of 4-valued logic, as 'true and known to be true', 'true but not known to be true' etc.

And, again, it seems that Kleene so interprets '*u*' ('undecidable') that sentences which take *u* are nevertheless either true or false, though it is not possible to tell which. Thus, we have:

t = true (certainly)
u = true or false (but undecidable which)
f = false (certainly)

so that once again 'true' and 'false' are jointly exhaustive.

In these cases I have suggested that, on certain interpretations of their intermediate value(s), many-valued systems are innocent of commitment to new truth-values. I now consider a related but instructively different case.

One motivation for thesis (4) was consideration of the use of such locutions as 'partly true', 'half true', etc. which seemed to show that there are 'degrees of truth'. Now, at least sometimes when one says that an assertion is 'partly true', what one has in mind is, that the assertion is a compound one, and some but not all of its components are true. We might paraphrase 'A is partly true', when 'partly true' is used in this way, by 'part of A is true'. (cf. Waismann [1946], p. 87. This is not the only way in which 'partly true' is used. Sometimes 'A is part of the truth' might be a better paraphrase. I shall not consider that use here. For an alternative approach to the problem of partial truth, cf. Bunge [1963].)

Suppose, then, that one treats sentence letters as standing, not for sentences, but for sequences of sentences: then the ascription of 'true' to some but not all members of the sequence would amount to the ascription of 'partly true' to the sequence itself.

There is a calculus already available which may be exploited to work out the details of this suggestion. Consider the following interpretation of an m-valued logic:

(1) The sentence letters $P, Q, R \ldots$ are to stand for $m - 1$ tuples of ordinary, 2-valued sentences $p, q, r \ldots$ with the true members occurring before the false.

(2) P is to take the value i when exactly $i - 1$ elements of P are false.

(3) $\frac{m}{\mathbf{1}} P$ is to stand for the result of replacing the first false element p_1 of P by its (ordinary, 2-valued) negation; if there is no false element, $\frac{m}{\mathbf{1}} P$ is to stand for the result of replacing all elements of P by their (ordinary, 2-valued) negations.

(4) When $P = <p_1, \ldots P_{m-1}>$ and $Q = <q_1, \ldots q_{m-1}>$, then $P \overset{m}{\underset{\mathbf{v}}{}} Q = <p_1 \text{ v } q_1, \ldots, P_{m-1} \text{ v } q_{m-1}>$ where the disjunction on the right-hand side is ordinary, 2-valued disjunction.

This interpretation satisfies Post's [1921] matrices. It will be shown, for the case $m = 3$, that one can justify the following interpretation of the values:

1 = wholly true; 2 = half true; 3 = wholly false.

The number of members of each sequence of sentences is $m - 1$, i.e. $3 - 1$, i.e. 2. When $|P| = i$, the number of false members of $P =$

$i - 1$. So the number of true members of P is $2 - (i - 1)$. Hence the proportion of true members of P is

$$\frac{2 - (i - 1)}{2}.$$

Now, suppose $|P| = 1$. Then the proportion of true members of P is

$$\frac{2 - (1 - 1)}{2} = \frac{2}{2} = 1 \quad \text{i.e. } P \text{ is } \textit{wholly true.}$$

Suppose $|P| = 2$. Then the proportion of true members of P is

$$\frac{2 - (2 - 1)}{2} = \frac{1}{2} \quad \text{i.e. } P \text{ is } \textit{half true.}$$

Suppose, finally, that $|P| = 3$. Then the proportion of true members of P is

$$\frac{2 - (3 - 1)}{2} = \frac{0}{2} = 0 \quad \text{i.e. } P \text{ is } \textit{wholly false.}$$

It is easy to verify that equally suitable interpretations of the values (e.g. $1 =$ wholly true, $2 = \frac{2}{3}$ true, $3 = \frac{1}{3}$ true, $4 =$ wholly false) are available for $m > 3$.

Thus, one can use Post's system to provide a logic of 'partial truth' without having to suppose that there are more than two truth-values. The need to ascribe intermediate truth-value(s) to a sentence is avoided by assigning, instead, one of the ordinary truth-values to components of that sentence. So, whereas in the cases I considered earlier commitment to intermediate truth-values was avoided by interpretation of the extra values as epistemological, in this case a similar effect is achieved by reinterpretation of the kind of item to which the intermediate values are applied. It may be worth observing that this strategy has certain affinities with thesis (2), though what is involved here is a new specification of the kind of item for which sentence letters stand, rather than straightforward retranslation of English sentences into the formalism.

This suggestion has certain philosophical affinities with Popper's treatment (e.g. in [1972]) of 'verisimilitude'. Popper's aim is to express formally the idea that one theory may be closer to the (whole) truth than another, even though both theories are false. But unfortunately his definition of 'nearer the truth':

$$B < A \text{ iff } \begin{cases} Ct_T(A) \subset Ct_T(B) \;\&\; Ct_F(B) \subseteq Ct_F(A) \\ \text{or} \\ Ct_T(A) \subseteq Ct_T(B) \;\&\; Ct_F(B) \subset Ct_F(A) \end{cases}$$

('$<$' is read 'is nearer the truth than', 'Ct_T', 'the truth-content of', 'Ct_F', 'the falsity-content of', '$\subset$', 'is included in', and '$\subseteq$', 'is properly included in'), has the consequence:

$$B < A \vdash Ct_F(B) = 0.[1]$$

No two false theories stand in this relation, which cannot, therefore, represent the idea Popper intended to capture. In view of this failure, the formalisation of partial truth suggested above may not be totally lacking in philosophical motivation.

A suggestion of Scott's ([1973]), that sense can be made of many-valued logics by interpreting assignment of intermediate value i to a statement A as corresponding to assignment of 'true' or 'false' to the statement 'A is true to within degree of error i', has some formal analogy in that assignment of non-classical values is interpreted via assignment of classical values to related statements.

2. Consequences for the theory of truth

The use of a many-valued system does not, necessarily, commit one to a belief in new, non-classical truth-values. This observation, however, raises as many questions as it answers. When is an intermediate value to count as a *truth*-value, for instance? And, in general, what can be said about the consequences for the theory of truth of the adoption of a many-valued system?

Some writers think that 'true' and 'false' are inevitably used in a non-standard way if we move to many-valued logic. Thus, Quine:

> we must remember . . . that the terminology 'true', 'false' and 'negation' carries over into [3-valued logic] from our logic only by partial analogy.
>
> ([1970], p. 84.)

Others maintain, on the contrary, that certain essential features of 'true' and 'false' are preserved in many-valued logic. Thus, Putnam:

> the words 'true' and 'false' have a certain 'core' meaning which is *independent* of *tertium non datur*
>
> ([1957], p. 74.)

[1] I owe this point to D. Miller.

The question, whether, or, to what extent, the classical conception of truth is violated in the move to Deviant logics is relevant to the decision whether to count such system as rival *logics*, or merely as perhaps mathematically interesting, but anyway philosophically sterile formalisms. So it should be no surprise that the quotation maximising the change in the concept of truth comes from a work I have already recognised as conservative in tendency, and the quotation minimising the change from a radical paper.

I shall approach the question of the consequences of Deviance for the theory of truth, by investigating the effect of the adoption of Deviant systems on three principles: the principle of bivalence, the principle that every wff is either true or false (hereafter, PB); the law of excluded middle, the wff '*p* or not *p*' (hereafter, LEM); and Tarski's material adequacy condition for definitions of truth, the principle that '*A*' is true iff *A* (hereafter, (*T*)).

(i) *The principle of bivalence*

I argued above that *some* proposed interpretations of the intermediate values of many-valued systems are such that 'true' and 'false' remain (mutually exclusive and) jointly exhaustive. It is sometimes said, more radically, that many-valued logics *never* really violate PB, but inevitably keep it in a disguised form.

For instance, Quine considers the suggestion that taking '*f*' and taking '*m*' could be thought of as simply different ways of being false. (cf. Dummett [1959].) Quine objects to this suggestion on the grounds that if $t =$ true and $f = m =$ falsity, and falsity is defined as truth of negation, then, if negation is to be a truth-function, the law of double negation must be forfeited. So that:

> Try what we will, three-valued logic turns out true to form; it is a rejection of the classical true – false dichotomy, or of classical negation.
> ([1970], p. 84.)

One may also rebut this suggestion from another angle. If '*f*' and '*m*' are both to count as 'false', it is inexplicable why wffs taking either '*f*' or '*m*' or uniformly '*m*' for all assignments to their variables should not be counted as contradictions. And yet '*m*' is not antidesignated in Bochvar's or Łukasiewicz's 3-valued logics.

But this reply might provoke another counter-suggestion. Does not many-valued logic inevitably preserve PB, albeit in a disguised form, via the distinction between designated and antidesignated values?[2] (A wff which takes only *designated* (truth-like) values is a tautology; by analogy, a wff which takes only antidesignated (false-like) values is a contradiction. (See Rescher [1969], pp. 82–3.) Against this suggestion, one might argue as follows. First, it is not necessarily the case that every value of a many-valued system is either designated or antidesignated; in many such systems, the middle value(s) is (are) neither. So even if one identified 'designated' with 'true' and 'antidesignated' with 'false', one would not have PB. Second, in a 3-valued logic such as Łukasiewicz's, there is a very good reason why the middle value can be neither designated nor antidesignated. If 'm' were designated, the unacceptable result that 'p & $\sim p$', which takes 'm' when $|p| = |\sim p| = m$, might have a designated ('true') value would follow: and if 'm' were antidesignated, the unacceptable result that 'p v $\sim p$', which takes 'm' when $|p| = |\sim p| = m$, might have an antidesignated ('false') value would follow.

However, one can agree that given a many-valued system in which the values were so interpreted that it was plausible for every value to be either designated or antidesignated, it *would* be plausible to think that PB was being preserved in a disguised form. But it is plausible to designate or antidesignate *all* the values only when the values are so interpreted that we are inclined to say that the true/false distinction remains exhaustive, i.e. only in those cases, discussed above, where I had already suggested that PB was preserved.

(ii) *The law of excluded middle*

Many philosophers use the expressions 'law of excluded middle' and 'principle of bivalence' interchangeably, or take for granted that these principles are equivalent. Taylor, for example, in [1962], speaks of the principle that 'any proposition is, either true, or, if not true, false, i.e. "p v $\sim p$"'.

I, however, wish to distinguish between the questions:

(a) whether every wff of the system is either true or false (whether PB holds)

and

(b) whether 'p v $\sim p$' is a theorem of the system (whether LEM holds).

[2] A suggestion made by Professor Anscombe.

I place no particular weight on the use of the terminology 'PB' and 'LEM' to mark this distinction; I adopt it only because it happens to be used by those (e.g. van Fraassen, Lambert, McCall) who are careful about the distinction. I do not make any claims about the historical propriety of this terminology; on which question cf. Routley [1969].

What *is* important, is that the answer to question (a) may be negative, and the answer to (b) affirmative. This might come about:

(i) in a many-valued system in which only one value is designated, but 'p v $\sim p$' is assigned that value even when $|p| = |\sim p| = m$. (Such a matrix would not be entirely lacking in motivation – compare Łukasiewicz's assignment of t to '$p \to p$' for $|p| = m$.)

(ii) in a non-truth-functional system in which some wffs are assigned neither 'true' nor 'false', but in which 'p v $\sim p$' is assigned 'true' even when 'p' is assigned neither 'true' nor 'false', though 'p v q' is not assigned 'true' if its disjuncts are assigned neither 'true' nor 'false'. (Van Fraassen's 'supervaluation' semantics are of this kind.)

Conversely: the answer to question (a) may be affirmative, and the answer to (b) negative. For instance, LEM is not a theorem of Kleene's 3-valued system ($|p$ v $\sim p|$ for $|p| = |\sim p| = u$ is u). But, as we argued above, if one understands 't' as 'certainly true', 'f' as 'certainly false', and 'u' as 'true or false but undecidable which', PB is seen to be true of this system.

It is to be observed that it is not a simple matter to say whether or not these principles are true of a system. It is relatively straightforward to say whether a system has a 2-valued, or only a many-valued, characteristic matrix; but a tricky matter to decide, if the system is many-valued, whether the intermediate values are to count as *truth*-values, and so, whether PB is dropped. And it is straightforward to say whether or not the wff 'p v $\sim p$' is a theorem of a system; but a tricky matter to decide whether the analogy between the 'v' and '$\sim$' of the system in question, and the classical 'v' and '$\sim$', is strong enough to justify the inference that LEM is (is not) a theorem of the system.

But anyway: LEM and PB are distinct principles, and, indeed, either may be true of a system without the other also being so. PB and LEM are however connected, in the following way. If LEM is a theorem of a system, and if Tarski's (T) schema holds for that system, PB must also hold. Thus:

(1) $Tp \equiv p$ (T)

(2) p v $\sim p$ (LEM)

(3) p assumption
(4) Tp from (1), (3), by df. of '$\equiv$' and MPP
(5) $\sim p$ assumption
(6) $T \sim p$ from (1), $\sim p/p$, (5), by df. of '$\equiv$' and MPP
(7) $Tp \vee T \sim p$ from (4), by vel introduction
(8) $Tp \vee T \sim p$ from (6), by vel introduction
(9) $Tp \vee T \sim p$ from (2), (3), (5), (7), (8) by vel elimination
(10) $Tp \vee Fp$ from (9) by df. of 'F'.

So I now ask whether (T) may be expected to hold for many-valued logics.

(iii) *The (T) schema*

Tarski argues in [1931] that the semantic definition of truth entails what he calls 'the law of excluded middle', that is, the principle:

$$(x) \quad (x \in Tr \vee \bar{x} \in Tr)$$

('for all sentences x, either x belongs to the class of true sentences, or the negation of x belongs to the class of true sentences') – which I call PB.

Indeed, it looks as if PB can be derived, not only from the semantic definition of truth, but actually from Tarski's (T) schema:

(1) $Tp \equiv p$
(2) $p \supset Tp$ from (1) by df. of '$\equiv$'
(3) $\sim p \supset T \sim p$ from (2), $\sim p/p$
(4) $\sim Tp \supset \sim p$ from (2), $\vdash (p \supset q) \supset (\sim q \supset \sim p)$
(5) $\sim Tp \supset T \sim p$ from (3), (4) $\vdash (p \supset q) \supset ((q \supset r) \supset$
                                       $(p \supset r))$
(6) $\sim \sim Tp \vee T \sim p$ from (5) by df. of '$\vee$'
(7) $Tp \equiv \sim \sim Tp$ $\vdash p \equiv \sim \sim p$, Tp/p
(8) $Tp \vee T \sim p$ from (6), (7), substitution of equivalents
(9) $Tp \vee Fp$ from (8), by df. of 'F'

((8) is, of course, only notationally different from Tarski's formulation of bivalence.)

Now the (T) schema is intended by Tarski as a material adequacy condition; that is to say, it should be entailed by any definition of truth which is to be considered adequate. So if the derivation of PB from (T) is acceptable, it follows that rejection of bivalence entails rejection of (T), and thus a rather considerable modification of classical theories of truth.

Putnam, however, maintains just the contrary. He claims to have shown, in [1957], that:

(a) there are certain 'core' properties of 'true' and 'false' in 2-valued logic, which

(b) are preserved when 'true' and 'false' are used in 3-valued logic, and which

(c) also characterise the intermediate value, 'middle' of 3-valued logic, and so justify its claim to be called a truth-value.

So I must look at his arguments.

The first strand in the alleged 'common core' meaning of 'true' is its *tenseless* character. That is, it is to be supposed that 'true' and 'false' have, as Putnam says they ordinarily have, the characteristic that if they once apply to a statement, they always apply to it; and that 'middle' shares this characteristic. Putnam's procedure seems rather questionable; he begins by claiming that he will *show* that 'true' has a core of meaning preserved in 3-valued logic, but immediately goes on to *assume* that 'true' is, in 2- and 3-valued logic, tenseless. Worse, it is doubtful whether this assumption is correct. It is arguable that, if one says of a *tenseless* statement, that it is true, then one must say that the statement always was and always will be true. But it doesn't follow from this that 'true' is tenseless. (Similarly, it doesn't follow from the fact that if one calls a 'colour-invariable' object 'blue' at one time, then one must call it 'blue' at all times, that 'blue' is a temporally invariable predicate.) Perhaps, then, Putnam is supposing both that 'statement' must be so used that statements are tenseless, and that 'true' must be applied only to statements, so that the use of 'true' would be temporally invariable. But, in the first place, the word 'statement' is not always restricted to tenseless items (e.g. Prior [1957]); and, second, the motivation for so restricting 'statement' generally arises from a conviction that 'true' is timeless, and so cannot be used in support of that conviction.

Not only does Putnam fail to establish the tenseless character of 'true' in 2-valued logic; he also entirely fails to offer any argument why 'true' should retain this characteristic in 3-valued logic, or why 'middle' should share it. And there is reason to doubt both these claims. For Łukasiewicz originally intended his system (which is the one

Putnam discusses) as a formalisation of Aristotle's solution to the problem of fatalism; thus, the sentences which the system was to handle were, specifically, tensed sentences, and the sentences which were to take the intermediate value were, specifically, future-contingent sentences. So on the original intended interpretation of the very system which Putnam discusses, it was not assumed either that 'true' or 'false', or that 'middle', applied timelessly.

Much more interestingly, the second strand in the alleged 'common core', appealed to in the last section of Putnam's paper, is that 'true', in both 2- and 3-valued logic, satisfies the Tarski (*T*) schema. This contention is surprising, in view of the argument above, which apparently showed that PB can be derived from (*T*), and hence that rejection of PB would entail rejection of (*T*).

How, in view of this argument, can Putnam maintain that the (*T*) schema still holds even in 3-valued logic? Well, one may observe that the argument employs principles – the definition of '*A* v *B*' as '~ *A* ⊃ *B*' at line (6), and the law of double negation at line (7) – which may not hold in a 3-valued logic. Neither principle is valid in Bochvar's system, for instance, and only the latter in Łukasiewicz's.

So if it were supposed that a 3-valued, rather than a classical, *meta*-language is appropriate to a 3-valued object language, then, since the proof of PB from (*T*) would be blocked, (*T*) might be retained.

To put essentially the same point in a different way: if one thinks that the predicate 'true', as it applies to 3-valued logic, is itself 3-valued, so that it would have the matrix:

$$
\begin{array}{cc}
T & A \\
\hline
t & t \\
m & m \\
f & f \\
\end{array}
$$

then the (*T*) schema will be verified:

$$
\begin{array}{cccc}
T & A & \equiv & A \\
\hline
t & t & t & t \\
m & m & t & m \\
f & f & t & f. \\
\end{array}
$$

But if one thinks that the predicate 'true', as it applies to 3-valued logic, is 2-valued, so that it would have the matrix:

T	A	or	T	A
t	t		t	t
f	m		t	m
f	f		f	f

then the (T) schema will not be verified:

T	A	$\equiv$	A		T	A	$\equiv$	A
t	t	t	t		t	t	t	t
f	m	f	m		t	m	f	m
f	f	t	f		f	f	t	f

Whether one chooses a 2- or 3-valued 'T' will presumably depend upon the way one interprets the middle truth-value. If, for instance, 'm' is interpreted as 'indeterminate', one would set $|\,T\,A\,| = f$ for $|\,A\,| = m$. If, on the other hand, 'm' were interpreted as 'undecidable', one might set $|\,T\,A\,| = m$ for $|\,A\,| = m$.

I cannot, then, accept Putnam's claim in a fully general form. I am only entitled to conclude that even if a 3-valued system drops PB, it *may* still be consistent with (T), if the intended interpretation of its third value is such as to motivate a 3-valued 'T'.

The consequences for the theory of truth of the adoption of a non-standard logic are not, then, by any means straightforward or obvious. How much or how little modification of the classical concepts of truth and falsity is necessary will depend on the particular non-standard system in question. But certain conclusions can be drawn from the above considerations.

The adoption of a many-valued system may not be inconsistent with PB: the interpretation of the intermediate value(s) may be such as to leave 'true' and 'false' mutually exhaustive. This is likely to be the case if but not only if the interpretation is such as to motivate the designation or antidesignation of all the values.

PB and LEM are distinct principles, either of which may be true of a system and the other false. If, however, LEM is a theorem of a system, and (T) holds for that system, PB must also hold.

If (T) is true of a system, PB will also be true of it, *unless* the interpretation of the intermediate value(s) of the system is such as to motivate adoption of a non-classical metalanguage, in which case (T) may be true but PB false.

PART TWO

4

Future contingents

The 'problem of future contingents' provided the motivation for one of the pioneer investigations of many-valued logics. Łukasiewicz writes:

I can assume without contradiction that my presence in Warsaw at a certain moment of next year, *e.g.* at noon on 21 December, is at the present time determined neither positively nor negatively. Hence it is possible, but not necessary, that I shall be present in Warsaw at the given time. On this assumption the proposition 'I shall be in Warsaw at noon on 21 December of next year', can at the present time be neither true nor false. For if it were true now, my future presence in Warsaw would have to be necessary, which is contradictory to the assumption. If it were false now, on the other hand, my future presence in Warsaw would be impossible, which is also contradictory to the assumption. Therefore the proposition considered is at the moment *neither true nor false* and must possess a third value, different from 'o' or falsity and '1' or truth. This value we can designate by '½'. It represents 'the possible' and joins 'the true' and 'the false' as a third value.

The three-valued system of propositional logic owes its origin to this line of thought.

([1930], p. 53.)

The line of thought is an old one. Łukasiewicz derived it from Aristotle; a version appears in Diodorus Cronus, another in medieval and subsequent discussions of the consequences of God's omniscience. And the argument, though old, is still very much alive, for instance in the numerous discussions provoked by Taylor's [1962].

1. Aristotle's argument: exposition

An argument like the one which provoked Łukasiewicz to construct a 3-valued logic is, arguably at least, to be found in Aristotle's *de Interpretatione* ix. The interpretation of this passage is, indeed, disputed. But many commentators, including Ross, Bocheński, the Kneales, Prior and Cahn find there the argument which Łukasiewicz found; and this interpretation is, I think, plausible.

More important to the present enterprise than the interpretation of Aristotle, is the question, whether the argument attributed, rightly or wrongly, to Aristotle is sound, and whether, if it is, it points to a need for a modified logic. So, although I shall offer textual support for my interpretation of Aristotle, I shall not devote a great deal of time to close examination of rival interpretations.

Aristotle seems to argue as follows:

(1) If every future tense sentence is either true or false, then, of each pair consisting of a future tense sentence and its denial, one must be true, the other false.

(2) If, of each pair consisting of a future tense sentence and its denial, one must be true, the other false, then, everything that happens, happens 'of necessity'.

(3) But not everything that happens, happens of necessity; some events are contingent.

∴ (4) Not every future tense sentence is true or false.

Clearly, this argument is a valid one. But, equally clearly, Aristotle's arguments for the premisses, particularly (2), need examination.

Premiss (1)

It may seem puzzling why Aristotle thinks he needs an elaborate argument to establish this. But the need becomes clear from the argument itself. Aristotle observes that, in the case of general sentences and sentences predicating something of an individual, if each sentence must be true or false, then of each sentence/denial pair, one must be true, the other false. (18a 30–2.) But with sentences predicating something of some but not all members of a class, this is not the case. (18a 32–3.) This is presumably because such pairs as:

Some men are white

and

Some men are not white

may be both true. So Aristotle needs an argument to show that a future-tense sentence and its denial cannot be both true and cannot be both false, so that if both have a truth-value, one is true and the other false; for he does not mean by 'denial' what modern logicians mean by 'negation', which guarantees that a sentence and its negation are contradictories, but rather, something like 'The sentence denying the predicate of the subject'. Aristotle proceeds to argue (18a 39–40) that a future tense sentence and its denial cannot be both true, and (18b 17–25) that they cannot be both false.

So if such sentences have a truth-value at all, they must have opposite truth-values. But whereas Aristotle is confident that present and past tense sentences are bivalent (18a 28–30), he is doubtful whether this is the case with future tense sentences (18a 32–3).

Premiss (2)

If future tense sentences are bivalent, then whatever happens, happens necessarily:

it is necessary for the affirmation or the negation to be true. It follows that nothing either is or is not happening, or will be or will not be, by chance or as chance has it, but everything of necessity and not as chance has it.

(18a 44–8)

Two arguments are given for this premiss, the first, at 18b 9–16:

if it is white now it was true to say earlier that it would be white; so that it was always true to say of anything that has happened that it would be so. But if it was always true to say that it was so, or would be so, it could not not be so, or not be going to be so. But if something cannot not happen it is impossible for it not to happen; and if it is impossible for something not to happen, it is necessary for it to happen. Everything that will be, therefore, happens necessarily.

The structure of this argument seems to be:

(i) If '*e* is happening' is true [false] '*e* will happen' was always true [false].

(ii) If '*e* will happen' was always true [false], *e* cannot not happen [cannot happen].

(iii) If *e* cannot not happen [cannot happen], it is necessary [impossible] for *e* to happen.

So (iv) If '*e* will happen' was always true [false], *e* is necessary [impossible].

The second argument, at 18b 34–8, elaborates on the first:

> there is nothing to prevent someone's having said ten thousand years beforehand that this would be the case, and another's having denied it; so that whichever of the two was true to say then, will be the case of necessity.

However, as Aristotle observes (18b 38–40 and 42–4), neither the fact that the future tense sentence was actually uttered, nor the particular time of the utterance, is strictly relevant. And so this argument collapses into the first, on which, therefore, I shall concentrate in what follows.

Premiss (3)

But, Aristotle argues, it is just not the case that everything that happens, happens necessarily:

> in general, in things that are not always actual there is the possibility of being and of not being; here both possibilities are open, both being and not being, and, consequently, both coming to be and not coming to be. Many things are obviously like this.

(19a 7–23)

His argument is that if everything that happens *were* necessary [impossible], then there would be no point in human deliberation and action with the object of preventing or bringing about some event; but human action *can* affect what happens, so it cannot be the case that everything that happens is necessary, nor that everything that does not happen is impossible.

Conclusion

Since, if future tense sentences are true or false, what happens, happens necessarily, but not everything that happens does happen necessarily,

Aristotle concludes that future tense sentences cannot be true or false:

> Clearly then, it is not necessary that of every affirmation and oppo-site negation one should be true and the other false. For what holds for things that are does not hold for things that are not but may possibly be or not be.
>
> (19a 39–42)

A sentence:

> With these [future contingents] it is necessary for one or the other of the contradictories to be true or false.
>
> (19a 35–6)

which might be thought inconsistent with this interpretation, is shown by the immediately following remark:

> – not, however, this one or that one, but as chance has it; or for one to be true *rather* than the other, yet not *already* true or false.
>
> (18a 36–8)

to be explicable as follows: it *is* necessary that one or other of a future tense sentence and its negation *turn out* true, but not necessary that either in particular should be the one that so turns out; nor is either true *yet*.

Comments

I shall not, here, question premiss (1) or premiss (3), though (3) is, I think, doubtful. I shall concentrate, rather, on premiss (2), since it is central to Aristotle's, and to others', fatalist arguments.

For example, the long tradition (from Boethius to Pike [1965]) of arguments for fatalism, which argue from God's foreknowledge to the present truth of future tense sentences, and then to their necessity, employs centrally what is essentially Aristotle's argument for premiss (2). (See Haack [1974] for a more detailed discussion of these arguments.)

I shall show that this crucial argument of Aristotle's is invalid, and that, in consequence, both his and others' fears that bivalence must be abandoned if free will is to be secured, are unfounded.

The fallacy in the argument can be seen on an examination of steps (ii) and (iii) in its schematic form (p. 76 above):

(ii) If '*e* will happen' was always true [false], *e* cannot not happen [happen].

(iii) If *e* cannot not happen [happen], it is necessary [impossible] for *e* to happen.

The first of these steps is true, if interpreted as

(ii)′ *L* (If '*e* will happen' is true [false] then *e* will happen [not happen])

so that the 'cannot' which appears in the consequent is taken as corresponding to the '*L*' governing the *whole* conditional: 'necessarily (if . . ., then it won't happen)' = 'if . . ., then it can't happen'. But in the second step the consequent of this conditional, with its 'cannot', justified by the necessity of the whole conditional, is detached; and this is illegitimate. The argument would work only if the inference from

$$L (p \supset q) \quad \text{to} \quad p \supset Lq$$

were valid. But it is not — it is a straightforward modal fallacy. If this is Aristotle's argument, it is invalid. And if Aristotle's argument is invalid, there is not, as he thought, any need to modify logic.

Two questions immediately arise: how plausible is this as an interpretation of Aristotle's argument? And, is there any *other* interpretation of his argument which is reasonably plausible but which makes it valid?

This interpretation is, I think, quite plausible *as an interpretation of Aristotle's argument at 18b 9–16*. But it does have one rather serious drawback, which is that later in *de Interpretatione* ix, Aristotle appears to be at pains to warn against certain modal fallacies, one of which is, arguably, precisely the one which, on this interpretation, Aristotle is supposed to have committed. The relevant passage is 19a 23–36. The first part of this passage:

> What is, necessarily is, when it is; and what is not, necessarily is not, when it is not. But not everything that is, necessarily is; and not everything that is not, necessarily is not. For to say that everything that is, is of necessity, when it is, is not the same as saying unconditionally that it is of necessity.

looks much as though it points out the invalidity of the reference from

$$L (p \supset p) \quad \text{('what is, necessarily is, when it is') to}$$
$$p \supset Lp \quad \text{('everything that is, necessarily is')}$$

And if this *is* the point of this passage, it would be curious that Aristotle should have used, so shortly before, this very form of inference. This interpretation of the passage is, furthermore, given some support by the fact that the immediately following passage:

> everything necessarily is or is not, and will be or will not be; but one cannot divide and say that one or the other is necessary.

could be read as warning against another modal fallacy, that of inferring from

$$L (p \vee q) \quad \text{to} \quad Lp \vee Lq.$$

However, it is possible to interpret the awkward passage (19a 23–8) in another way, this time more consistently with Aristotle's having committed the modal fallacy I have ascribed to him: to interpret it, that is, as saying that *once an event has happened*, it is necessary, i.e. irrevocable, although not all events are, before they happen, necessary, i.e. inevitable.

So it is possible to interpret Aristotle as I have done without being *forced* to suppose that he uses a form of inference which only very shortly afterwards he (correctly) claims to be invalid.

Still, it remains to be asked whether any other interpretation is available. A clue to a possible alternative interpretation can perhaps be found in the claim, sometimes rather plausibly argued in the literature, that fatalism is a harmless logical truth. Ayer, for instance, writes:

> recognition of *the tautology that what will be will be* is not at all a ground for concluding that our activities are futile. They too, indeed, are what they are and their consequences will be what they will; but it does not follow . . . that whatever they were their consequences would be the same.

So the answer to the fatalist is that his bogy is a fraud.

([1956], p. 170, my italics.)

This suggests an alternative point of view: that there is indeed a valid argument for fatalism, but the conclusion of that argument is not, as Aristotle thought, a thesis which is inconsistent with the pointfulness of human action, but a perfectly harmless truism. Ayer's arguments suggest that the appropriate interpretation of Aristotle's argument would exploit the fact that it is analytically the case that what happens cannot be prevented.

Perhaps, then, the argument could be re-interpreted like this: if it is true [false] that *e* will happen, then *e* is inevitable, for it cannot be prevented [impossible, for it cannot be brought about]. So if it is either true or false that *e* will occur, *e* is either inevitable or impossible, i.e. either unpreventable, or unbring-aboutable. The first thing to see is that even if this interpretation is such as to make Aristotle's argument valid, it *still* won't show a need for a change of logic. For the suggestion is that its conclusion is *true*, in fact logically true. And if that is so, the conclusion can be accepted, so that the argument would *not* constitute a *reductio* of PB.

And anyhow I shall argue that this interpretation, though it may *appear* to yield a valid argument, in fact collapses into the first interpretation. For this interpretation too can be shown to involve the modal fallacy I diagnosed in the first. The claims that

(1) If *e* is going to happen, it can't be prevented

and

(2) If *e* is not going to happen, it can't be brought about

are, admittedly, true. For if *e* happens, nothing could count as preventing it, and if it doesn't, nothing could count as bringing it about. So (1) and (2) are true because the weaker claims

(3) If *e* is going to happen, it won't be prevented

and

(4) If *e* is not going to happen, it won't be brought about

are (logically) necessary. That is, (1) = L(3), and (2) = L(4): 'If *e* is going to happen, then it *can't* be prevented' is equivalent to 'Necessarily, if *e* is going to happen, then it *won't* be prevented'; and similarly for (2) and (4). But this means that the argument is not of the (valid) form

$$p \supset Lq$$
$$\sim p \supset Lr$$
$$p \vee \sim p$$
$$\therefore \quad Lq \vee Lr$$

but of the *invalid* form

$$L\,(p \supset q)$$
$$L\,(\sim p \supset r)$$
$$p \vee \sim p$$
$$\therefore \quad Lq \vee Lr$$

As Ayer says, that if *e* is going to happen, it won't be prevented, and that if it is not, it won't be brought about, are harmless truisms. But the conclusion of the re-interpreted argument, which is, not that either *e* *won't* be prevented or it *won't* be brought about, which is also a truism, but that either *e* *can't* be prevented or it *can't* be brought about, is *not* a harmless truism.

I claim, therefore, that an alternative interpretation which makes Aristotle's argument valid, but his conclusion harmless, is not possible; what looks like such an interpretation turns out to collapse into the first, which makes Aristotle's conclusion strong but his argument invalid.

There are, furthermore, general reasons which might lead one to think that no interpretation of Aristotle's argument could be found which *both* is valid, *and* has a non-trivial conclusion. For the only assumption Aristotle uses is the Principle of Bivalence. That, indeed, is why, if his *reductio* were accepted, the only possible conclusion to draw would be the one he does draw, namely, that logic must be changed. But if Aristotle's argument is valid, and if its only assumption is purely logical, its conclusion must be purely logical too; and if its conclusion is not purely logical, it must be invalid.[1]

It might therefore be plausible to conclude, even independently of my attempt to show that Aristotle's argument is invalid, that no interpretation of his argument *could* be given which would provide any reason for a change of logic, since, if any interpretation could be found on which the argument is valid, its conclusion, on that interpretation, would be one which could be accepted with equanimity, and not one it was necessary to alter logic to avoid. However, this argument is not totally conclusive in the context of an argument of which the possible upshot is rejection of a formerly accepted logical principle. For in the case, e.g., of the set-theoretical antinomies an apparently valid argument from apparently logically true premisses yields a contradiction, forcing the conclusion that the premisses cannot have been logically true after all. But it does have some plausibility.

---

[1] Cahn sees this. But unfortunately he responds to it, not by recognising that Aristotle's argument cannot create a need for change of logic, but by drawing a distinction, which I find very confused, between an 'analytic' and a 'synthetic' version of the Law of Excluded Middle.

2. The issue about truth-bearers

I have rejected Aristotle's argument on the grounds that it involves a modal fallacy.

It has sometimes been thought, and is argued at some length in Kneale [1962], that Aristotle's argument should be rejected for a quite different reason: that it rests on a mistake about the bearers of truth and falsity. Now I have argued already (ch. 3) that there are general reasons to think that this kind of manoeuvre is not likely often to be successful. And so it turns out in this case. It is instructive to see what goes wrong.

Mrs Kneale writes:

> [Aristotle's] argument . . . is faulty because [he] thinks of the predicates 'true' and 'false' as applicable to something (probably a sentence) at a certain time. What puzzles him is the fact that we can *now* say that there will be a naval battle tomorrow. But the 'now' is superfluous . . . By introducing the phrase 'it is true that' we make no assumption about determinism which is not made by the use of the simple sentence in the future tense. We mislead ourselves, however, when we speak, as Aristotle does, of its being true *now* that there will be a naval battle tomorrow, for we thereby induce ourselves to suppose that *this* will not be true tomorrow evening, when the battle is over, but something else will, *i.e.* 'There has been a naval battle today'. Two different *sentences* are plainly involved here, but they both express the same proposition.
>
> ([1962], p. 51.)

Part of the trouble with this passage is that it is far from clear exactly what the diagnosis of Aristotle's mistake *is*. Some sentences suggest that the diagnosis is as follows: Aristotle wrongly supposes that the predicates 'true' and 'false' can be significantly applied to (tensed) sentences, whereas they can in fact only be significantly applied to (tenseless) propositions. Aristotle's premiss that 'There will be a sea-battle tomorrow' is either true or false is therefore nonsensical, and so his argument does not even get off the ground. If this is the diagnosis, however, it fails. In the first place, no argument is offered *why* it is nonsensical to apply 'true' and 'false' to sentences; and the only one suggested by the passage is the one Strawson uses in [1952] p. 4, that if sentences could significantly be called 'true' or 'false', it would follow that they are sometimes true and sometimes false, which is totally inconclusive. (See Lemmon [1966], or Haack [1970], if this is not obvious.) And second, it is in fact conceded (p. 53) that 'true' and 'false' *may* be significantly, though derivatively, applied to sentences.

Perhaps, then, the diagnosis is, not that 'true' cannot be applied to sentences, but that '*now* true' cannot be applied to propositions. On this account, Aristotle's 'mistake' would be to have used 'true' of sentences, rather than propositions, and hence to have been led to suppose, wrongly, that 'now true' is a pointful locution. However, if it were granted that 'true' applies primarily to propositions, and that propositions do not change their truth-values, it would not follow that 'now true' could not be significantly used. For if a proposition is true, it is, on the no change of truth-value thesis, always true. And if a proposition is always true, it is, in particular, *now* true.

Perhaps, finally, the diagnosis is, not that 'now true' is senseless, but that it is misleading, because *it* is responsible for introducing the worry about fatalism, which would not have arisen had Aristotle stuck to the plain future tense. On this account, Aristotle's 'mistake' would be to have supposed that 'It is now true that there will be a sea-battle tomorrow' has some significance over and above 'There will be a sea-battle tomorrow', in virtue of which it, but not the plain future tense assertion, entails fatalism. But actually the two sentences are logically equivalent. However, this diagnosis of Aristotle's 'mistake' is inadequate, for, in order to avoid the force of his argument, it would at least be necessary to show that 'There will be a sea-battle tomorrow' does not entail fatalism; since otherwise a supporter of Aristotle could reply that since 'It is now true that there will be a sea-battle tomorrow' entails fatalism, if 'There will be a sea-battle tomorrow' is logically equivalent to it, *it* must entail fatalism too.

So the attempt to show that Aristotle's argument rests on a mistake about truth-bearers is, as the general considerations of ch. 3 suggested, unsuccessful. Nevertheless, the last interpretation of Mrs Kneale's diagnosis does raise an interesting question.

3. An inadequacy in Aristotle's 'solution'?

That question is, whether Aristotle's own solution, which is to reject PB but accept LEM, is adequate to his (supposed) problem; for although his argument uses PB rather than LEM, could it not be reconstructed using only the latter? and if it could, wouldn't this show that if Aristotle's arguments had been acceptable, LEM as well as PB would have been threatened?

As it turns out, an argument which seems to be as good as (or rather, no worse than) Aristotle's can indeed be formulated using, as premiss, LEM rather than PB. For

If *e* will [not] happen, *e* cannot not happen [happen]

i.e.

L (If *e* will [not] happen, then *e* will [not] happen)

is, like the premiss Aristotle uses

If '*e* will happen' is true [false], *e* cannot not happen [happen]

i.e.

L (If '*e* will happen' is true [false], then *e* will [not] happen)

true; and so it looks as if Aristotle might as well (or ill) have derived the conclusion, that *e* is either necessary or impossible, from

Either *e* will happen or it won't   (LEM)

as from

Either '*e* will happen' is true, or it is false.   (PB)

Whether Aristotle's solution can be saved, in view of this, is a question which will require attention.

4. The inadequacy of Łukasiewicz's 'solution'

I have argued that Aristotle does *not* give a good reason to drop bivalence, and so, that no change of logic is called for, at least, not on account of future contingents. But it may nevertheless be worth pointing out how, even if Aristotle's argument were accepted, Łukasiewicz's 3-valued logic, which was designed to accommodate Aristotle's difficulty, would be quite inadequate.

Aristotle draws from his argument the conclusion that future contingent sentences are neither true nor false, although the disjunction of a future tense sentence and its negation is invariably, indeed, necessarily, true (19a 41–4). PB is to be dropped but LEM retained. But it is evident that while Łukasiewicz's proposal embodies the first proposal (some sentences are neither true nor false but 'intermediate'), it does *not* embody the second (LEM is not a theorem, since $|p \text{ v} \sim p| = i$ when $|p| = |\sim p| = i$).

Nor could this inadequacy be easily remedied. LEM could be retained if *either* the matrix for disjunction were changed so that $|p \text{ v} q| = t$ when $|p| = |q| = i$, *or* 'i' were designated as well as 't'. But either of these modifications would have the side-effect that '$p \text{ v} q$' would take a designated value when $|p| = |q| = i$, and this would surely be contrary to Aristotle's intentions. There is no evidence that Aristotle thought that *every* disjunction of future contingents was true; he thought only that the disjunction of a future contingent sentence *and its negation* was true, in spite of the lack of truth-value of its disjuncts.

An alternative proposal

These considerations suggest that any system appropriate to formalise Aristotle's conclusions would have to be non-truth-functional. Such a system could allow, what Quine refers to as 'fantasy' on Aristotle's part, that LEM should hold even though PB fails. In fact, I shall argue that if it had been the case that Aristotle's argument *did* call for a change of logic, then the appropriate logic would be, not Łukasiewicz's, but van Fraassen's.

Although van Fraassen's 'presuppositional languages' were primarily devised, not for the formalisation of Aristotle's solution to the supposed 'problem' of future contingents, but for the formalisation of a roughly Strawsonian solution to the problem of non-denoting terms, they turn out to have exactly the features which Aristotle's position requires.

For these languages allow that some sentences may be neither true nor false, but nevertheless assign 't' to all sentences, including LEM, which would be assigned 't' by all classical valuations. LEM is saved, however, without, as side effect, giving a designated value to *all* disjunctions of truth-valueless disjuncts: for though '$p \text{ v} \sim p$' would be assigned 't' by all classical valuations, '$p \text{ v} q$' would be assigned 't' by some and 'f' by others, and therefore is assigned *no* value by a supervaluation.

Van Fraassen claims that his languages are appropriate to truth-value gaps rather than intermediate truth-values. And it seems clear that if this claim were acceptable this would be another point in favour of their appropriateness to Aristotle's position. Aristotle's discussion tends to the conclusion that future contingent sentences have *no* truth-value, rather than the conclusion that they have some *intermediate* truth-value. For in view of his argument why 'There will be a sea-battle tomorrow' and 'There won't be a sea-battle tomorrow' cannot be both false:

> if it neither will be nor will not be the case tomorrow, then there is no 'as chance has it'. Take a sea-battle; it would *have* neither to happen nor not to happen.
>
> (18b 24–6)

Aristotle would presumably reject the suggestion that 'There will be a sea-battle tomorrow' is indeterminate, on the grounds that if it were, it would follow that the sea-battle was *necessarily* indeterminate.

As I argued in ch. 3, the reasons van Fraassen gives for the appropriateness of his languages to truth-value gaps are inadequate. But as it happens, these reasons work more successfully in the present case than in general. According to Aristotle, future contingent sentences do not yet have, but will eventually acquire, truth-values; and thus supervaluations, the principle of which is that a sentence whose components lack truth value should be assigned that value (if there is a unique such value) which it would be assigned whether its components were true or false, seem entirely appropriate.

At this point, however, another question arises. I have argued that Łukasiewicz's logic is inadequate as a formalisation of Aristotle's solution, because in it LEM as well as PB fails. But I have argued above that Aristotle's argument can be reconstructed using LEM instead of PB as premiss. If this is the case, is Łukasiewicz not, to some extent, vindicated? For his system, though indeed inadequate as a formalisation of Aristotle's solution to his own problem, may embody a solution more adequate than Aristotle's own.

As it turns out, the suggestion that Aristotle's solution be formalised using van Fraassen's system avoids this difficulty. In van Fraassen's system, the form of inference

$$\frac{A \vdash C, \quad B \vdash C}{A \vee B \vdash C}$$

fails, and with it the special case

$$\frac{A \vdash C, \quad \sim A \vdash C}{A \vee \sim A \vdash C}.$$

So if, as suggested above, such a system could be used to formalise Aristotle's solution, it *would* ensure that the conclusion Aristotle wished to avoid would be blocked, even though LEM is retained. (Whether Aristotle can reasonably be assumed to have seen this difficulty, or its solution, is of course another matter!)

5. Modal interpretations of Łukasiewicz's system

I have so far paid no attention to Łukasiewicz's suggestion that his third truth-value — which I have called, in the interests of neutrality, 'intermediate' — should be interpreted as 'possible'. However, this suggestion is of some relevance to the question, whether Łukasiewicz's system is contrary to Aristotle's intentions in introducing a new truth-value rather than truth-value gaps. For, it might be argued, 'possible' is not really a third truth-value; being possible isn't a third alternative on a par with being true or being false.

However, it seems that Łukasiewicz *did* think of 'possible' as a third truth-value. 'This ['intermediate']', he writes, 'represents "the possible" and joins "the true" and "the false" as a third value.' And if Łukasiewicz's third value is simply read as he proposes, substantial difficulties arise. Among these is the following: since $|p \ \& \sim p| = i$ when $|p| = |\sim p| = i$, it looks as if '$p \ \& \sim p$' must be regarded as possible if its conjuncts are, individually, possible: a quite unacceptable consequence.

Prior suggests, in [1953], a more plausible way to construe Łukasiewicz's system as modal, by defining modal operators within it. M ('possible') is given the truth-table:[2]

M	A
t	t
t	i
f	f

[2] Tarski has pointed out that 'MA' could have been defined as '$\sim A \supset A$', which has this truth-table.

and

$$LA = \text{df.} \quad \sim M \sim A \qquad (\text{'necessary'})$$
$$CA = \text{df.} \quad MA \mathbin{\&} M \sim A \,(\text{'contingent'})$$
$$IA = \text{df.} \quad L \sim A \qquad (\text{'impossible'})$$

giving the truth-tables:

L	A		C	A		I	A
t	t		f	t		f	t
f	i		t	i		f	i
f	f		f	f		t	f

As a modal logic, this system has some rather odd features – features which, however, are not wholly unexpected in view of Dugundji's proof that the standard modal logics have no finite characteristic matrices. A sentence is necessary just in case it is true, impossible just in case it is false, contingent just in case it is intermediate. So it might be objected that this interpretation of the system would obliterate modal distinctions altogether. But this would not be an overwhelming objection, since the thrust of Aristotle's argument, had it been valid, would have been precisely to show that whatever is true is necessary (etc.).

Prior's suggestion is, therefore, reasonably successful as an attempt to make Łukasiewicz's system more acceptable. But in view of this it is curious to find that Łukasiewicz himself came to think that his 3-valued 'modal' system was mistaken, and to propose, instead, a 4-valued modal logic. He writes:

> If we accept with Aristotle that some future events, *e.g.* a sea-fight, are contingent, then a proposition about such events enounced today can be neither true nor false . . . On the basis of this idea . . . I constructed in 1920 a three-valued system of modal logic developed later in a paper of 1930. I see today that this system does not satisfy all our intuitions concerning modalities and should be replaced by the system Ł_4^m.
>
> ([1957], pp. 166–7.)

This new system, he claims,

> refutes all false inferences drawn in connexion with modal logic, explains the difficulties of the Aristotelian modal syllogistic, and

reveals some unexpected logical facts which are of the greatest importance for philosophy.

([1957], p. 169.)

The matrices of $Ł_4^m$ are formed as the product of the matrix for classical propositional calculus with itself. Its truth-values are ordered pairs of classical truth-values:

$$1 = \ <t, t>$$
$$2 = \ <t, f>$$
$$3 = \ <f, t>$$
$$0 = \ <f, f>.$$

Two functors, M and W, both representing possibility, are then introduced:

$$M <v_2, v_2> \ = \ <v_1, t>$$
$$W <v_1, v_2> \ = \ <t, v_2>.$$

Łukasiewicz's argument, why two functors for possibility are needed, goes as follows: if 'A is contingent' is defined as 'A is possible and not-A is possible', then given the thesis that 'if something is true of A and also true of the negation of A, then it is true of any arbitrary proposition B', it follows that there can be no true contingent propositions. To avoid this, two kinds of contingency are defined in terms of the two kinds of possibility: X-contingency (for 'A is M-possible and $\sim A$ is W-possible') and Y-contingency (for 'A is W-possible and $\sim A$ is M-possible'). In these senses of contingency, there can be true contingent propositions.

These arguments reveal that $Ł_4^m$ must fail *both* as a conventional modal logic, *and* as an 'Aristotelian' modal logic. In the first place, it is clear that the principle Łukasiewicz takes for granted, that

$$\text{if } \delta A \text{ and } \delta \sim A, \text{ then } \delta B,$$

is acceptable only for functors δ which are *truth-functional*. And 'possible', which does not satisfy this principle, is not, as usually understood, a truth-function. Thus $Ł_4^m$ is unlikely to be acceptable as a straightforward modal logic, precisely because insistence on this principle forces the modal operators to be truth-functional.

However, it could be, as was argued above, that a truth-functional rendering of the modal operators should yield an appropriately 'Aristotelian' modal logic. But $Ł_4^m$ does not succeed even as a non-conventional modal logic. For Łukasiewicz's argument for the two possibility operators depends upon the assumption that the conclusion, that there are no true contingent propositions, is to be avoided. But an Aristotelian modal logic should, not avoid, but embody, this conclusion. For the argument of *de Interpretatione* ix requires just this. A contingent proposition, if Aristotle were right, would be neither true nor false. $Ł_4^m$ is even less successful than $Ł_3$.

6. Conclusions

(1) Aristotle's argument in *de Interpretatione* ix, would show, if valid, that if all sentences were true or false, then it would follow that all events are necessary and all non-events are impossible. It would thus provide motivation for a non-bivalent logic.

(2) His argument is, however, invalid, since it employs a modal fallacy. An attempt to interpret his argument differently turns out also to involve the same fallacy. Although one passage might be interpreted as showing Aristotle's awareness of the invalidity of this form of inference, it can also be interpreted in another way, consistently with my diagnosis.

(3) The Kneale's attempt to show that Aristotle's argument rests on a mistake about the truth-bearers is unsuccessful. But discussion of this suggestion reveals that

(4) Aristotle's own solution to his problem, which retains LEM while dropping PB, may be inadequate.

(5) $Ł_3$, which drops LEM as well as PB, is inadequate as a formalisation of Aristotle's conclusion, though it can be re-interpreted more successfully as an Aristotelian modal logic. $Ł_4^m$, however, is adequate neither as a conventional, nor as an 'Aristotelian', modal logic.

(6) The most adequate formalisation of Aristotle's solution would use a non-truth-functional, non-bivalent logic along the lines of van Fraassen's presuppositional languages.

(7) But, since Aristotle's argument is invalid, no change of logic is in fact called for.

5

Intuitionism

[To the Intuitionist] the dogma of the universal validity of the principle
of excluded third is a phenomenon in the history of civilisation, like
the former belief in the rationality of π, or in the rotation of the
firmament about the earth.

(Brouwer [1952], pp. 141–2.)

1. The Intuitionist view of mathematics and logic

The Intuitionists represent themselves as critics of classical logic, which
holds to be true principles to which there are, they claim, counter-
examples. But it would be a serious mistake to suppose that their
disagreement with certain classical logical principles is the basic tenet
of Intuitionism. This disagreement, on the contrary, is a consequence
of a more fundamental difference; a difference about the nature and
status of logic itself.

While 'classical' logicians no doubt differ among themselves about
the status of logic, there is one point on which they are, I think, agreed:
that logic is the most basic, the most general, of theories. This idea is
crucial to the logicism of Frege and Russell; mathematics is to be
reduced to logic, and the epistemological value of the programme lies
in the presumed *fundamental* nature of the latter. Even pragmatists,
while wishing to treat logic as a theory like others, concede that its
extreme generality gives it a special status. But Intuitionists think
otherwise. On their view, mathematics is primary and logic secondary:
logic is simply a collection of those rules which are discovered, *a
posteriori*, to be true of mathematical reasoning. (Intuitionists would
therefore regard the logicist programme as hopelessly misconceived.)

But this alone would not account for their claim that certain of the
classical logical laws turn out not to be generally true, for the laws of
classical logic *do* hold true of classical mathematical reasoning. However, Intuitionists hold, in addition to their unusual views about logic,
an unusual view about mathematics. Their view has elements both of
psychologism and of constructivism. First, numbers are *mental* entities. They are constructed, according to Brouwer, out of 'the sensation

91

of time'. This seems to mean, from the idea of distinctness or plurality (Brouwer: 'two-ity') acquired thanks to the temporal nature of experience. Mathematics is, thus, a mental activity, and Brouwer stresses that mathematical formalisms are strictly inessential, useful only for communicating the real, mental mathematics. Second, only *constructible* mathematical entities are admitted, so that, for instance, it is not allowed that completed infinite totalities, which are not constructible, exist; and only constructive proofs of mathematical statements are admitted, so that, for instance, a statement to the effect that there is a number with such-and-such a property is provable only if a number with that property is constructible.

This view about the nature of mathematics has a radical consequence: not all of classical mathematics is Intuitionistically acceptable. And from this restriction of mathematics there follows a restriction of logic; some principles of classical logic are found not to be universally valid. The 'principle of excluded third' (LEM) has, for example, counter-instances.

So the structure of the Intuitionist critique of classical logic can be represented as follows:

(1) A subjectivist, constructivist view of mathematics

supports the thesis that

(2) some parts of classical mathematics are unacceptable,

and with

(3) a view of logic as a description of the valid forms of mathematical reasoning

supports the thesis that

(4) some parts of classical logic are mistaken.

The source of the Intuitionists' disagreement with classical logic thus lies deep.

For this reason, one natural reaction can be shown to disregard an important element of Intuitionism. Often the appeal of constructivism is recognised, but it is felt to be unnecessary, and undesirable, to allow it to affect *logic*; it would be sufficient, it is thought, to be constructivist just about mathematics. The situation seems, to someone who does not share the Intuitionists' view of the status of logic, much as if it were recommended that logic be modified in order to cope with set-theoretical paradoxes: surely any necessary modification could be confined to set-theory? But this reaction would be unacceptable to an Intuitionist; for it rests on the assumptions that modification should be made in the less fundamental rather than the more fundamental theory, *and* that mathematics is less fundamental than logic. The Intuitionists deny the latter assumption. This is why Quine's comment:

> one can practice and even preach a very considerable degree of constructivism without adopting intuitionist logic. Weyl's constructive set theory is nearly as old as Brouwer's intuitionism, and it uses orthodox logic; it goes constructivist only in its axioms of existence of sets . . . Constructivist scruples can be reconciled with the convenience and beauty of classical logic.

([1970], p. 88.)

is not wholly satisfactory. Of course, if one rejects the Intuitionists' view of the status of logic, one might sympathise with their constructivism and yet reject their critique of classical logic; but to be justified in adopting this position one really requires an argument against their conception of logic or their conception of mathematics, or both. This is not to say that there is no interest in investigation of what parts of classical mathematics can be retained consistently with constructivism; on the contrary, the very considerable interest of this question is sufficiently evidenced by the sympathy which many mathematicians and philosophers of mathematics (e.g. Poincaré, Kronecker, Borel, Lebesgue, Russell in his discussion of 'impredicative definitions') feel for constructivism. And the problems raised by the set-theoretical paradoxes and Gödel's theorem provide further incentive for this programme. But my present point is that in order to discover whether there is anything in the Intuitionist criticisms of classical logic it would be improper simply to take for granted a non-Intuitionist view of the status of logic, which would have the consequence that constructivist scruples can be accommodated without change of logic.

2. The Intuitionist critique of classical logic

It is necessary to see exactly how the Intuitionists think that certain classical 'laws' fail. This becomes clearer from an examination of Brouwer's argument against the 'principle of excluded third'.

Brouwer calls a property, *F*, of natural numbers, a *fleeing* property if

(a) for each natural number it can be decided either that it possesses
F, or that it cannot,

but

(b) no method is known for calculating a number which is F

and

(c) the assumption that there is such a number is not known to
lead to absurdity.

Then, according to Brouwer,

A natural number possessing F either exists or cannot exist

which is his reading of

$(\exists x)\ Fx \lor \lnot (\exists x)\ Fx$

fails to be true.

It may not be possible *either* to construct a number with F, *or* to
prove that no such number could be constructed. Derivation of a
contradiction from the assumption that there is no such number will
not count, by Intuitionist standards, as showing that there is such a
number, for on their view of the nature of mathematical objects a
number exists only if it is constructible. Hence in these circumstances
it is not true that the number either does or doesn't exist. And this is a
counter-example to the principle of excluded third.

It is somewhat ambiguous whether the principle is thought to be
false, or truth-valueless. Brouwer's argument suggests that he thinks
that both disjuncts, '$(\exists x)\ Fx$' and '$\lnot (\exists x)\ Fx$', and hence the whole
disjunction, are false, and he says this explicitly at least once in [1952].
The same position would be supported by Heyting's comment, that to
say that a number exists means the same as to say that it has been
constructed.

But there is some evidence for another interpretation. Menger raised
the objection that from an Intuitionist point of view such a definition as

$L =$ the greatest prime number such that $L - 2$ is also prime, or
$L = 1$ if there is no such number

would become a proper definition as soon as the twin prime problem
was solved, leaving the embarrassing question, whether '$L = 1$' was
true before the discovery of the solution; Heyting replied ([1966], p. 4)
that this allegedly embarrassing question makes sense only given the

metaphysical assumption, which the Intuitionist rejects, that there exists an independent realm of mathematical entities. This reply suggests that in the absence both of a constructive proof of the former or a *reductio* proof of the latter Heyting would think it nonsense to ascribe either 'true' *or* 'false' to '$(\exists x)\ Fx$' and '$\neg\ (\exists x)\ Fx$.'[1]

The principle of excluded third, of course, fails either way. But the question, whether the claim is that the principle is sometimes false, or sometimes truth-valueless, is of some importance to a further, and interesting, issue: whether Intuitionist logic is a rival, or only a supplement of classical logic; for on the first interpretation, the Intuitionist critique seems to depend on an idiosyncratic interpretation of negation as a contrary- rather than a contradictory-forming operator.

3. Intuitionist logic: rival or supplement?

Because they think of mathematical language as inessential to mathematics, simply a device for recording and communicating, Intuitionists also regard the formalisation of the valid logical rules as a matter of secondary importance. In consequence, there is not one, but a number, of Intuitionist logics. Of these, the Heyting and Johansson calculi are perhaps, in view of their relative entrenchment, the most serious candidates for the title 'Intuitionist logic'. Of the two, Heyting's calculus is the more generally accepted formalisation of the Intuitionistically acceptable logical principles. (I shall question, later, whether this is just.) Heyting himself, however, stresses the provisional nature of his logic; he is confident that all the principles he admits are Intuitionistically acceptable, but not confident that only the principles he admits are acceptable.

In what follows, therefore, the qualification, that the Heyting calculus may not be a wholly adequate formalisation of the Intuitionistically valid logical principles, should be borne in mind.

The Heyting calculus does, however, provide an excellent illustration of the difficulties, discussed in ch. 1, of deciding whether a non-standard system is a rival or a supplement of classical logic.

Some writers (e.g. Quine [1970], pp. 87–9; Hackstaff [1966], p. 221; Nelson [1959], p. 215) have argued that Intuitionist logic is not really, as its proponents, who take themselves to be radically critical of class-

---

[1] This interpretation throws some light on the motivation for Griss's negationless Intuitionist logic, in which all expressions are either true or ill-formed. (See Griss [1944].)

ical logic, think it to be, a rival system; for, they claim, Intuitionist logical constants differ in meaning from their classical (supposed) counterparts. Other writers (e.g. Kneale [1962], Parsons [1971]) think that the Intuitionist criticism cannot be simply deflected by alleging meaning-variance.

Part of the trouble is that those who do appeal to meaning-variance differ about just where the change of meaning is supposed to have taken place. McCall, for one, attributes the Intuitionists' deviance to 'the idiosyncracies of the intuitionist doctrine of negation' ([1970]). This reaction is, certainly, natural, in view of the evidence that Brouwer would take both disjuncts of some instances of '*A* v ⅂ *A*' to be false, and so must be using '⅂' as a contrary-forming operator; and it is also supported by his reading '(∃*x*) *Fx* v ⅂ (∃*x*) *Fx*' as 'A number possessing *F* either exists or *cannot* exist'.

But matters are not really so simple. For one thing, it is possible to interpret the Intuitionist criticism of LEM differently (the disjuncts may be truth-valueless, rather than both false). For another, if there is idiosyncracy in the Intuitionists' interpretation of the constants, it surely extends beyond the sentential connectives. Brouwer and Heyting both sometimes read '(∃*x*)' as 'A number has been constructed . . .', and Heyting quite explicitly says, in [1961], that Intuitionists have restricted the meaning of the existential quantifier. This is where Quine ([1970]) locates the meaning-variance.

The difficulty becomes acute when one looks at suggested translations of the Heyting calculus. The calculus can indeed be interpreted as an extension of classical logic. One way of doing this was suggested by Gödel: if the classical connectives 'v', ' ⊃ ', and '≡' are defined in the usual, classical way in terms of Intuitionist negation and conjunction, thus:

$$p \lor q \; = \; df. \quad \rceil_I (\rceil_I p \;\&_I \rceil_I q)$$
$$p \supset q \; = \; df. \quad \rceil_I (p \;\&_I \rceil_I q)$$
$$p \equiv q \; = \; df. \quad (p \supset q) \;\&_I (q \supset p)$$

then all classical theorems, plus theorems in *Intuitionist* disjunction, implication and equivalence, can be derived in the Heyting logic. It would be tempting to conclude that what Intuitionist logic amounts to is an extension of classical logic to include some new sentential operators. But there is something curious about this; for one of the arguments for change of meaning centred upon Intuitionist negation, yet this interpretation maps Intuitionist directly on to classical negation.

And there is disagreement remaining in spite of the agreement over theoremhood. The Intuitionist does not accept that the argument from A to B is valid iff '$\daleth_I (A \&_I \daleth_I B)$' is logically true, for '$\daleth_I (A \&_I \daleth_I B)$' is not equivalent to '$A \to_I B$'. (cf. van Fraassen [1969], p. 80.)

Another possibility is to interpret the Heyting calculus as a modal logic. Thus, if:

$$m(A) \quad = LA \text{ (for atomic sentences)}$$
$$m(A\vee_I B) = m(A)\vee_c m(B)$$
$$m(A\&_I B) = m(A)\&_c m(B)$$
$$m(\daleth_I A) \quad = L\sim_c m(A)$$
$$m(A\to_I B) = L(m(A) \supset_c m(B))$$

it is provable that a wff is valid in the Heyting calculus iff its translation is valid in $S4$. (See Fitting [1969].)

This translation, too, fails to preserve all deducibility relations. And, although it has the advantage over the previous suggestion that it does not exempt Intuitionist negation from meaning variance, the translation it offers of '$\daleth_I$' is not the one suggested by Brouwer's reading.

Of course, if the Heyting calculus is 'translated' homophonically, all its connectives being interpreted as their classical counterparts, it appears to be what Heyting took it to be, a restriction, not an extension, of classical logic. And in view of the variety, and the doubtful satisfactoriness, of non-homophonic translations, it hardly seems proper to assert that *all* of the Intuitionists' supposed disagreement with classical logic can simply be explained away. Meaning considerations are – as in ch. 1 I argued they would be – inadequate to bear such a weight. Parsons sums up the situation admirably:

> it would be too naïve to take [the disagreement about LEM] as a straight disagreement about a single statement whose meaning is clearly the same. On the other hand, it would not do either to take the difference as 'verbal' in the sense that each one can formulate what the other means in such a way that the disagreement will disappear.
>
> ([1971], pp. 152–3.)

4. Assessment of the Intuitionist criticism

I have argued that the Intuitionists' own claim to be critics of classical logic should be taken seriously; for the disagreement is not straightforwardly soluble by reference to meaning-variance. So the question, whether their criticisms of classical logic are justified, needs answering.

Since this criticism rests upon the Intuitionists' unusual views of mathematics and logic, it might seem to be essential to assess the tenability of these views before a verdict can be given. Fortunately, however, some comments can be made on the adequacy of their criticism without recourse to considerations of quite such a high degree of generality.

A crucial element in Intuitionist philosophy is its constructivism. But I have so far – deliberately – left vague exactly when a number is to count as 'constructible'. It seems to me that it is almost impossible to eliminate this vagueness. Possible interpretations of 'constructible' vary from the very restrictive to the very tolerant. The most restrictive interpretation, that a number is to be allowed to exist only if it has actually been constructed by the 'creating subject', is given some support by remarks of Brouwer and Heyting about the risky character of interpersonal communication of reports of mathematical activity, on account of the imperfection of mathematical language as a description of mathematical thought. A more generous interpretation, which would allow a number to exist provided it had been constructed by some member of the mathematical community, would still impose a temporal restriction. Heyting's negative reply to Menger's question, whether '$(\exists x)\ Fx$' was true *before* a number with F was constructed, lends some support to the restriction to actually effected constructions.

But it is perfectly clear that if either of these interpretations were intended, the Intuitionistically acceptable part of mathematics would be very restricted indeed. And in [1961] Heyting argues that the Intuitionist should not restrict himself to actually effected constructions, because to do so would mean restricting the acceptable part of mathematics to theorems concerning relatively small natural numbers. This is a curious kind of argument for an Intuitionist to use; for the Intuitionists are unusual among the schools of philosophy of mathematics for their insistence that those parts of classical mathematics which cannot be justified on their terms must be abandoned as illegitimate; whereas formalists, say, or logicists, take it for granted that an acceptable philosophy must provide foundations for the whole of classical mathematics. So one might have expected an Intuitionist to decide what constructions are permissible independently of how much of classical mathematics would be allowed by whatever account of constructibility he chooses.

However, Heyting proposes to allow, besides

(1) actually effected constructions

both

(2) general methods of construction

and

(3) hypothetical constructions.

Whereas (1) is sufficient for the proof of affirmative theorems about small natural numbers, (2) and (3) are required for the proof of *general* or *negative* theorems. Heyting's example is the proof of

$$\vdash \neg (2 + 2) = 5$$

which would go:

(i) and (ii) repeated construction of the number 2

(iii) construction of $2 + 2$

(iv) construction of 5

(v) *hypothetical construction* of a $1 - 1$ correspondence between the results of (iii) and (iv)

(vi) *general method* of deducing a contradiction from (v).

(2) and (3) would also, he argues, be required for the proof of a general theorem such as

$$\vdash a + b = b + a$$

The difficulty here is that both (2) and (3) require some sense to be given to 'possible but not actual construction'. This extension creates some problems. If he allows more than actually effected constructions, the Intuitionist is vulnerable to embarrassing objections from the strict finitist. Just as the Intuitionist criticises the classical mathematician on the grounds that incomprehensible metaphysics are involved in the supposition that a number might exist even though it is impossible, even in principle, to construct it, so the strict finitist would criticise the Intuitionist for allowing that a number might exist even though its construction might be too long or complicated ever to be carried out. (cf. Dummett [1970], p. 1.)

Furthermore, the sense of 'possible construction' is far from clear. Intuitionists disagree among themselves about what the proper sense of 'possible construction' should be. Griss, for example, evidently understands 'possible construction' more restrictively than Heyting, for he denies the possibility of hypothetical constructions. One cannot, he thinks, have 'a clear conception of a supposition that eventually proves to be a mistake' ([1944]). Doubt is, in consequence, thrown on the method of *reductio ad absurdum*: suppose p . . . then q and not q . . . so not p. For if p is, as it turns out, impossible, one wasn't supposing anything coherent at the outset. The result is an extremely restricted, negation free, logic. (cf. de Jongh [1949], Gilmore [1953].) Heyting himself manifests a certain unease about his 'hypothetical construction of a $1 - 1$ correlation between $2 + 2$ and 5'. In demonstrating the negation of a proposition p, he says, a construction satisfying part of the conditions imposed by p is described, and it is then shown that it violates another part.

However, it might be suggested that, although the notion of a 'possible construction' is left less than satisfactorily clear by Heyting, it can nevertheless be made clear, by identifying it with the *effectively decidable* in the technical sense of Church. This suggestion is somewhat unhistorical, since when Brouwer first criticised classical mathematics (in his doctoral dissertation of 1907) Church's thesis had not been proposed. Nevertheless it looks promising.

The proposal to interpret the crucial notion of 'possible construction' is made by Kleene in [1945]. The basic idea is that the Intuitionist understands '$(\exists x)\ Fx$', for instance, as an incomplete communication of a statement actually giving an x which is F, and '$(x)\ Fx$' as an incomplete communication of an effective general method for finding, for any x, the information which completes the communication 'Fx' for that x.

Exploiting the thesis that the effective general methods are the recursive ones, and the fact that since recursive functions can be enumerated they can be identified with integers via Gödel numbering, Kleene defines *recursive realisability* as follows: a natural number e *realises* a closed number-theoretic formula p (i.e. is the number of a construction which 'completes' p) if:

1. p is an atomic formula: $e = 0$ and p is true. (This clause makes use of the fact that primitive arithmetical predicates are decidable.)

2. p is of the form $A\ \&\ B$: $e = 2^a.\ 3^b$ where a realises A and b realises B.

3. p is of the form $A\ \text{v}\ B$: $e = 2.°\ 3^a$ where a realises A, or $e = 2^1.\ 3^b$ where b realises B.

4. p is of the form $A \supset B$: e is the Gödel number of a partial

recursive function ϕ of one variable such that, wherever a realises A, $\phi(a)$ realises B.

5. p is of the form $\neg A$: e realises $A \supset 1$: $1 = 0$.
(A, B any closed formulae.)

6. p is of the form $(\exists x) F(x)$: $e = 2^x \cdot 3^a$ where a realises $F(x)$.

7. p is of the form $(x) F(x)$: e is the Gödel number of a general recursive function ϕ of one variable such that, for every x, $\phi(x)$ realises $F(x)$

(x a variable, $F(x)$ a formula containing free only x.)

Kleene has shown that *all formulae which are provable in intuitionistic arithmetic are realisable by an arbitrary 'e'*.

However, Rose has proved ([1953]) that *it is not the case that only formulae which are provable in intuitionistic arithmetic are so realisable.*

So it looks as if the Intuitionists' understanding of 'constructible' is stronger than this interpretation allows. (Not vice versa, as Mostowski claims in [1960] p. 96.) And this supports the conclusion that Kleene's attempt to precisify the Intuitionist concept of 'constructibility' unfortunately does not succeed.

Heyting, I think, would not find this conclusion surprising, for he several times comments that 'constructible' cannot be defined, but must be taken as primitive. (See e.g. [1959], where he uses an argument derived from Péter [1959], to the effect that any definition would use an existential quantifier which would in turn require the notion of possible construction for *its* explication.) He suggests, that is, that 'possible construction' be taken as implicitly defined by the principles of Intuitionist logic.

But there seems to me to be an unavoidable difficulty in this procedure. The motivation for the restriction imposed by Intuitionist logic was that it allowed only those principles which hold of constructivist mathematics. The argument against LEM, for example, was that, given constructivist standards of proof, sometimes neither '$(\exists x) Fx$' nor '$\neg (\exists x) Fx$' might be true. But if what counts as a possible construction is not defined independently of Intuitionist logic, this sort of motivation would be impossible.

This difficulty becomes apparent when one looks at Heyting's own comments on his axioms. He feels the need to offer some justification for one of his axioms, the last:

$$X \vdash \neg p \to (p \to q).$$

It is rather significant, in itself, that Heyting should find only this axiom in need of justification. And the justification offered is very curious:

> Axiom X may not seem intuitively clear. As a matter of fact, it adds to the precision of the definition of implication. You remember that $p \to q$ can be asserted if and only if we possess a construction which, joined to the construction p, would prove q. Now suppose that $\neg p$, that is, we have deduced a contradiction from the supposition that p were carried out. Then, in a sense, this can be considered as a construction which, joined to a proof of p (which cannot exist) leads to a proof of q.
>
> ([1966], p. 102.)

Although Heyting represents axiom X as involving simply an extension of the sense of 'implies', what the proposal really amounts to is that the sense of 'construction' be extended, so that a construction of p plus a derivation of a contradiction from the assumption that there is such a construction, is to count as a construction of q. But the extended sense of 'construction' is so liberal that it hardly seems characteristically *Intuitionist* at all. Now of course if Heyting's axioms implicitly define 'constructible', this would be an absurd objection to make. But in that case too it is hard to see how Heyting's comments could possibly justify the inclusion of the axiom.

If the tenth axiom is dropped, the resulting system is Johansson's 'minimal calculus'. Interestingly enough, a system equivalent to the minimal calculus was proposed as a formalisation of Brouwer's ideas by Kolmogorov as early as 1925. Kolmogorov had commented that Heyting's axiom X

> does not have and cannot have any intuitive foundation.
>
> ([1925], p. 421.)

In view of the inadequacy of Heyting's 'justification', this comment is, I think, entirely fair. The minimal calculus represents the set of Intuitionistically valid formulae better than the Heyting calculus. Heyting would say that the minimal calculus simply formalises a slightly different, but still possible, sense of 'construction'. But if this were accepted, it would be inexplicable why Heyting does not allow that classical logic formalises yet another, but still possible, sense ('consistent').

To sum up the argument of this section. The Intuitionist criticism of classical logic depends upon a notion of 'possible construction' which is susceptible of a wide variety of interpretations. If it is interpreted very narrowly, the parts of classical mathematics which would be ruled acceptable are very restricted indeed, too restricted to be acceptable to most Intuitionists. If it is interpreted more broadly, the Intuitionist becomes vulnerable to criticisms from the strict finitist analogous to his own criticisms of the classical mathematician. Furthermore, how exactly to specify a broader interpretation poses problems; the most promising suggestion, an interpretation in terms of effective decidability, turns out to be broader than the Intuitionists wish. And Heyting's suggestion, that 'possible construction' can be taken as implicitly defined by his axioms, fails because, if it were accepted, it would make the motivation for the Intuitionists' rejection of certain principles quite obscure.

The criticisms I have made centre upon the notion of constructibility, which, I have argued, is not, and cannot, consistently with traditional Intuitionist views about what parts of mathematics are acceptable, be made precise. But although these criticisms do some damage to traditional Intuitionism, they leave open the question, whether, if Intuitionist views on the status of logic and mathematics were accepted, and constructibility were interpreted in terms of realisibility, something *like* the Intuitionist criticisms of classical logic might not still be possible?

In order to rebut this suggestion it would be necessary to attack the more basic tenets of Intuitionism – the thesis that mathematical entities do not exist independently or the thesis of the dependence of logic on mathematics. So I propose in the next section to examine the arguments offered by Dummett in support of the first of these theses. Dummett's arguments make admirable sense of much that is fragmentary in earlier Intuitionist work; so that if *they* can be shown to be inadequate, this thesis will be quite seriously discredited.

5. An 'Intuitionist' theory of meaning

According to Dummett:

> The strongest arguments [for Intuitionism] come from the insistence that the general form of explanation of meaning, and hence of the logical operators in particular, is a statement not of the truth-conditions but of the assertibility-conditions.

([1959a], p. 347.)

The most powerful form of argument in favour of . . . a constructivist view is that which insists that there is no other means by which
we can give meaning to mathematical expressions. There is no means
by which we could derive . . . a notion of truth and falsity for mathematical statements independent of our means for recognising their
truth-value.

([1970], p. 1.)

Dummett's argument seems to be that an *assertibility-condition*
theory of meaning is preferable to a *truth-condition* theory, and that
such a theory of meaning has as consequence an Intuitionist view of
mathematical truth.

First, then, Dummett's arguments against a truth-condition theory
of meaning. (See especially [1959].)

The truth-condition theory of meaning cannot be held in conjunction with a redundancy theory of truth. For, according to the redundancy theory, the meaning of a statement S is the same as the meaning
of 'It is true that S'. So the meaning of S cannot without circularity be
given in terms of its truth-conditions, since the truth-conditions of S
are in turn given in terms of S. This objection looks rather like a
statement of the 'paradox of analysis'.

Since, therefore, a truth-condition theory cannot be held with a
redundancy theory of truth, it must be supported by a correspondence
theory, a theory, that is, according to which a statement is true only if
there is something in virtue of which it is true. And this entails that a
truth-condition theory of meaning is acceptable only if, for any statement S, there is something in virtue of which either S or its negation
is true; otherwise it would fail to give any meaning to some statements.
It is apparently assumed that the redundancy and the correspondence
theories are the only available theories of truth.

However, this 'realist' assumption is false; many statements are
such that there is nothing in virtue of which either they or their
negations are true. Dummett mentions three kinds of example:

(1) Suppose Jones is now dead and never faced danger in his life.
And suppose there are 'ordinary grounds' neither for 'If Jones had
faced danger he would have acted bravely' nor for 'If Jones had faced
danger he would not have acted bravely'. The realist must insist,
Dummett argues, that there must all the same be something, perhaps a
mysterious psychological or physiological something called 'character',
in virtue of which either 'Jones was brave' or 'Jones was not brave' is

true. There is some reason to think that Dummett is treating 'Jones was not brave' as, not the contradictory, but the contrary, of 'Jones was brave'.

(2) Consider 'A city will never be built on this spot'. If, as the realist claims, there is something in virtue of which it is true (or false), that something will have to be an infinite collection of facts: that there will be no city here in 1981, 1982, 1983 . . . etc. Yet one might be unable either to be sure that there will be a city here in the year *n*, for some specified *n*, or to find a general proof that there will never be a city here. Dummett would apparently reject ordinary, inductive evidence, since he insists that only an *infinite* set of facts would justify 'There will never be a city on this spot'.

(3) If the realist is to maintain that a mathematical statement of the form '(∃x) Fx' is either true or false, then, since he must concede that one might be unable either to produce a number which is *F*, or to prove that there can be no such number, he must claim that there exists a mathematical reality, independent of human knowledge of it, in virtue of which '(∃x) Fx' is either true or false.

And the position to which the realist is forced is, Dummett thinks, not just implausible, but impossible. If a statement *S* is true, it must be true in virtue of some fact of a kind which one was taught as justifying one in asserting it. Anyone who claims that *S* is true in virtue of some other kind of fact, must understand *S* in an idiosyncratic sense. The truth-condition theory of meaning, plus the correspondence theory of truth, has the consequence that certain sentences don't mean what, in fact, they do mean. So it fails.

Dummett proposes, therefore, to replace the truth-condition by an assertibility-condition theory of meaning: the meaning of a statement *S* is given by the conditions in which it is justifiably assertible. And he proceeds to argue that the virtue of this theory is that it allows that a statement may have a clear sense, but no truth-value. His argument goes: the meaning of a sentence is learnt by learning the conditions in which it can justifiably be asserted. But a sentence with quite definite assertibility-conditions may nevertheless not be assertible, and its negation, also with quite definite assertibility-conditions, may not be assertible either. So the sentence can have sense without truth-value.

These arguments are most ingenious. But they are not, I think, satisfactory.

The first question I want to raise is, what, exactly, *are* assertibility-conditions? Dummett describes them as the conditions in which one would be justified in asserting the sentence concerned, and stresses that they are distinct from the truth-conditions, those, that is, in which the sentence would be true. This suggests that he must hold *either*:

(a) that a sentence S may be true but not assertible

or

(b) that a sentence S may be assertible but not true

since otherwise the distinction between assertibility- and truth-conditions would be in danger of collapse. However, Dummett's discussion of case (2) makes it pretty clear that he would not allow (b); he takes 'A city will never be built here' not to be assertible on the strength of any finite amount of inductive evidence in its favour, and so presumably intends that S be assertible only if there is *conclusive* evidence for it, in which case S will be true. And it also seems that Dummett can't allow (a) either; for the burden of his attack on the truth-condition theory is, that a person who insists that S *is* true (or false), though it is not assertible (or refutable) must understand S in an idiosyncratic sense.

If both (a) and (b) are rejected, it begins to look as if Dummett has not so much replaced truth-conditions by assertibility-conditions, as assimilated the two. Truth-conditions and assertibility-conditions turn out to be equivalent.

But if this is right, another question arises. Why, if truth-conditions and assertibility-conditions are equivalent, does Dummett think that a truth-condition theory cannot, while an assertibility-condition theory can, allow that a sentence may be meaningful but truth-valueless? Apparently because he thinks that the truth-condition theory will give a sentence a meaning only if the sentence has a truth-value, and, further-more, that some sentences in fact lack truth-value.

But the second of these claims is surely out of place here, since the point of the whole argument was to establish just that – that some sentences are neither true nor false. That a question is being begged becomes clear when one recalls Dummett's discussion of case (3); the claim that '$(\exists x)\, Fx$' is invariably either true or false is rejected on the grounds that it may not be possible either to construct a number which is F, or to prove that there can't be such a number. But this is to assume what was to be proved: that the Intuitionist view of mathematics is correct. The classical mathematician would disagree with

Dummett about what the assertibility conditions of '($\exists x$) Fx' *are*; a derivation of a contradiction from '$\neg$ ($\exists x$) Fx' would, for him, make '($\exists x$) Fx' assertible.

But even if it were granted that some sentences are neither true nor false, would a truth-condition theory really be unable to cope? Dummett's argument why an assertibility-condition theory could allow this, is that the assertibility-condition theory of meaning says that a sentence is significant if there are conditions in which it *would be* assertible. However, a sentence with quite definite assertibility-conditions may not be assertible, and thus the assertibility-condition theory allows significant but truth-valueless sentences. But exactly the same argument would show that a truth-condition theory can also allow this possibility. The truth-condition theory says that a theory is significant if there are conditions in which it *would be* true. However, a sentence with quite definite truth-conditions might nevertheless fail to be true or false. If one accepted Dummett's view of case (3), for instance, one could very well say that '($\exists x$) Fx' has quite definite truth conditions (it would be true if a number with F had been constructed, false if it had been proved that there is no such number) but yet, in some circumstances, it may be neither true nor false.

The theory of truth (Tarski's) which is used by one notable exponent of a truth-condition theory of meaning (Davidson) is, indeed, bivalent. But this is not the inevitable accompaniment of a truth-condition theory. It can be avoided by the adoption of a liberal definition of negation:

D1. $\sim A$ is true if A is false, false if A is true

in place of the more restrictive:

D2. $\sim A$ is true if A is false, false otherwise

and then it can allow the possibility of significant but truth-valueless sentences.

Not only is an assertibility-condition theory not necessary (as I have just shown) to allow this possibility; it is not sufficient, either. Further assumptions, about what the assertibility-conditions of certain statements are, are also needed. For instance, a classical mathematician would think that '($\exists x$) Fx' is assertible if there is a proof of a contradiction from its negation, and that '$p \lor \sim p$' is assertible in all circumstances whatever. (Dummett virtually admits this in [1959a], pp. 337–8.)

A strict finitist would presumably find Dummett's account of assertibility conditions too liberal. He would argue that we learn the meaning of a sentence only in circumstances in which it can be shown, can actually, that is, not, 'in principle', be shown, to be assertible. It is hard to see what resources remain to Dummett to answer him.

Nor, of course, is the admission that a sentence may be significant but truth-valueless sufficient to establish Intuitionism. The most it does is leave open the possibility of denying PB. Indeed, it could even be thought that Dummett's arguments, if they were successful, would actually throw doubt on Intuitionism. For his aim was to show that classical logic is in some respects mistaken, and to do so in a way which made no special appeal to the subject-matter of mathematics. But this means that if his arguments were sufficient to establish the Intuitionists' view of mathematics, they would also be sufficient to establish anti-realism with respect to any subject-matter. Anti-realism is, however, *less* plausible when applied to other subject matters – e.g. geography – than when applied to mathematics. Dummett seems to recognise this:

> After all, the considerations do not apply only to mathematics but to all discourse; and while they certainly show something mistaken in the realist conception of thought and reality, they surely do not imply outside mathematics the extreme of subjective idealism – that we *create* the world.
>
> ([1959a], p. 348.)

So, on the confession of its advocate, the 'strongest argument' for Intuitionism is less than conclusive.

6. Conclusions

Traditional Intuitionism, then, runs into difficulties because of unclarities in its central concept of 'constructibility'. Motivation for a form of neo-Intuitionism to which this concept is given a precise interpretation in terms of realisibility would, however, still exist if the Intuitionists' conception of mathematics were accepted. But Dummett's arguments for this conception, which are the most explicit and the strongest I know, seem to fail.

6

Vagueness

1. Location of the problem

Some advocates of non-standard logics have appealed to the alleged
vagueness of ordinary language by way of justification; and some
philosophers who have considered the problems created by vagueness
have appealed to non-standard logics by way of solution. Much of this
discussion is, however, confused by a failure adequately to specify
what is meant by 'vagueness'. This failure has led to a number of
difficulties. I mention, for illustration, two of the kinds of problem
which are liable to arise.

Some writers (e.g. Pap [1949], p. 116; Black [1963], p. 10) define a sentence as vague just in case PB (or LEM or both) fails for it. This kind
of definition has the unsatisfactory consequence that sources of failure
of PB *other than* vagueness cannot be allowed. I shall therefore avoid it.

Other writers discuss, under the title 'vagueness', phenomena which,
on close inspection, turn out doubtfully to fall in this category. C. S.
Peirce, for instance, who thought that:

> Logicians have been at fault in giving Vagueness the go-by
>
> ([CP] 5.446, p. 298.)

and who claimed (5.506, p. 358) to have worked out a complete 'logic
of vagueness', seems from his examples, to have had a somewhat
eccentric conception of vagueness. In 5.506, pp. 355–6, he contrasts
vague with general sentences; and he gives examples which suggest
that he understands by a 'general' sentence, one which is universally
quantified, and by a 'vague' sentence, one which is existentially quantified. In view of this, his claim that general sentences violate LEM, and
vague sentences the law of non-contradiction, becomes comprehensible; for it is indeed the case that '$(x) Fx$' and '$(x) \sim Fx$' may be both
false, and that '$(\exists x) Fx$' and '$(\exists x) \sim Fx$' may be both true. But the
connection of Peirce's work with later claims that sentences containing
expressions whose application has borderline cases require a non-
standard logic, now looks rather tenuous.[1] I don't mean that Peirce is

[1] The analogy with MacColl's work, incidentally, now looks rather strong. cf pp
54–5.

necessarily *misusing* the term 'vagueness'; Alston in [1964], p. 85, points out that 'vague' and 'unspecific' are commonly, though he thinks unfortunately, used interchangeably. Nor do I mean that Peirce's comments on the logical properties of the sentences he calls vague are without interest. But this example does make clear the need to beware that differences in the use of 'vague' are not unnecessarily clouding the issue. A definition of vagueness which is not too far out of line with prevalent usage is, surely, desirable.

The examples discussed in the literature under the heading 'vagueness' are of an extraordinary variety, and it is not easy to specify what they have in common. The examples are most often of predicate expressions, a vague sentence being taken to be one containing one (or more) vague predicates. And one feature which most examples share is that the predicate in question is such that, for some subject(s) there is uncertainty whether the predicate applies. Uncertainty of application is not, however, coextensive with vagueness, since there are, or appear to be, quite precise expressions, e.g. '3·001 cm. long' the application of which in some cases may be uncertain, say because of the inadequacy of available measuring techniques. (I am for the moment assuming – as ordinary usage suggests – that whereas some predicates are vague, others are quite precise, and that a definition of vagueness should allow for this distinction. Later, however, it will be necessary to examine the view that there are, in fact, no precise predicates.) So I distinguish two ways in which uncertainty about the applicability of a predicate might arise:

(1) The qualifications for being F are imprecise.

(2) The qualifications for being F are precise, but there is difficulty in determining whether certain subjects satisfy them.

(By 'the qualifications for being F' is understood: the filling of a true sentence-scheme of the form 'Necessarily (x is F iff...)'. This, because of the 'necessarily', is very rough and ready, but should be adequate for present purposes.) I take it that only uncertainty of the first kind would normally be thought of as amounting to vagueness. But, of course, (1) can hardly be taken as a definition of vagueness, since it employs the expression 'imprecise', and so would be, as a definition, objectionably circular. (1) can, however, be improved somewhat by specification of some of the ways in which the qualifications for being F could be imprecise:

(a) The qualifications are complex (in the form of an open conjunction, or conjunction of disjunctions) and it is *indeterminate how many of the qualifications* must be satisfied, and how the qualifications are to be weighted. Alston gives ([1964], p. 88) the example of the qualifications for a cultural entity counting as a religion; does, e.g. a culture which embodies belief in supernatural beings but lacks ritual, count as religious?

(b) The qualifications are complex, and in certain cases *conflicting*. Quine gives ([1960], p. 128) the example of the qualifications for one river's being a tributary of another; does, e.g. a river which is shorter, but greater in volume than another which it joins, count as a tributary? Mellor in [1965] takes something like this as his *definition* of 'conceptual imprecision'.

(c) The qualifications are simple (in the form of a single condition, or of a straightforward conjunction all of whose conjuncts must be satisfied), but in certain cases it is *indeterminate whether the condition, or one of the conditions, is satisfied*. An example, which occurs in a number of writers, might be colour predicates; how closely, e.g. does an object have to resemble an English pillar-box if it is to count as red? To avoid confusion with uncertainties of type (2), it is necessary to add, that the indeterminacy about whether the qualifications are satisfied should not be due to any lack of information about the object in question.

I shall count predicates of any of those kinds and predicates the qualifications for which involve such predicates as vague. Predicates of type (c) are perhaps the commonest in the literature, but predicates of types (a) and (b) are also quite often classified as vague. Wittgenstein's 'family resemblance' concepts seem to be of type (a), (see Wittgenstein [1953], and cf. Campbell [1965]); type (b) is included in the class of 'law-cluster' concepts (see Gasking [1960], and Putnam [1962]). It is not claimed that these types are exclusive – some predicates may fall into more than one category, perhaps having qualifications in the form of an open-ended conjunction of conditions, thus falling into type (a), some one or more than one of which is indeterminate in application, thus falling also into type (c). It is also possible that a predicate should suffer both type (1) and type (2) uncertainty; for instance, it could be argued that 'red', which falls in category (1)(c), *also* suffers type (2) uncertainty, since in some cases it may be impossible to tell, or impossible to get observers to agree, whether one object matches another in colour. (Waismann, in [1946], takes colour words to be subject to both kinds of uncertainty.)

I have restricted myself, in this rough delineation of the types of predicate to be counted as 'vague', to *static* features of a language. Waismann's notion ([1945], p. 123) of 'open-texture' seems to be partly a *dynamic* one. The underlying idea is that predicates adequately defined for present circumstances might appear quite *in*adequately defined for quite different circumstances – it is open, e.g. whether one should call a creature, in other respects feline, a cat, if it suddenly grew to 12ft high. This bears some analogy to category (1)(a); but in so far as Waismann's concept involves reference to the possibility of *change* in the qualifications for application of a predicate in response to hitherto unforeseen circumstances, it is not covered by my classification.

I have also restricted the classification in a way which takes vagueness to be (primarily) a linguistic matter (words can be vague, not the things to which words apply), and furthermore, (primarily) semantic rather than pragmatic ('vague' is treated as a predicate of predicates, and sentences, rather than of uses of sentences). I hope no relevant questions are begged by these restrictions.

2. The consequences of vagueness: arguments for the failure of classical logic

It has frequently been suggested that vagueness threatens the acceptability of classical logic (see e.g. Alston [1964], p. 96). Some writers explicitly claim that the existence of vagueness therefore creates a need for a non-classical logic (see e.g. Körner [1960], ch. 8; [1966], ch. 3; Waismann [1946]). Others draw only the perhaps less radical conclusion, that classical logic is 'not applicable' to vague sentences (see e.g. Russell [1923], pp. 85, 88–9): just what *this* means, is a question which will need further attention.

The arguments used, *why* vague sentences constitute a difficulty for classical logic, differ from writer to writer. The following arguments are derived from the writers mentioned, but modified, with the intention of maximising their plausibility.

(1) Classical logic is bivalent; it is assumed, that is, that its sentence-letters stand only for sentences which are either true or

false. But vague sentences may be neither true nor false. For a vague predicate is such that it may be indeterminate whether it applies to certain subjects, and so, those sentences in which a vague predicate is ascribed to a borderline subject will fail to be either true or false.

It is not only that it may be irremediably uncertain whether the sentences are true or whether they are false – as it might be uncertain, in the absence of adequate measuring techniques, whether 'This object is 3·001 cm. long' is true or false; they *are* neither true nor false. The distinction between type (1) and type (2) uncertainty is important here. In the case of uncertainty of type (2) the failure is epistemological, the failure to discover the truth-value of a sentence; whereas with uncertainty of type (1), the failure is more radical, the failure of the sentence to *be* true or false. Not all the writers I have mentioned (e.g. Waismann, Russell) are very careful to observe this distinction. But I think the argument depends for its plausibility on the distinction's being observed.[2]

(2) This direct line of argument, why vagueness threatens bivalence, is sometimes supplemented by an indirect argument appealing to the Sorites paradox. A traditional form of the paradox goes: given that *one* grain of sand doesn't amount to a heap, and given that adding one grain to something less than a heap doesn't make it a heap, it follows that *no* amount of sand is a heap: a most implausible conclusion. But, if, in view of the implausibility of the conclusion, it is assumed instead that *one* grain of sand doesn't amount to a heap, but 1 million grains (say) do, then it follows, by reasoning equally impeccable classically, that there is some number, 800,000, say, such that 800,000 grains of sand are *not* a heap: but 800,001 grains *are* a heap: an equally implausible conclusion.

Similar paradoxes are constructed, using other vague predicates – 'short' by Black in [1963], 'bald' by Russell in [1923], 'small' by Dummett in [1971]; a particularly charming version, using 'is a tadpole', is given by Cargile in [1969]. And each of these writers considers the possibility that a proper reaction to the paradox might be to deny the correctness, or the applicability, of the classical logical principles employed in the paradoxical arguments.

[2] This could be denied. Passages in [1970] suggest that Dummett would deny it. But Dummett's willingness to infer the existence of a truth-value gap from an epistemological failure rests upon his assertibility-condition theory of meaning, which has already been criticised in ch. 5.

A non-classical logic for vague sentences?

Even if it were agreed that these arguments showed that vagueness creates a need for a non-classical logic, it would be rather unclear what kind of modification of logic would be called for. The direct argument, if correct, presumably leads to the conclusion that a logic suitable for manipulating vague sentences should not be bivalent. The calculi proposed by Waismann and Körner are 3-valued, and LEM as well as PB fails. However, the first, direct argument considered leaves open the question whether LEM as well as PB is threatened.

Dummett has an argument that LEM should be retained: consider a vague sentence which fails to be true or false, such as:

O is orange

where 'O' stands for an object borderline with respect to 'orange'. Now, Dummett argues, O must be on the border between orange and some other colour, say, red. Then

Either O is orange or O is red

is true. But

O is red

entails

O is not orange

and so

Either O is orange or O is not orange

is true, in spite of its disjuncts lacking truth-value. If this argument were accepted, it suggests that a logic, like van Fraassen's, conventional so far as theoremhood is concerned but non-bivalent, might be required. (However, though Dummett's reasoning is sound, it may not apply to *all* vague sentences; it is possible that the choice of a predicate which is a determinate of a determinable is essential to the argument.)

Most writers, too, assume that LEM, as well as PB, is threatened by the indirect argument, the argument via the Sorites paradox. Dummett, however, suggests that the paradoxical argument could be blocked, if PB were dropped, *without* dropping LEM, by denying the principle that, if '($\exists x$) Fx' is true, then there must be some definite, specifiable object which is F; then 'There is some number of grains such that that many isn't a heap, but one more is' can be admitted,

without there being any definite answer to the question *which* number?
(p. 11). This is a very curious concession for one of Dummett's Intuitionist leanings to make, for it is typical of the Intuitionist to refuse to
allow '($\exists x$) Fx' in the absence of a proof, with respect to some specific
number, that *it* is *F*. But Dummett's suggestion bears considerable
analogy to van Fraassen's claim,[3] that his system disallows the inference,
'A v B, $A \supset C$, $B \supset C \vdash C$'; so it is possible that Dummett's suggestion could be worked out in sufficient detail to yield the desired
consequences, or rather, not to yield the undesired consequences.

There are, then, arguments which, if correct, show that vagueness
creates some difficulty for classical logic. One possible reaction would
be to attempt to devise, perhaps exploiting the suggestions discussed
above, a suitable *non*-classical logic. But this reaction would be somewhat hasty. At least two questions need answering before such a radical
step is taken: are the arguments discussed sound? and, if they are, is
there any way of coping with vagueness short of modification of logic?

3. Are the arguments against classical logic sound?

Some arguments to be found in the literature would, if correct, show
that the arguments why vague sentences create a need for non-standard
logic are simply mistaken. Odegard, for instance, in [1965] attempts to
show that it is only tempting to suppose that vague sentences are
neither true nor false, if the distinction between contraries and contra
dictories is neglected. Unfortunately, he nowhere gives an argument
which establishes that such pairs of sentences as

Socrates was bald

and

Socrates was not bald

are contraries rather than contradictories; and in the absence of such
an argument, merely pointing out the difference between contraries
and contradictories goes no way towards showing the argument
against bivalence to be mistaken. Odegard also tries to show that the
proponents of this argument have confused object- and meta-languages;
but his argument rests on assimilating 'not true' and 'false', which, of

[3] cf. the comments made in ch. 4 on the adequacy of van Fraassen's calculus to
block Aristotle's fatalist argument.

course, begs precisely the question at issue, since 'not true' = 'false' only if PB is accepted. The arguments, why vague sentences require a non-standard logic, have not been shown to rest on any simple *mistake*.

4. Are vague sentences within the scope of logic?

But it might be suggested that adoption of a non-standard calculus would be doubtfully satisfactory as a solution to the problems allegedly created by vagueness. Suppose that instead of dividing sentences exhaustively into the true and the false, one divided them into three categories, the true, the false, and those which, from vagueness, fail to have any truth-value at all. A new problem, analogous to the original problem motivating the adoption of the threefold categorisation, would now arise. The original problem was that some sentences could be assigned neither 'true' nor 'false', because they ascribed vague predicates to borderline cases. But exactly *which* cases are borderline, is itself indeterminate. (It is not that a man with fewer than 500 hairs on his head is clearly bald, a man with 1,000 clearly not bald, and a man with between 500 and 1,000 hairs clearly borderline. It is indeterminate whether a man with, say, 505 hairs is bald, or borderline.) It is as counterintuitive to draw the boundaries of the borderline precisely, as to draw the boundaries between cases whether the predicate is true and cases where it is false precisely. This line of thought tends to the conclusion that the Sorites problem is hardly less acute if a *non*-bivalent logic is adopted.

And this conclusion is in harmony with a less radical reaction to the threat to classical logic.

Consider the *insouciance* with which Russell comments that

All traditional logic habitually assumes that precise symbols are being employed. It is therefore not applicable to this terrestial life, but only to an imagined celestial existence . . . logic takes us nearer to heaven than most other studies.

([1923], pp. 88–9.)

It is notable that Russell does not entertain the possibility that the language of *Principia*, which excludes vagueness, might need modification; it is just 'not suitable for public occasions'. Russell thinks that vagueness shows that logic is 'not applicable' to ordinary language, and by 'not applicable' he evidently means, not 'false', but something more like 'inappropriate'.

This suggests that Russell would advocate a version of what was dubbed, in ch. 3, the 'no-item' strategy. Such a strategy would argue that vague sentences are *outside the scope* of logic, so that logic need not be modified to cope with them.

A common version of this strategy proceeds by arguing, in support of the exclusion of vague sentences from the scope of logic, that vague sentences fail to express propositions, or, to make statements (or, etc.), and that logic is concerned with propositions, or statements, rather than sentences. It became clear in ch. 3, however, that this strategy rather easily lends itself to triviality. Thus, in Lewy's [1946] 'proposition' is used to mean 'item of which classical logic is true', with the result that vague sentences are, in a wholly trivial way, ruled not to express propositions, and not to be within the scope of logic. The argument used by Jeffrey in [1967], p. 7, employing the locution 'statement' rather than 'proposition', seems similar in structure.

But not all arguments to the effect that vague sentences are outside the scope of logic are, necessarily, trivial. For it could be suggested that vague sentences are not the kind of item to which logic *ought* to apply, perhaps on the grounds that precision is one of the aims of formalisation. This idea seems to lie behind Russell's comments; the language of *Principia* was devised, he says, in order to *avoid* vagueness.

This kind of reaction has its attractions.

If its attractions are not obvious, it may be helpful to consider a – possibly analogous – case. It has sometimes been suggested (e.g. in Halldén [1949], Goddard [1966], Routley [1966], [1969]) that a 3-valued logic is needed to handle *meaningless* sentences. Considerable effort has been expended on devising a suitable calculus. And yet it seems to me perfectly clear that meaningless sentences really have no business in logic; for their meaninglessness unfits them for any interesting role in (valid) inference.[4] (That is why, in this book, no attention is paid to 'logics of meaninglessness'.)

Although it is not so obvious, it is at least arguable that vague sentences, also, ought to be excluded from logic, rather than logic's being modified to cope with them. Now, the reason I gave, why the argument that logic ought not to be modified to handle meaningless sentences, is plausible, was that such sentences do not normally figure in

---

[4] If, exceptionally, a meaningless sentence occurs essentially in an argument, its detection is surely sufficient to warrant rejection of the argument.

argument; so the relevant question, with respect to vague sentences, is whether *they* normally so figure?

However, on the face of it at least, it looks as if vague sentences can indeed occur in valid arguments – so that, since validity is *par excellence* the province of logic, vague sentences should be admitted within its scope. But the answer to the question, whether vague sentences occur in valid arguments, will of course depend on the definition of validity which is employed. The definition of validity might be either syntactic or semantic. An argument is (syntactically) valid-in-L iff its conclusions follow from its premisses via the axioms and/or rules of inference of L; the question, whether an argument is syntactically valid-in-L, can be checked by a purely formal procedure. However, the syntactic definition of validity is not very relevant to the present issue, since merely to show that vague sentences do not occur as premisses or conclusions of arguments syntactically valid in some language L, would in no way show that there is, or should be, no language L' in valid arguments of which vague sentences *could* occur. (For instance, in [1970] Cleave argues for the *formal* feasibility of the definition of validity for systems including vague predicates proposed by Körner in [1966]. But this formal feasibility is at best a necessary, not a sufficient, condition for the acceptability of Körner's proposal to modify logic to handle 'inexact predicates'.)

The question, whether vague sentences might occur in valid arguments, where 'valid' is defined *semantically*, looks more interesting. An argument is (semantically) valid iff it is logically impossible for its premisses to be true and its conclusion false. And presumably vague sentences *could* feature in arguments which are semantically valid, since it could be true of an argument the premisses and/or conclusion of which, through vagueness, lacked truth-value, that if its premisses *were* true, its conclusion *would* be true. So, although the semantic definition of validity which I have used errs, if anything, on the side of narrowness – it might exclude e.g. imperative logic – it allows vague sentences. Such sentences cannot be excluded from logic on the grounds that their vagueness prevents their standing in interesting logical relations.

5. Can vagueness be eliminated?

If, as it now appears, vague sentences are not obviously outside the scope of logic, and if, furthermore, there are sound arguments why, if

logic is to handle vague sentences, it must be modified, does any
alternative remain to the radical step of adoption of a non-standard
logic? Well, one alternative which suggests itself is that it might be
more economical to precisify[5] vague discourse, so that standard logic
could be used. This proposal is still in the spirit of Russell's comment
that logic is 'not applicable' to vague discourse. Its acceptability
depends in part upon the view which is taken of the aim of formalisation. For if it were supposed, as sometimes, e.g. in Strawson's [1952],
it is, that the object of constructing formal systems is simply to systema-
tise the valid inferences of informal argument, then the discrepancy
between classical propositional calculus, which is bivalent, and the
vague sentences of ordinary language, which are not, would be a
conclusive reason to resort to a non-bivalent logic. (If, at least, it was
not thought to be a reason for giving up formalisation altogether.
Strawson – as I shall argue in detail in ch. 7 – is apparently undecided
between these two conclusions.) But the view that 'ordinary language'
is the final arbiter of the correctness of formal systems is unacceptable.
I do not maintain, as Frege might have, and as Tarski sometimes seems
to, that logic is important solely, or even, necessarily, primarily, for its
service to mathematics. I admit that a legitimate aim of the construction
of a formal calculus is to formalise arguments which occur in ordinary,
non-mathematical discourse. I only suggest that it may be necessary,
and desirable, for the logician to tidy up – or, as Quine more elegantly
puts it, to 'regiment' – this discourse. Given this view of the aims
of formalisation, it becomes relevant to the question whether vagueness creates a need for a non-standard formalism, to ask how
common a phenomenon vagueness is, and to what extent it can be
eliminated?

An analogy may help. The English expressions 'and', 'not', 'if', etc.
are generally agreed not to be, at least in all uses, truth-functional. To
the extent that this is the case, the sense of the sentential connectives of
classical propositional calculus fails to coincide exactly with that of
their usual ordinary-language readings. But this fact does not, of itself,
show that the classical truth-functional propositional calculus should
be replaced by a non-truth-functional system. The truth-functional
connectives capture *a* central use of 'and', 'not', etc.

If, however, vagueness were shown to be a very pervasive feature of
ordinary discourse, and if, furthermore, there was difficulty in tidying

[5] Peirce argued that the word should, by analogy with *decision/decide*, be
'precide'; but the more cumbersome usage has gained currency.

up ordinary discourse so as to eliminate vagueness, then the motivation
for a non-standard calculus would be increased.

Carnap proposes ([1950], ch. 1) that, before formalisation, vague
should be replaced by precise expressions, for example, qualitative by
comparative, or, better, quantitative, predicates. Normally, this is to
be done in such a way that the precise terms coincide with the vague
ones they replace in all the previously clear negative and positive
instances, but either definitely do, or definitely do not, apply to those
cases which, for the vague term, were borderline. In certain cases,
however, Carnap envisages allowing a change of extension; one
example, which is related to the 'law-cluster' concepts mentioned above,
is the use of the term 'fish' to exclude, unlike 'pre-scientific' usage,
whales or other marine mammals.

Carnap seems to assume that vagueness is a problem which arises in
'ordinary', non-scientific discourse, and that it can be completely
avoided in a suitably regimented language for science. Some writers
however, have argued that vagueness cannot so easily be excluded
even from scientific discourse. Such writers think, not just that precisification cannot be achieved without loss, without loss, that is, of the
advantages that vague ways of speaking undoubtedly possess (cf.
Quine [1960], §26; Alston [1964], p. 86); but that precisification cannot be achieved at all. This would be the consequence of the view –
held by Russell in [1923] and echoed in Black's [1937] – that the
whole of language is vague, so that there is no hope of replacing
vague by precise terms, since there are no precise terms to serve as
replacements.

Russell does not give a general argument for his claim that all words
are vague, but proceeds instead via consideration of examples of words
from different categories. *Qualitative* predicates (his examples are 'red'
and 'bald') are vague, because the extent of their application is 'essentially doubtful'. *Quantitative* predicates, by which scientists tend to
replace them, are also vague, because they can never be measured with
complete precision. *Proper names* are vague, because their bearers are
born, and die, and being born and dying are gradual processes. And
logical words are vague, because the sentence connectives are defined in
terms of their truth-conditions, and 'true' and 'false' are themselves
vague. (There is a detailed discussion of Russell's arguments in Kohl
[1969].)

The first two categories of words are the crucial ones for present
purposes. Proper names can be excluded from formal calculi without

loss (see Quine [1960], §38). The truth-conditions of the sentential connectives can be given quite precisely (as Russell concedes); and there is no reason to suppose that 'true' and 'false' cannot be precisely defined *for formal languages*. (See Tarski [1931].)

This leaves two issues: whether, as Russell claims, all qualitative predicates are vague, and whether, as he further argues, the quantitative predicates by which science aims to replace them are vague too.

Some writers have argued that any predicate with any title to be considered empirical is bound to be vague. Science must have an empirical vocabulary; and so it is necessarily infected with vagueness. Benjamin's argument, in [1939], rests upon the premiss that empirical words are learned, ostensively, by reference to some finite sample of objects having or lacking the relevant property, but apply to new objects not present in the learning sample. A 'fringe of indefiniteness' is, he claims, inevitable in any symbol possessing this 'future reference'. And the idea of a *construct* – a precisified analogue of a vague expression – is incoherent, since constructs are supposed *both* to be precise, *and* to have future reference, which is impossible.

The same argument is employed by Burks in [1946], p. 480. The fact that at least some words which would presumably count as 'empirical', such as, say, 'square', could be learnt otherwise than ostensively, e.g. via the definition 'equi-sided rectangle' is not a conclusive objection to this argument. For the weaker thesis is available that all empirical words either are learned ostensively, or are learned via definitions, the terms of which are themselves learned ostensively, or . . . etc.

It is tempting to reply to Benjamin and Burks' argument, that not only vague, but even quite precise, predicates can be taught ostensively ('pillar-box red' as well as 'red'); but this would be question begging. Perhaps a better reply is possible. Ostensive teaching of a word may, and perhaps must, fail to fix how that word is to be used in future. But it may fail in more than one way: it may be that ostensive teaching leaves the qualifications for the predicate imprecise ('red', say, taught with reference to clear cases, is left with an indeterminate borderline); or it may be that although ostensive teaching leaves the qualifications precise, there remains difficulty in determining whether the qualifications are fulfilled ('pillar-box red', say, is to apply only to objects matching certain standard samples, but there may still be uncertainty whether some object *does* match the sample). But this reply *still* begs the question, in assuming that ostensive teaching may make the qualifications for the predicate precise. It is necessary to attack the argument more directly.

The fact that the predicates with which Benjamin is concerned are learned with reference to a sample which is, *ex hypothesi*, only a subset of the objects to which they apply, entails that their fields of application are not, as it were, completely specified by the learning sample. The predicates apply to the objects in that sample and to all other objects bearing a certain relation to them. In the case of, say 'red', the relation is 'similar in colour', and this relation is so broad as to leave the qualification for being red imprecise. But in the case of, say 'pillar-box red', the relation is 'matching in colour', and this relation is narrow enough to leave the qualifications for being pillar-box red precise.

It might be thought that even then vagueness remains, because there may be difficulty in establishing whether the objects match exactly in colour. But this, as I shall try to show, is a quite different argument – and one which, unlike the previous one, does not bear directly on the issue about change of logic.

This, different, argument is employed by Swinburne in [1969], where his thesis is that replacement of what he calls *A* concepts (roughly: qualitative concepts) by *B* concepts (roughly: quantitative concepts measured on a dense scale) will leave ineradicable 'imprecision'. His way of putting the matter is rather confusing, since he refers to *B* concepts, his examples of which include 'exactly 9 volts', as 'imprecise', when they are actually paradigms of precision! But the point is fair enough; replacing vague qualitative predicates (like 'red') by precise, quantitative ones (like 'wavelength of 7,000 Å') may serve only to replace the uncertainty generated by vagueness by type (2) uncertainty. And this is inevitable if the 'scientific' predicates are such as to be measured on a dense scale, for there are limits to the possible discriminations observers can make.

Are *all* quantitative predicates by which vague qualitative predicates might be replaced subject to this kind of uncertainty? Swinburne thinks not, since, he argues, there might be good reasons for thinking that some property could take only a discrete set of values, so that the dense could be replaced by a non-dense scale. Such reasons, he thinks, could be either theoretical, or straightforwardly empirical. His example of the latter is Balmer's discovery that the frequencies of radiation of hydrogen are discrete. But clearly one could only have theoretical reasons to believe that some property took only a discrete set of values, since if a dense scale is employed the values cannot be precisely determined, and so it could not be discovered in a straightforwardly observational way that the values are, in fact, discrete.[6]

The idea that the attempt to avoid vagueness by resort to quantitative predicates may lead to uncertainty of another kind is by no means new. In [1904] Duhem makes a distinction between theoretical facts, which are expressed in precise, quantitative language, and practical facts, which are expressed in vague, qualitative, 'ordinary' language. And he argues that theoretical statements, *because* they are precise, are less certain than commonsense statements. Confidence in the truth of a vague assertion may be justified, just because of its vagueness, which makes it compatible with a whole range of observed facts. But scientific statements, being precise, are less certain, because available observations may be too coarse to discriminate between them. One could be sure of the truth of

Jones is tall

but unsure of the truth of

Jones is 6ft 4·0625 in. high.

In general, Duhem comments:

The laws of physics can acquire this minuteness of detail only by sacrificing some of the fixed and absolute certainty of common-sense laws. *There is a sort of balance between precision and certainty: one cannot be increased except to the detriment of the other.*

([1904], pp. 178–9, my italics.)

Duhem's confidence in the certainty of vague sentences is not inconsistent with the claim I have advanced, that the truth-value of some vague sentences, those, namely, whose subjects are borderline, may be subject to (type (1)) uncertainty. For truth-values of vague sentences whose subjects belong to the *central* field of application (positive or negative) of the predicate *are*, as Duhem stresses, certain.

[6] As might be expected, in view of this argument, Swinburne's account of Balmer's discovery is misleading. Balmer discovered a formula yielding values *approximately* fitting those Ångström had measured, and from which it followed that the values are discrete. Amusingly enough, Balmer's own account of his discovery goes thus: 'The variations of the formula from Ångström's observation amount in the most unfavourable case to not more than 1/40,000 of a wavelength, a variation which very likely is in the limits of the possible errors of observation and is really a striking evidence for the great scientific care and skill with which Ångström must have gone to work.' (Balmer [1885], p. 80.)

I accept that replacing vague by precise predicates will not avoid uncertainty, but will only exchange uncertainty of type (1) for uncertainty of type (2). But – and this is a crucial point – nevertheless the replacement of vague by precise predicates avoids the arguments for a Deviant logic. For those arguments apply only to predicates which give rise to type (1), and not to predicates which give rise to type (2), uncertainty. For, as I argued above, vague sentences may fail to be true or false, and this failure threatens classical logic. But with precise sentences the problem isn't failure to have, but failure to discover, truth-value.

Duhem himself believes that bivalence fails for theoretical statements. This is for two reasons, only one of which is to the present point. The irrelevant reason is that Duhem inclines towards instrumentalism. The relevant reason is that Duhem thinks of 'approximate' as an *alternative* to 'true' and 'false'. But I see no reason why the locution '*p* is approximately true' should not be explicated in terms of the two, classical truth-values. If '*p*' has the form 'The value of property *F* is *n*' and if $\in$ is some (small) number which corresponds to the degree of approximation, then what ' "The value of property *F* is *n*" is approximately true' amounts to is ' "The value of property *F* is $n \pm \in$" is true'. (A suggestion of this kind made by Scott was briefly discussed in ch. 3.)

But while I have opposed Duhem's claim that the uncertainty to which precise sentences are vulnerable threatens bivalence, I do not think that this uncertainty is without interesting consequences. Far from it. Duhem goes close to the heart of the matter when he observes that, given this uncertainty, a mathematical deduction can be useful scientifically only if, if its premises are approximately true, then its conclusion, too, is approximately true. If, in particular, a hypothetico-deductive model of scientific explanation is to be satisfactory, it must allow some place to the notion of approximation. (See Feyerabend [1963], pp. 20–5, for an exposition of the difficulty for the classical empiricist model of explanation, and Mellor [1965], for an attempt to deal with this difficulty.)

6. Conclusions

(1) Vague sentences may not be bivalent.

(2) They are, furthermore, within the scope of logic.

(3) However, a division of vague sentences into three classes – true,

false and neither, is liable to give results as counterintuitive as those consequent on the use of a bivalent logic.

(4) And the programme advocated by Carnap, of 'precisifying' ordinary language arguments, *is* feasible. For though replacing vague by precise expressions may lead to uncertainty due to inadequacies of measuring techniques, this uncertainty does not threaten bivalence. (5) So it seems most economical *not* to modify logic to cope with vagueness, but rather to regard classical logic as an idealisation of which arguments in ordinary discourse fall short, but to which they can be approximated.

7

Singular terms and existence

1. The problem

Classical logic appears to be committed to some existential claims. The troublesome assumptions are:

(a) that all singular terms denote

and

(b) that the universe of discourse is non-empty

which are apparently embodied in such theorems as

$\vdash Fa \supset (\exists x)\,Fx$
$\vdash (x)\,Fx \supset Fa$

and

$\vdash (\exists x)\,(Fx \vee \sim Fx)$
$\vdash (\exists x)\,(x = x)$

respectively. If it be admitted that existential assumptions are not purely logical, and that these assumptions are nevertheless made in classical logic, then some modification of classical logic might seem to be called for. The purpose of this chapter is to investigate whether, and if so, what, modification is necessary.

The first of the issues raised – how to handle non-denoting terms – has long been debated. The second issue has received rather less attention until relatively recently. But the two issues are, obviously, not altogether independent; for if the universe of discourse were empty, there would thus be nothing for the singular terms to denote, so that an adequate solution to the second problem would have to solve the first as well.

2. Some possible reactions

Among the proposals which have been canvassed are the following, placed in order of radicalness:

126

(1) Exclude the recalcitrant sentences from the scope of logic, hence make *no* modification ('no-item' strategy).

(2) Translate the recalcitrant sentences in the formalism in such a way as to make them amenable to standard treatment ('misleading form' strategy).

(3) Modify logic at predicate calculus level.

(4) Modify logic at propositional calculus level.

(i) *It could be admitted that classical logic embodies some existential assumptions, but denied, nevertheless, that any modification is called for*

I examine first some arguments why the first problem, non-denoting terms, does not create a need for modification, and then some argu ments why the second, the empty universe, does not.

(a) This reaction to the problem of non-denoting terms is the one favoured by Frege.[1] Denotationless singular terms are, he argues, an imperfection to which natural languages are prone, but one which should not be allowed to mar the logical perfection of a formal language:

> A logically perfect language should satisfy the conditions, that every expression grammatically well-constructed as a proper name out of signs already introduced shall in fact designate an object, and that no new sign shall be introduced as a proper name without being secured a reference.
>
> ([1892], p. 70.)

The way he proposes to achieve this is, not to insist that a definite description be well-formed only if it demonstrably has a denotation (which would have the unhappy consequence that the formation rules would be ineffective), but to insist that a denotation be provided, arbitrarily if necessary, for all well-formed expressions:

> [a definite description] must actually always be assured of reference, by means of a special stipulation, e.g. by the convention that o shall count as its reference, when the concept applies to no object or to more than one.
>
> ([1892], p. 71n.)

---

[1] His work contains arguments for a more radical proposal, which I shall consider later. But Frege himself clearly favours this, the most conservative position.

So Frege regards failure of denotation as an imperfection of natural
languages which it is the task of formalisation to eradicate rather than
embody. Denotationless singular terms *ought not* to be allowed within
the scope of logic.

Some writers – including Russell ([1905]) and Scott ([1967]) find
Frege's proposal objectionably artificial. However, it is not uncommon
for economical formalisation of informal argument to involve certain
artificiality (cf. '(∃x)' and 'some'.) And its intuitiveness aside, the
feasibility of Frege's proposal seems to be unquestioned.

(b) Strawson employs an argument which, though using entirely
different premises, seems to support a not dissimilar proposal.[2] This
argument goes as follows. The use of a sentence whose subject-term
is non-denoting is 'spurious', and does not constitute a statement. But
logic is concerned with statements, rather than with sentences as such;
and so such sentences are outside the scope of logic.

While this argument is not clearly distinguished from another, with
the more radical conclusion that utterances of 'reference failure' sentences constitute statements which are neither true nor false, it is clear
that it is present. For Strawson places great stress on the distinction
between expressions and their uses, and claims that Russell's theory of
descriptions is mistaken *because it ignores the sentence/statement distinction*; which very strongly suggests that Strawson thinks that Russell's
mistake lay in his failure to realise that no statement is made by an
utterance of 'The king of France is bald'.

Strawson's conclusion – by contrast with Frege's, which is that
denotationless terms *ought not* to be within the scope of logic – is that
sentences containing such terms *are not* within its scope. In order to
establish this, Strawson needs to argue for two premisses: that logic is
concerned only with statements; and that uses of 'reference-failure'
sentences do not constitute statements. Neither premiss is very adequately supported. The first, which is heavily stressed in [1952], seems
to be supported by the – quite inconclusive – observation that sentences
cannot be ascribed truth-values, because if they were it would have to
be admitted that they can change their truth-value. This is insufficient
even to establish that sentences cannot be true or false, and even more
inadequate to establish that logic cannot be about sentences as such,

---

[2] Strawson's work contains *two* lines of argument, which are not clearly distinguished by Strawson himself; the other argument supports a more radical
alternative. It will be discussed later. The two views are distinguished, and care-
fully traced through Strawson's work, in Nerlich [1965].

which would require the further premiss, that logic is concerned only with truth-bearing items.

The argument for the second premiss is much more complex, but not much more convincing. The first step is to argue that an utterance of 'The king of France is bald' *fails to refer*, since there is no king of France. The motivation for this claim springs from an account of reference according to which it is a necessary condition of successful reference that an expression be employed which has denotation. It is of interest that Strawson does not consistently propose such a 'semantic' theory of reference, but sometimes favours a 'pragmatic' theory, according to which it is a sufficient condition of successful reference that the speaker use an expression which brings to the attention of the hearer the item which the speaker has in mind, regardless, that is, of whether the expression used actually denotes that item. (cf. [1959], ch. 1, §1, and [1964], for this ambiguity in Strawson's theory of reference.)

The second step is to argue that someone who fails to refer, by the use of a sentence, makes a 'spurious use' of that sentence, and thus, does not make a statement by its utterance.

The motivation for supposing that a spurious use of a sentence is not a statement at all seems to spring from the fact that the characteristic feature of Strawson's paradigm cases of 'spurious use', overtly fictional utterances and utterances on the stage, is apparently that they are not *assertive*; and since Strawson seems, in [1950], to use 'statement' and 'assertion' interchangeably, the conclusion, that a spurious use of a sentence isn't a statement, is inviting. But this line of thought – which may influence Strawson – is unacceptable; there is no reason why an utterance of 'The king of France is bald' should not be made assertively, e.g. by a French monarchist, or by someone who wrongly believed Pompidou to be king; so that such utterances need not share the most prominent feature of Strawson's other examples of 'spurious' uses. There are, furthermore, well-known objections to the suggestion that the items with which logic deals are assertions – it can hardly be maintained, for instance, that the antecedent of a conditional is an assertion.

So Strawson's arguments for the conservative, no-modification, position are, I think, less acceptable than Frege's, which are more frankly pragmatic.

(c) Quine puts forward, in [1954], an argument which supports the conclusion that no modification of logic is really called for to cope with the second problem, the possibility of an empty universe. The argument rests upon the formal convenience of a predicate calculus valid only in non-empty domains. For, as Quine observes, where D is any non-empty domain, any quantificational wff which comes out true under all interpretations in all domains larger than D, also comes out true under all interpretations in D; that is, all small domains *except* the empty domain can be included at no extra cost. Furthermore, as Quine points out, there is a simple test for detecting those wffs of predicate calculus which are invalid in the empty domain; write 't' for every wff beginning with a universal quantifier, 'f' for every wff beginning with an existential quantifier, and perform a truth-table test. Quine's position could perhaps be put like this: classical predicate calculus may not be *quite* right, but it is less cumbersome than any modification which would cope with the empty domain, and it is, after all, always possible to tell *where* it is not quite right. (As a scientist might argue: this theory is correct only within a certain range of applications, but the range in question is that most commonly encountered, and a more comprehensive theory would have to be more complicated. And there is no danger that use of the strictly incorrect theory will lead into error, for one can tell in which cases the theory doesn't work.)

Cohen evidently sees this attitude of Quine's as the thin end of a rather undesirable wedge:

> If economy may be purchased here at the cost of comprehensive-
> ness, then why not elsewhere also? The road seems open to those
> who would wish to disregard the logic of non-extensional discourse
> because all classical mathematics is extensional, and to advocates of
> other similar economies . . . *The problem of systematisation is being
> shirked, not solved, once the ideal of comprehensiveness is sacrificed to
> considerations of economy.*
>
> ([1962], p. 260, my italics.)

The italicised comment suggests that Cohen's view of Quine's suggestion is that it opens the way to abuses. And the fact that, although his
epistemology is such as to admit the possibility in principle of change
of logic, Quine invariably balks at allowing any change in practice,
suggests that this 'slippery slope' argument may not be wholly mis-
directed.

There is one question, however, which requires attention before
Quine's position can be properly assessed; viz. to what extent predicate
calculus would need to be complicated in order to apply to the empty
domain. The cost in terms of simplicity may or may not outweigh the

gain in terms of comprehensiveness; it is not possible to decide whether it does, without some knowledge of what sacrifice of simplicity would be required. There is a danger that Quine's conservatism may lead him to overestimate the loss of simplicity involved in a change of logic.

Cohen himself, however, though he objects to this argument of Quine's, would apparently agree with the conclusion, that no modification is required in order to make logic valid in the empty universe. For Cohen thinks that the empty universe is self-contradictory – i.e. that the theorems which rule it out *are* purely logical after all. As I understand it, Cohen's reason for thinking that an empty universe is contradictory, is that assertions such as 'There are no winged horses' are always, as it were, elliptical ('There are no winged horses *on earth*'), containing an implicit reference to a domain. But he offers no argument why, but only asserts that, there cannot be (true) assertions of the form 'There are no winged horses (at all, anywhere)'.

It must be confessed that it is hard to give very clear reasons for the intuition, which underlies the feeling that existential theorems are 'troublesome', that that there is something is not a logical (or necessary, or analytic) truth. Lambert argues that it is not, because it is not true in all possible worlds; in particular, it is not true in an empty world. But of course this argument, while it has an intuitive appeal, has little compelling force in view of the unclarity of 'possible' in 'possible world'. Part of the difficulty is that one can hardly, in the present context, try to answer the question, whether that something exists is a logical truth, by reference to a formal system, classical or otherwise; while any relevant non-formal considerations are inevitably vague.

The reactions considered so far are very conservative – they involve *no* modification of logic. A slightly more radical possibility is:

(ii) *Accommodation of non-denoting terms could be achieved by changes in the manner of translation into logical formalism*

Russell's solution is effectively of this kind, since the theory of descriptions requires that English sentences containing definite descriptions, or ordinary proper names, which are construed as disguised definite descriptions, should be translated, according to the contextual definition of the description operator, into formal sentences in which no singular terms appear. This solution corresponds to what was called, in ch. 3, the 'misleading form' thesis; Russell, indeed, comments that his theory shows that the grammatical form of certain sentences is 'misleading as to their logical form', and it is from him that I borrowed this terminology.

Russell's arguments for his theory – which I have 'rationally re-constructed' somewhat – go as follows:

(1) If an expression is a logically proper name, there must be some object of acquaintance which it denotes. Logically proper names are *guaranteed* denotata.

Given the limitations Russell imposes upon acquaintance, the class of logically proper names turns out to be very restricted. According to [1910], acquaintance is only of sense-data, and so only 'this' and, possibly, 'I', count as logically proper names. On this account, *no* ordinary proper names are logically proper; though Russell sometimes uses 'logically proper name' more loosely, to include names of persons (or places etc.) with whom (which) one is 'acquainted' in the non-technical sense. A logical subject, according to Russell, is an expression which stands for a particular to which, in the whole proposition or judgement, a property is attributed. But Russell accepts as a 'funda-mental epistemological principle', that any proposition which can be understood must be composed wholly of constituents with which one is acquainted. And logically proper names are by definition expressions which stand directly for objects of acquaintance. So

(2) Only a logically proper name can stand as the logical subject of a sentence.

(3) So if 'The king of France' were the logical subject of 'The king of France is bald', it would have to be a logically proper name. (From (2).)

(4) But, if 'The king of France' were a logically proper name, there would have to be some object which it denotes. (From (1).)

(5) But 'The king of France' does not denote a real object.

(6) And *unreal* objects are inadmissible

so that

(7) 'The king of France' is not a logically proper name, nor, there-fore, the logical subject of 'The king of France is bald'. (From (4), (5) and (6).)

So that

(8) The 'logical form' of 'The king of France is bald' differs from its grammatical form; only *grammatically* is it a subject-predicate

sentence. 'The king of France' is not a *logically* proper name, but an 'incomplete symbol', to be contextually defined.

Russell supports premisses (5) and (6) by arguing *against* the theories of Frege (who proposed to provide a real object, e.g. the number 0, for otherwise non-denoting terms to denote) and Meinong (who allowed 'non-denoting' terms to stand for unreal objects) respectively.

In [1905] Russell brings two objections to Frege. The first is that his theory is artificial – which, though true, is inconclusive, especially in view of the fact that other writers, e.g. Strawson, find Russell's own theory artificial. The second objection takes the form of a very confused argument against Frege's sense/reference distinction. However, since Frege's suggestion that otherwise non-denoting terms be arbitrarily assigned denotata, so far as I can see, in no way depends upon his sense/reference theory, it is not necessary to examine this argument in detail. Russell has no very strong argument against Frege's conservative position.

One objection Russell has to Meinong is that his theory manifests an inadequate sense of reality – a criticism which looks rather ironic when one remembers that Meinong had complained about metaphysicians' unjustifiable prejudice in favour of the actual! More seriously, Russell objects that Meinong's theory is 'apt to infringe the law of contradiction', for it allows:

(i) that the existent king of France exists, and also does not exist

and

(ii) that the round square is round, and also not round.

Later, in his review of Meinong's *Untersuchungen zur Gegenstandstheorie und Psychologie* (Russell [1905a]) he charged, further, that the theory entailed

(iii) that the existent round square exists.

For some time Russell's vigorous attack effectively prevented further discussion of Meinong's theory, but it has recently been suggested that Russell's criticisms are based on a misinterpretation. Linsky, for instance, argues in [1967] that Russell's criticisms fail because Meinong never said that round squares, chimeras, etc. exist. However, although it is true that Meinong did not say this, this is not what Russell accused him of saying, either. The matter requires closer attention.

Russell's criticisms seem to focus on consequences of Meinong's theory of *Sosein* (see Meinong [1904]). According to the principle of the independence of *Sosein* from *Sein*, objects (by which Meinong means, intentional objects), have characteristics whether or not they exist; the golden mountain, for instance, *is* golden, even though it is unreal. (ii) above follows from this principle – indeed Meinong states it himself:

> Not only is the much heralded gold mountain made of gold, but the round square is as surely round as it is square.
>
> ([1904], p. 122.)

As this passage would lead one to expect, Meinong was little impressed by Russell's criticism on *this* score. Exceptions to logical principles which are confined to impossible objects are, he replied ([1915], p. 278), nothing to be alarmed at. (cf. Findlay [1933], p. 104.) Meinong denied, however, that his doctrine of *Sosein* entailed either (i) or (iii); for existence, he argued, cannot be 'part of the nature of an objectum', by which he apparently meant that existence isn't a property, and therefore the doctrine of *Sosein* doesn't apply to it. Whatever one might think about Meinong's claim that existence isn't a property, it is, certainly, a view which has many supporters, and, furthermore, in view of Meinong's doctrine of the 'indifference of pure Objects to being' (*Aussersein des reinen Gegenstandes*), his appeal to it is hardly *ad hoc*.

The issue turns, then, on thesis (ii), which does indeed follow from Meinong's theory. The question is, is (ii) really objectionable, as Russell thought, or harmless, as Meinong thought? The answer, I think, is rather complicated: that if Meinong's theory is taken (as he did not intend it) as proposing a solution to the problem of handling 'non-denoting' terms formally, it *is* objectionable. For if contradictory definite descriptions were allowed, and the usual rules of inference employed, inconsistency would result, in the form of theorems like:

$$\vdash F\{(\imath x)\, Fx\, \&\, \sim Fx\}\ \&\ \sim F\{(\imath x)\, Fx\, \&\, \sim Fx\}.$$

So Russell is right to reject the solution to his formal problem which Meinong's theory suggests. I am not saying, of course, that Meinong's theory is informally all right, but formally inconsistent; but that, although his theory is consistent, the proposal that it might be thought to support, that all singular terms, denoting and non-denoting, and even contradictory, should be allowed in a formal system (since all Objects have being in at least the weakest, *Quasisein* or *Aussersein*, sense), results in an inconsistent system.

Russell's own conclusion – that the grammatical subjects of sentences like 'The king of France is bald' are not logically proper names, but incomplete symbols – follows immediately once the alternatives, Frege's – that such expressions denote real objects, and Meinong's – that they denote unreal objects, have been rejected. In Russell's analysis of

(a) $G \ \{(\imath x) \, Fx\}$

viz

(b) $(\exists x) \, (Fx \ \& \ (y) \, (Fy \equiv x = y) \ \& \ Gx)$

no singular term appears: the subject-predicate form of the English sentence has vanished.

Given this analysis,

(c) $(\exists x) \, Fx$

is a logical consequence of (a); and so it becomes necessary for Russell to distinguish two senses of the negation of (a):

(d) $(\exists x) \, (Fx \ \& \ (y) \, (Fy \equiv x = y) \ \& \ \sim Gx)$

and

(e) $\sim (\exists x) \, (Fx \ \& \ (y) \, (Fx \equiv x = y) \ \& \ Gx).$

The logical principles which apply to constants (which are the formal analogue of logically proper names) do not apply to definite descriptions. This enables Russell to solve the problems he had set himself at the outset of 'On Denoting'. (It also means that Russell's theory involves some, though minor, modification to the rules of inference.)

It is worth observing that Russell's theory solves only the first of the problems, the problem about non-denoting terms; it does not affect the exclusion of the empty universe. It is possible to tackle the second problem as well as the first if a more radical position is adopted.

(iii) *Modification of deductive apparatus could be allowed, but confined to the predicate calculus level*

That is, only axioms or rules essentially involving quantifiers would be changed. This reaction is, in a sense, the most straightforward, in that it is admitted that its existential assumptions constitute a genuine

problem for the classical predicate calculus, and so the calculus is modified in such a way as to avoid them. That is perhaps why no *special*
argument is felt to be needed why this kind of modification should be
adopted. Less radical reactions treat the problem created by the existential assumptions as *less* serious than it appears so as to avoid the need
for modification; more radical reactions treat the problem as *more*
serious than it appears, in order to motivate modification beyond the
predicate calculus.

The modifications of classical predicate calculus which have been
proposed are discussed rather thoroughly in Schock [1968], so I shall
give no more than the briefest sketch of the possibilities which have
been explored.

Appropriate modifications might cope with one of the original
problems (of empty terms and of the empty universe) or – and this
would surely be preferable if it is feasible – both. Some systems have
been proposed (by Jaśkowski [1934], Mostowski [1951], Hailperin
[1953], Quine [1954] and Schneider [1961]) which are valid in the
empty domain, but which, having no constants, are such that the first
problem simply fails to arise.

But systems have also been devised intended to cope with both
problems. The idea used is one which goes back to Leonard, who
proposed, in [1956], that the rule of existential generalisation:

$$Fa \vdash (\exists x)\, Fx$$

should be replaced by a weaker rule:

$$Fa, a \text{ exists} \vdash (\exists x)\, Fx.$$

Leonard used a complex and rather unsatisfactory modal definition of
'exists'. The formal analogue

$$(\exists x)\,(x = a)$$

– '*a* is something' as Quine neatly puts it – is commonly used by later
writers.

Hintikka's system, in which the existential generalisaton rule is
replaced by

$$Fa, (\exists x)\,(x = a) \vdash (\exists x)\, Fx$$

can, he claims,

truly be said to be a *logic without existential presuppositions*

([1959], p. 135.)

lacking all the problematic theorems – those invalid in the empty universe as well as those invalid if empty terms are allowed. Belnap, however, argues that Hintikka is mistaken about this – sentences are provable in his system which are false in the empty domain. Thus, like the system of Hailperin–Leblanc ([1959]), his system is not successful in solving the second problem. Schock claims that his [1968] system, which not only restricts universal and existential generalisation to existents, but makes other changes in the quantifier rules, *is* successful in excluding *both* theorems false for empty terms *and* theorems false in the empty domain.

It might be thought that modification on any larger scale than this, modification that is extending as far as the propositional calculus, could not possibly be justified, since the troublesome theorems essentially involve quantifiers. But more than one writer has argued that the problems arising in the predicate calculus are symptoms of more deep-seated difficulties.

(iv) *The most radical reaction requires modification at the propositional calculus level*

Bivalence is dropped, since sentences containing non denoting terms are claimed to be neither true nor false. Resort to such radical modification is not necessarily perverse. It has been argued that such sentences stand in the logical relation of *presupposition* to the corresponding existential sentences; and presupposition, according to Frege's definition:

S_1 presupposes S_2 = df. S_1 is neither true nor false
unless S_2 is true

can only be adequately formalised in a non-bivalent logic.

Although the word 'presupposition' had been used before in this context (e.g. Land [1876]), Frege was the first to give it a clear sense and a substantial theoretical support. The theoretical backing comes from Frege's theory of sense and reference. The sense/reference distinction was devised in order to solve a puzzle about identity statements: how could

(i) The Evening Star = The Morning Star

differ in 'cognitive value' from, i.e. be more informative than,

(ii) The Evening Star = The Evening Star

given that (i), like (ii) is true? For, if the Morning Star is the Evening Star, ought not (i) and (ii) to amount to the same thing? Frege's solution is that while the *reference* of 'The Morning Star' is the same as the reference of 'The Evening Star' (which is why (i) is true), these expressions have different *senses*, and this difference accounts for the different cognitive values of (i) and (ii).

The sense/reference distinction, the original motivation for which applies to subject expressions, is extended to cover all expressions:

Expression	*Sense*	*Reference*
Proper name (= ordinary proper names *and* definite descriptions)	Meaning of denoting phrase	Object
Predicate	Meaning of predicate expression (?)	Concept
Sentence	Proposition	Truth-value

That the reference of a sentence should be its truth-value is a consequence of Frege's assumption that the sense/reference of a compound expression depends upon the sense/reference of its parts. Frege argues as follows: if some component of a sentence is replaced by another with a different sense but the same reference, as in:

(a) Elizabeth II has four children
(b) The Queen of England has four children

then the proposition expressed by the sentence (its sense) is altered, but its truth-value remains the same. So the truth-value, which is invariant under co-referential changes of components, must be the reference of the sentence.

In the case of non-extensional sentential operators, such as the verbs of propositional attitude, there are apparent counter-examples to Frege's theory: for instance, although '$2 + 2 = 4$' and 'Arithmetic is incomplete' are presumably co-referential, being both true, they cannot be interchanged without change of truth-value in the context:

Every schoolboy knows that . . .

But Frege avoids this difficulty by distinguishing between the direct and the indirect reference of expressions, identifying the indirect reference with the customary sense, and ruling that in oblique contexts expressions have, not their customary, but their indirect, reference. So in

Every schoolboy knows that $2 + 2 = 4$

the reference of the contained sentence is its customary sense, viz, the proposition that $2 + 2 = 4$; and so, since the indirect reference of 'Arithmetic is incomplete', viz, the proposition that arithmetic is incomplete, differs from this, the apparent counter-example fails, because it is not an example of co-referential substitution after all.

The consequences of the sense/reference theory for the question of non-denoting terms can be derived[3] from the principles:

(1) that all expressions, both sentences and their components, have both sense and reference,

(2) the reference of a proper name being the object denoted, and the reference of a sentence being its truth-value, and,

(3) that the reference of a compound expression depends on the references of its parts.

It follows from these principles that if a sentence contains a singular term which lacks a reference, then the sentence itself must lack reference, that is, must be without a truth-value.

On Frege's semantic theory, then, a sentence containing a non-denoting term, though having a perfectly good sense, lacks truth-value. So neither a sentence, nor its negation, has a truth-value, unless its components denote. As Frege puts it, both

(a) Kepler died in misery

and

(b) Kepler did not die in misery

presuppose that 'Kepler' denotes something, that is, are neither true nor false unless 'Kepler' denotes something. For otherwise, he argues, the negation of (a) would be, not (b), but

(c) Either Kepler did not die in misery, or 'Kepler' denotes nothing.

(On Russell's theory, of course, where 'Kepler died in misery' implies rather than presupposes '"Kepler" denotes something', there is just

---

[3] Frege himself does not use the sense/reference theory to establish this conclusion, but, rather, appeals to the intuitiveness of the claim that such a sentence as

Odysseus was set ashore at Ithaca while sound asleep

while having a perfectly good sense, cannot be assigned either truth-value, in support of his thesis that the reference of a sentence is its truth-value. This difference of procedure is not, however, important for the present purpose.

such an ambiguity in its negation. But Frege takes this consequence to be unacceptable.)

Frege himself did not favour the position which his theory supports; rather than develop a non-bivalent calculus in which presupposition could be formalised, he preferred to disallow non-denoting terms altogether, and thus retain bivalence.

Strawson also uses an argument which would motivate adoption of a non-bivalent logic. He claims, in opposition to Russell, that 'The king of France is bald', does not entail, but presupposes, 'The king of France exists'. In [1950] it is left unclear how 'presupposes' is to be understood, and ambiguous even whether presupposition is intended as a logical or an epistemological relation; but in [1952] and [1954] Strawson adopts Frege's definition.[4]

Since presupposition, so defined, cannot be interestingly formalised in a bivalent system – where all wffs would presuppose just the tautologies – a non-bivalent system appears to be called for. Just what kind of non-bivalent system is appropriate has been disputed. Three systems have been proposed, each with the intention of formalising Frege's 'presupposition', two of them (Smiley's and Woodruff's) many-valued, the third (van Fraassen's) non-truth-functional.

A major difference between Smiley's and Woodruff's 3-valued calculi is that the former, but not the latter, obeys the principle that whenever a component of a compound wff lacks truth-value, so does the whole wff. (This holds, to speak more strictly, for Smiley's *primary* connectives.) This, prima facie, is a point in favour of Smiley's system; for it is a principle of Frege's sense/reference theory that the reference of a sentence depends upon the reference of its parts, so that it lacks reference if they do. Woodruff has two arguments against the truth-valueless input – truth-valueless output principle. The first is that Bochvar and Halldén, who employ matrices in accord with this principle, identify truth-valuelessness with meaninglessness, an identification which would certainly have been unacceptable to Frege. This argument is quite inconclusive, since the fact that some writers who use these matrices did so for a reason Frege would have rejected, does

---

[4] In view of Strawson's stress that logical relations hold only between statements, this requires that he admit that utterances of 'The king of France is bald' *do* constitute statements (*contra* his no-item argument), but statements which are neither true nor false. [1950] is thoroughly ambiguous between the 'no-item' and the 'truth-value gap' theses; [1964] is more, although not entirely, clearly in favour of the latter.

not at all show that the matrices are not the most appropriate to Frege's position. Woodruff's second argument is that, if it is assumed that the language has the structure of a lattice, then, if matrices on the truth-valueless input – truth-valueless output principle were used, then 'true', 'false' *and* 'truth-valueless' collapse into each other. But this argument is inconclusive too, for the assumption that the language has the structure of a lattice amounts to the assumption that

$$A \vdash A \vee B$$

which could be false given Bochvar–Halldén–Smiley matrices, where if 'A' is true but 'B' truth-valueless, '$A \vee B$' will be truth-valueless.

Van Fraassen claims for his proposal the advantage that it, being non-truth-functional, formalises truth-value gaps rather than intermediate truth-values. But, as I argued in ch. 3, this claim fails. The other alleged advantage of his proposal is its conservatism – all classical tautologies remain as theorems. But Lambert (who is in favour of his suggestion) realises that this may not be, in the present context, an unmixed blessing. For it could be doubted whether it is intuitive to keep LEM for sentences containing denotationless terms. (See Lambert [1969].)

So the most promising system to formalise presupposition seems to be Smiley's. The intention is that assignment of 'u' is to be taken as *lack* of truth-value, rather than of some intermediate value. In this system the primary connectives obey the Fregean principle, though the secondary ones – defined in terms of the primary connectives and 't' ('it is true that') do not. 'Presupposes' is defined as

$$A \text{ presupposes } B = \text{df. } A \vdash B \text{ and } \sim A \vdash B$$

which has the (desirable) consequences that

(i) if a has primary occurrence in A, A presupposes 'a exists'

and

(ii) if $(\imath x)A$ has primary occurrence in B, B presupposes '$(\exists_1 x) Ax$'.

3. Some comments on these alternatives

It has become apparent, I think, that the alternatives considered tend to be *either* conservative, rather simple, and somewhat restricted in scope, *or* radical, more complex, and broader in scope. They could be ordered in terms of increasing complexity and decreasing scope:

simplest, most restricted	$\longrightarrow$		most complex, widest scope
refuse any modification	'misleading form' strategy	modify predicate calculus	modify propositional calculus
(1)	(2)	(3)	(4)

In view of this, deciding between them is likely to be difficult, since two *desiderata*, simplicity and comprehensiveness, conflict. If the loss of scope due to the failure of classical logic in the empty domain is felt not to be very serious, it will be cheerfully accepted as the price of simplicity. This, I think, is the position Quine adopts in [1954]. If this loss, and the loss due to failure to cope with empty terms, is felt to be important, an increase of complexity will be cheerfully accepted as the price of adequate scope. This is Schock's attitude. And if it were thought that presupposition is an interesting logical relation, especially if it had application beyond the case of sentences containing non-denoting phrases, this might motivate the further complexity involved in carrying modification to the propositional calculus level. Van Fraassen, who hopes (see [1968]) that the notion of presupposition may also be used to provide a solution to the semantic paradoxes, takes something like this attitude.

The prospects for a firm and soundly motivated conclusion, that one of these alternatives is clearly preferable to the others, do not, therefore, look very promising.

So it is something of a relief to find a new alternative which promises to combine conservatism with breadth, and would therefore be, presumably, preferable both to the conservative but narrow, and to the radical but broad proposals.

4. A rather conservative proposal

Classical logic – as I observed with what may have seemed to be excessive caution – *appears to be* committed to some existential assumptions. It appears to be committed to these assumptions because it has certain theorems, which, if the existential quantifier is read, as it generally is read, 'there is (at least one) object such that . . .' explicitly make existence claims.

This reading of the quantifier, which Quine calls the 'objectual' interpretation, is standard. But there is an alternative, the 'substitutional' interpretation. On *this* interpretation

$(\exists x)\ Fx$

is to be read: some substitution instance of 'Fx' is true, and

$(x)\ Fx$

is to be read: all substitution instances of 'Fx' are true. This interpretation is sometimes employed by Russell, e.g. in [1905]. It is suggested by – though it differs somewhat from – Lejewski's [1955], which, in turn, drew inspiration from Leśniewski's ontology. Its clearest proponent, however, is Marcus, who presents arguments in its favour in [1962] and [1963].

It is clear that if the 'troublesome theorems' are interpreted in this way, they cease to be troublesome; and so there no longer appears to be a need for modification of logic to avoid them. But before one can conclude that this interpretation is the solution, or rather the dissolution, of the problems, the question of the feasibility of the substitutional account needs to be investigated.

In favour of the substitutional account, besides its success in defusing the problem of existential commitment, Marcus mentions two arguments. The first argument is that it avoids problems which are thought to arise concerning the tense of 'there is' if the existential quantifier is given the objectual interpretation. This problem is discussed at some length by Strawson in [1952], pp. 150–1. But this argument in favour of the substitutional interpretation is not very convincing, since *if* there is really a problem about the tense of the 'is' if '$(\exists x)\ Fx$' is read '*There is* at least one object which is F' (which, I confess, I doubt), then there is surely also a problem about the tense of the 'is' if '$(\exists x)\ Fx$' is read 'Some substitution instance of 'Fx' *is* true'.

The second argument, however, seems to have more force. It is, that the substitutional account avoids difficulties in quantified modal logic. Quine, of course, is sceptical about whether the notion of necessity can be made clear and to that extent has doubts about the intelligibility even of modal propositional logic. But at least when modal operators are confined to the role of sentence operator they can be understood within the scope of Quine's 'first grade of modal involvement', where 'necessary' and 'possible' are treated as predicates of sentences. But when *quantified* modal logic is envisaged, with modal operators allowed to govern *open* sentences, it becomes even more doubtfully intelligible. For example, the sentence:

(1) L (The Evening Star $=$ The Evening Star)

entails

(2) $(\exists\, x)\, L(x =$ The Evening Star)

and this ('There is some object which is necessarily identical with the Evening Star') raises some very embarrassing questions: *which* object? The Evening Star? but *that* is the same as the Morning Star, and the Morning Star isn't *necessarily* identical with the Evening Star – questions which Quine is not slow to exploit to the detriment of quantified modal logic. (See Quine [1947], [1953], [1960].) Professor Marcus argues, however, that (2) raises *no* such embarrassing questions if it is read substitutionally ('Some substitution instance of '$L(x =$ The Evening Star) is true'). Of course, this proposal does not solve the problem of the failure of Leibniz' law, which concerns formulae with no quantifiers. And it could be argued that any really satisfactory solution should apply to both quantified and unquantified formulae.

It has also been suggested that the substitutional account might shed some light on problems created by quantification into belief contexts. For example, the apparent failure of existential generalisation from

(3) Tom believes that Mr Pickwick is the Vice-Chancellor

to

(4) $(\exists x)$ (Tom believes that x is the Vice-Chancellor)

is *only* apparent if (4) is read, not 'There is someone whom Tom believes to be Vice-Chancellor', but 'some substitution instance of 'Tom believes that x is the Vice-Chancellor' is true'. The same qualification as was made above, however, needs to be made here: the substitutional interpretation will leave untouched problems concerning unquantified formulae.

The substitutional interpretation also offers, prima facie, a simplification in the truth definition, avoiding the usual detour via satisfaction of open sentences by infinite sequences by a direct definition of the truth conditions of quantified sentences in terms of the truth of atomic sentences. But the resulting definition has given rise to criticism. Wallace argues in [1971] that for theories with infinite domains the simplified truth definition has a drawback: it does not satisfy Tarski's material adequacy condition. That is, not all instances of (T) can be derived from it. For consider how one might try to prove:

$$T \text{ '}(x) Fx \text{'} \supset (x) Fx$$

(one half of one instance of (T)). Assuming the antecedent, one can derive, from the relevant clause of a 'substitutional' truth definition:

$$T \text{ '}Fa\text{'} \ \& \ T \text{ '}Fb\text{'} \ \& \ T \text{ '}Fc\text{'} \ \& \dots \text{ etc.}$$

For a theory with an infinite domain, this conjunction will be infinitely long. But the desired conclusion can only be derived from the whole conjunction, and not from any finite segment of it. So the derivation cannot be completed in a finite number of steps. Nor, in the case of arithmetic, can the derivation be saved by adjoining all theorems. (See Wallace [1971], especially pp. 204–5.) This is without question a drawback in the present proposal. But in view of the fact that (as I argued in detail in ch. 3) modification of logic also sometimes involves sacrifice of the (T) schema, it is not, perhaps, an overwhelming objection.

There is another objection, though, which is made by Quine. Since, given its consonance with his 'linguistic' view of necessity, one might have expected Quine to have welcomed substitutional quantification, his objection should be given serious consideration. It is that the substitutional interpretation differs from the objectual in an important way, which is liable to give rise to difference of truth-value. It works only so long as every object in the universe of discourse has a name. But suppose that some member of the universe of discourse has no name, but is the only member to have a certain property F; then

$$(\exists x) Fx$$

is true on the objectual interpretation, but false on the substitutional interpretation. Since the natural numbers can serve, denumerably many names are available, but substitutional quantification threatens to break down in theories with indenumerable domains. If the situation Quine envisages were to arise, this would indeed count against the substitutional interpretation. However, his objection can be met by pointing out that the Skolem–Löwenheim theorem, which states that any theory which has a model has a denumerable model, guarantees that this situation does *not* arise.[5] It could not be the case, as Quine fears, that:

> an existential quantification can come out true when construed in the ordinary sense, thanks to the existence of appropriate real numbers, and yet be false when construed in Prof. Marcus' sense, if by chance those appropriate real numbers happen to be severally unspecifiable.
>
> ([1962], p. 181.)

I think, then, that this objection of Quine's fails. It is perhaps important to emphasise that Quine's opposition to substitutional quantification is connected with his criterion of ontological commitment: to be is to be the value of a variable. (See e.g. [1951].) This criterion is clearly supported by the usual, objectual reading of the existential quantifier, and threatened by the substitutional reading. Quine himself does not use his ontological criterion to combat the substitutional interpretation, but rather, uses the (alleged) failure of the substitutional account to support his ontological criterion. But since his objection to the substitutional account fails, it is worth asking whether there are convincing reasons in favour of his ontological criterion, other than this rejection, which might therefore be used against the substitutional interpretation. Quine's major argument in favour of his ontological criterion is that ontological commitment must be carried by the variables of quantification because the other candidates, singular terms, are eliminable ([1950]). This argument is inconclusive in view of the fact that variables are – as Quine himself explains in [1960] – themselves eliminable in favour of combinatory operators. Furthermore, serious doubt about whether Quine's criterion can be put precisely without yielding quite unacceptable consequences has been raised by the criticisms of Cartwright [1954], and Scheffler and Chomsky [1959]. And Quine's indeterminacy of translation thesis, which also strikes at the apparatus of reference, has led to a relativisation of the ontological criterions which lessens its usefulness. So it is doubtful in the extreme whether the feasibility of the substitutional interpretation is threatened by any very clear success on the part of Quine's ontological criterion.

---

[5] I find that this reply to Quine's objection is also made by Wallace.

5. Conclusions

I do not claim to have established beyond doubt that the substitutional interpretation of the quantifiers is 'the solution' to the problems considered. I claim only that it is a promising suggestion, offering both simplicity and scope, and that it is, furthermore, an interpretation for which there are other reasons besides its usefulness in the present context. The alternative suggestions, though each has its virtues, suffer from the drawback that, in each case, the *desiderata* of simplicity and comprehensiveness seem to conflict.

8

Quantum mechanics

1. The problem

A number of writers have suggested that adoption of a non-standard logic would provide a solution to certain problems raised by quantum mechanics: among them are Birkhoff and von Neumann in [1936], Destouches-Février in [1937] and [1951], Reichenbach in [1944], Lambert in [1969]. These writers differ among themselves, however, in respect of the details of the Deviant systems proposed, and also in respect of the reasons offered, why a non-standard system should be needed at all.

I have heard it argued that the question, whether any of the arguments offered in this context in favour of a non-standard logic, are acceptable, is now a dead one. It could be suggested that developments in quantum mechanics since the 1940s, in particular the development of the quantum field theory, have dealt adequately, within physics itself, with the problems which, in the 1930s and 1940s, seemed, to some, severe enough to call for a change of logic. Continued interest in the proposals of Deviant logics (e.g. Piron [1964], Finkelstein [1969], Putnam [1969], Gardner [1971], [1972], Scheurer [1972]) is evidence that this view is, at least, controversial. And even if this view were correct, this would not rob the earlier dispute of its interest; for that dispute, viewed as an episode in the history of the philosophy of science, well repays present study. (So the reader who feels wholly satisfied with the present state of quantum theory is asked to read this chapter as an investigation of that episode.) Many of the general issues which are apt to arise in connection with any proposal for a change of logic arise in particularly clear form in this instance. And so, although there is a great deal of physical detail which I shall have to put aside, I think it worthwhile to try, using the results of Part One, to make clear some of the major issues raised by the arguments used by the proponents, and the opponents, of a new 'quantum logic'. I shall try, in what follows, to avoid unnecessary technicalities, without, I hope, evading necessary ones.

2. The arguments for a change of logic

Not all of the proponents of Deviant logics for quantum mechanics feel it necessary to offer any very serious argument *why* a change of logic is called for. Birkhoff and von Neumann, for instance, claim at the very beginning of their paper that:

> One of the aspects of quantum theory which has attracted the most general attention, is the novelty of the logical notions it presupposes.
>
> ([1936], p. 823.)

though later they mention that they think there are 'quasi-physical and technical' reasons (which they do not specify) for this assumption. Dishkant begins his paper with equal confidence that:

> The question what is the logic of the atomic world, belongs to . . . empirical science. It can be solved only by ways of hypotheses framing and testing.
>
> ([1972], p. 23.)

Destouches-Février concludes that:

> Il n'y a pas une logique unique indépendante de tout contenu, mais dans chaque domaine une logique se trouve adéquate. Il y a inter-dépendance du logique et du physique, du formel et du réel.
>
> ([1951], p. 88.)

on the strength of her investigations into non-standard logic for quantum physics, rather than offering any independent argument for the assumption that there may be physical reasons for a change of logic. (Her advocacy of *local* reform is interesting, however, in view of the arguments of ch. 2.) Lambert, too, offers rather little in the way of argument for a change of logic: his main concern is to propose a different kind of Deviant system which, he claims, is simpler and more conservative than those favoured by other writers.

Reichenbach's argument

Reichenbach, however, goes to some trouble to present an argued case for a change of logic. His proposal, that a 3-valued logic should be adopted, is presented as more acceptable than the suggestion, which he attributes to Bohr and Heisenberg, that certain quantum mechanical sentences be treated as meaningless.[1] ([1944], p. 144.) He argues that the only justification of the Bohr–Heisenberg proposal is that it eliminates certain 'causal anomalies' from quantum theory (p. 41), but that it is an unacceptably cumbersome way of achieving this, since it makes contingent information about what measurements have been made relevant to whether or not an expression counts as well-formed. In view of this it is reasonable to suppose that Reichenbach sees the elimination of these 'causal anomalies' as the justification of his own proposal. This is confirmed by the trouble he takes to argue that, using his 3-valued logic, the anomalous sentences will never take the value 'true' (pp. 160–6).

So Reichenbach's argument has this general structure: if classical logic is used, quantum mechanics yields some unacceptable consequences, the 'causal anomalies'. But if 3-valued logic is used, these anomalies can be avoided, and this is, furthermore, the least cumbersome way of avoiding them.

By a 'causal anomaly' Reichenbach means a statement which 'contradicts the laws established for observables' (p. 26). The introduction of this idea is prefaced by a discussion of problems about unobserved objects in the microcosm (pp. 17–20); there is, Reichenbach argues, a class of *equivalent descriptions* of unobserved objects, from which one picks out as 'true' the one which is *normal*, i.e. which is such that both (1) the laws of nature are the same whether or not the objects are observed, and (2) the state of the objects is the same whether or not the objects are observed. The distinction between *phenomena* – occurrences 'easily inferable from macrocosmic data', e.g. coincidences between electrons, etc. – and *inter-phenomena* – occurrences 'introduced by inferential chains of a much more complicated sort', e.g. occurrences between coincidences, such as movements of electrons – is then introduced in analogy to the observable/unobservable distinction in the macrocosm. It is argued that the wave and particle interpretations provide equivalent descriptions of interphenomena, but neither constitutes a normal description; for in both certain sentences are derivable which state that events occur which are contrary to laws established for observables (i.e. (1) fails); these sentences are the *causal anomalies*.

---

[1] This suggestion bears an interesting analogy to the proposal that definite descriptions be treated as well-formed only if demonstrably denoting. Like that suggestion, it has unfortunate effects on the formation rules.

One such 'anomaly' is illustrated by a discussion of certain inter-ference experiments (pp. 24–32). Reichenbach considers first a set-up consisting of a diaphragm containing one slit *B* through which radia-tion of light passes towards a screen, giving an interference pattern which, in the case of very low intensities of radiation, will consist of individual flashes in a certain area, say *C*, of the screen. (See fig. 1.)

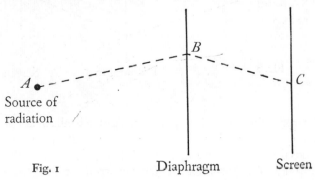

A •
Source of
radiation

Fig. 1   Diaphragm   Screen

In this experiment the phenomena are the flashes on the screen. If the interphenomena are introduced using a particle interpretation, a normal description is obtained; individual particles are emitted from the source of radiation, at *B* interact with the particles of which the diaphragm is composed, thus deviating from their paths in such a way as to hit the screen in the given pattern. Thus there is a certain probability $P(A, B)$ that a particle leaving *A* will arrive at *B*, and a certain probability $P(A, B, C)$ that a particle leaving *A* and passing through *B* will arrive at *C*. But now suppose the interphenomena are introduced using a wave interpretation: spherical waves leave *A*, a small part of these waves passes through *B*, and spreads towards the screen, this part of the waves consisting of different trains of waves, each with a centre lying on points within *B*. So long as the wave has not reached the screen, it covers an extended surface (a hemisphere with its centre in *B*); but when it reaches the screen it produces a flash at only one point, *C*. So one has to say that the wave disappears at all other points. But this constitutes a causal anomaly; the wave interpretation fails to give a normal description.

Then Reichenbach considers a set-up like the first except that the diaphragm has two slits.

In this experiment the phenomena are, again, flashes on the screen, though the pattern is different from that in the first experiment. A

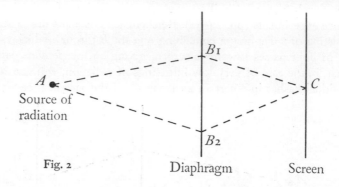

Fig. 2   Diaphragm   Screen

wave interpretation of the interphenomena, Reichenbach argues, provides a normal description (p. 30). But a particle interpretation gives
rise to causal anomalies. Some particles leaving A pass through B_1 and
some through B_2 (some also being absorbed or reflected by the
diaphragm), and the probability that a particle reaches C can be given
by

$$P(A, C) = P(A, B_1).\ P(A.\ B_1,\ C) + P(A, B_2).\ P(A.\ B_2,\ C)$$

However, if B_1 is closed and the process of radiation allowed to go on
for a certain time, and then B_2 is closed and the process allowed to go
on for the same time, the patterns being superimposed on the screen,
the resulting pattern is not the same as the pattern resulting when both
slits are opened together. Thus the probabilities $P(A.\ B_1,\ C)$ and
$P(A.\ B_2,\ C)$ must have changed; that is, the probability with which a
particle passing through B_1 reaches C depends upon whether B_2 is
open or not, a conclusion which violates the principle of action by
contact, and thus constitutes a causal anomaly.

So, for either interpretation, there is some experiment the description of which, on that interpretation, gives rise to causal anomalies.
Furthermore, Reichenbach argues, there is reason to think that there
is no interpretation which involves no causal anomalies (p. 44).

Reichenbach later discusses another causal anomaly, the 'barrier-
penetration paradox' (p. 165), which he thinks his proposal can avoid
as well.

In view of the considerations of ch. 2, this argument looks initially
promising – it is the *kind* of argument which, if I am right, could show
a need for a change of logic. Of course, it by no means follows that it

does establish such a need: there are a number of points at which it can be challenged.

3. Objections to Reichenbach's argument

Objection (i): it is methodologically improper to modify logic in response to physical difficulties

Popper claims that:

> we should (in the empirical sciences) use the full or classical or two-valued logic. If we do not use it but retreat into the use of some weaker logic – say, the intuitionist logic, or some three-valued logic (as Reichenbach suggested in connection with quantum theory) – then, I assert, we are not critical enough; it is a sign that something is rotten in the state of Denmark (which in this case is the quantum theory in its Copenhagen interpretation).
>
> ([1970], p. 18.)

Feyerabend feels equally strongly:

> this sly procedure is only one (the most 'modern' one) of the many devices which have been invented for the purpose of saving an incorrect theory in the face of refuting evidence and . . . consistently applied, it must lead to the arrest of scientific progress and to stagnation.
>
> ([1958], p. 50.)

This kind of objection is quite general: it would apply to *any* proposal to modify logic in the face of difficulties in science.

The claim is that change of logic would hold up the progress of science. Why is this so? One answer is suggested by the fact that Popper offers a criterion of demarcation of science which excludes logic. But this criterion excludes logic *on the grounds that it is not revisable.* If this is the basis of his argument, it is circular. It was discussed at some length in ch. 2, and need not be pursued further here.

The question arises, whether there might not be any other arguments why change of logic would impede the progress of science, which would conceivably be acceptable to Popper, and which might be more satisfactory than this. Perhaps one possible argument is this: certain *kinds* of change of theory are to be preferred, as more conducive to the progress of science, than others. In particular, the kind of change to be recommended replaces the theory in difficulty by a stronger theory, the kind of change to be deplored replaces it by a weaker one. And in view of the completeness of propositional calculus, it is to be expected that a change of logic would be of the second, undesirable kind. But this argument, though an improvement on the previous one, still fails. First, a change of logic need not be of the kind suggested. The 3-valued logic which Reichenbach proposes adds new connectives, and hence new theorems, as well as dropping some classical theorems. (cf. the definition of quasi-deviance in ch. 1.) Second, it is not obvious why a bolder should always be preferred to a more timid change. One example: Buridan entertained, but rejected, the hypothesis of the rotation of the earth, considering it falsified because a consequence to be expected if it were true, that if an arrow were shot in the air it would fall to the ground some distance to the west, is not confirmed by experience. (See Grant [1971], pp. 66–7.) This seems as clear an example as could be wished of a case of premature abandonment of a theory; 'timid' modification to avoid falsification would have been more conducive to scientific progress. One is reminded of Duhem's comment that it is sensible neither to hang on to a theory already overcomplicated in reaction to massive contrary evidence, *nor over-hastily to drop a theory, which could be saved* ([1904], p. 217).

Feyerabend supports *his* allegation of methodological viciousness against Reichenbach and Putnam, only by the claim that modification of logic would prevent the development of fruitful new theories ([1958], p. 50). I confess I cannot share his confidence. It is not true in general that an attempt to *save* a theory might not produce fruitful results. An example: Darwin retained the theory of evolution, in spite of the fact that it was very imperfectly corroborated by fossil findings, and argued that the failure of corroboration must be due to the inadequacy of the geological record. This resulted in an undeniably fruitful revision of geology. (See Darwin [1859], especially chs 6 and 9.) Feyerabend himself subsequently recognises ([1970], §9) that *ad hoc*ness is not undesirable in itself. And it could be argued that Reichenbach's proposal has given rise to fruitful research in logic: Reichenbach himself argues, interestingly enough, that a drawback of the Bohr–Heisenberg proposal is that it protects *logic* from a test it ought to face!

Any remaining unease about the methodological propriety of change of logic may be allayed somewhat by the following considerations. First, although one might agree that if one always reacted to recalcitrance by a change of logic the consequences would be most undesirable, it by no means follows that the consequence of *ever* reacting in this way would also be undesirable. It would be undesirable always to appeal to experimental error, but it is not undesirable *ever* to do so. Second, change of logic is, of course, no more irrevocable than any other theory change, so it need not be feared that it would prevent any subsequent change in physics.

So I think that the methodological objections to Reichenbach's procedure are not successful. His position is, thus far, defensible.

Objection (ii): modification of logic to avoid difficulties in quantum theory involves too great a sacrifice of simplicity

Quine's verdict on Reichenbach's proposal is that it is too costly. He writes:

> let us not underestimate the price of a deviant logic. There is a serious loss of simplicity . . . And there is a loss, still more serious, on the score of familiarity . . . The price is perhaps not quite prohibitive, but the returns had better be good . . .
> when one begins to consider complicating logic to cut fat from quantum physics, I can begin to believe that other things are far from equal.
>
> ([1970], p. 86.)

The cost, in terms of simplicity, is, certainly, relevant to the question, whether a change of logic should be contemplated. But it is necessary to see what Quine takes the costs and benefits of such a change to be, and to ask whether his assessment is reasonable.

Quine takes it that the main advantages of adopting a non-standard logic for quantum theory is that 'any exorbitant excess of admissible questions over possible answers' will be avoided. Thus, he takes the motivation to arise from Heisenberg's uncertainty principle: when the position of a particle is measured to a high degree of accuracy, the momentum cannot be measured accurately, and vice versa, this failure of measurability being a consequence of the theory. Since it is theoretically impossible to measure both the position and the momentum (of the one particle at the one time), classical logic 'accommodates . . . empty questions'.

The major disadvantages of adopting a non-standard logic, according to Quine, are losses of familiarity and simplicity.

Quine's estimate of the costs and benefits seems questionable.

Reichenbach, at least, claims for his proposal not only, or even mainly, that it provides a more economical framework for describing quantum mechanical reality (though he does mention this advantage on p. 43); but also, that it makes it possible to maintain quantum theory unmodified while eliminating causal anomalies, and so is a way of squaring theory with evidence. Indeed, this merit of his proposal could be admitted even by critics, like Feyerabend, who accuse Reichenbach of adopting a dishonest device for saving an incorrect theory from refuting evidence – if they admit that his proposal would save the theory, and that the theory would, otherwise, be refuted. Quine's estimate of the benefits is, arguably, too low.

Quine's estimate of the costs may also be questioned. The main reason Quine offers why adoption of a new logic for quantum mechanics will involve substantial loss of simplicity, is that the logic proposed by Birkhoff and von Neumann is not even truth-functional. In the absence of an adequate test of simplicity it is hard to say whether a truth-functional logic is or is not simpler than a non-truth-functional one; but, supposing for the moment that Quine were right, that a non-truth-functional logic is inevitably more complex, it must be pointed out that two of the proposed systems for quantum mechanics, Reichenbach's, and one of Destouches-Février's, *are* truth-functional, so that their adoption would involve a lesser sacrifice in simplicity.

There are other difficulties. One is that Quine places excessive weight on loss of familiarity, and even goes so far (in Quine and Ullian [1970]) as to identify simplicity and conservatism.[2] Another is that he considers only the loss of simplicity in logic, disregarding the possible gain in physics. (cf. my remarks on the 'Poincaré fallacy' in ch. 2.)

So I suggest that Quine's estimate of the possible benefits may be too low, and of the possible cost, too high. This by no means shows that Quine's verdict is wrong. But it does show that the question is much more complex than his brisk treatment suggests. I mention only some of the difficulties. Birkhoff and von Neumann, and also Putnam, claim for their system the advantage of its isomorphism to the mathematics of quantum mechanics. Lambert claims for the system (van Fraassen's) which he proposes the merit of conservatism, since it

[2] Duhem's comment that neither dogmatic conservatism nor dogmatic radicalism is consonant with 'good sense' seems relevant to Quine as well as to Popper and Feyerabend.

retains the classical set of logical truths. Quine associates simplicity both with familiarity and with truth-functionality; would he count Lambert's system, which is non-truth-functional, even if more conservative, as less simple than Reichenbach's? There are two kinds of difficulty: to find criteria by which to judge relative simplicity, conservatism, etc., and to find some means whereby to balance a loss in conservatism, say, against a gain in simplicity or generality, or vice versa. And a more elementary difficulty still: that the cost of a change of logic cannot possibly be estimated until it is certain *what* change of logic would avoid the anomalies. This, as will shortly become apparent, is still very far from clear.

Objection (iii): Reichenbach is wrong to think that causal anomalies are derivable in quantum mechanics

Feyerabend claims that the anomalous statements are not derivable from quantum mechanics *alone*:

> those difficulties arise only if we use the laws of quantum mechanics *together with* assumption *C* (which is not a law of quantum mechanics)
>
> ([1958], p. 53.)

Feyerabend aims to show that the derivation of causal anomalies from quantum theory requires a classical assumption, *C*, which he explains as follows:

> (a) Divide the class of all the properties which the entities in question may possess *at some time* into subclasses comprising only those properties which exclude each other. These subclasses will be called the *categories* belonging to the entities in question. Then each entity possesses *always* one property out of each category. (b) The categories to be used are the classical categories. Applied to the case of an electron *C* asserts that the electron possesses always a well-defined position and a well-defined momentum.
>
> ([1958], p. 51.)

Feyerabend suggests that *C* is smuggled into Reichenbach's argument under cover of an ambiguity in Reichenbach's definition of an *exhaustive interpretation*. According to Reichenbach's [1944], p. 33, an exhaustive interpretation is one which 'includes a complete description of the interphenomena'; according to [1948], p. 342, an exhaustive interpretation is one which 'attributes definite values to the unobservables'. Reichenbach intends to show that the use of an exhaustive interpretation in the first sense (an E_1) must lead to causal anomalies, but only succeeds in showing that the use of an exhaustive interpretation in the second sense (an E_2) does so. And, Feyerabend continues, to assume that all E_1 are E_2 is precisely to take C for granted.

But C, Feyerabend argues, can be shown to be false even for macroscopic objects. For example, water does not possess a well-defined surface tension unless it is in its liquid state. Thus, the derivation of the causal anomalies requires an assumption which there is independent reason for thinking false, and which, therefore, should be rejected rather than sacrificing quantum theory.

The question is, whether Reichenbach's argument does, as Feyerabend claims, require C. I shall try to show that it does not.

To show this, I must first get clear Reichenbach's distinction between *exhaustive* and *restrictive* interpretations. It seems clear that what Reichenbach regards as the crucial difference between them is that the former do, whereas the latter do not, provide a description of interphenomena. He writes:

> We shall call conceptions of this kind *restrictive interpretations* of quantum mechanics, since they restrict the assertions of quantum mechanics to statements about phenomena ... Interpretations which do not use restrictions, like the corpuscle and the wave interpretation, will be called *exhaustive interpretations*, since they include a complete description of interphenomena.
>
> ([1944], p. 33.)

Later (p. 43) he makes it clear that he counts his own proposal for the assignment of a third truth-value to statements about interphenomena as constituting, like the Bohr–Heisenberg proposal, a restrictive interpretation.

Distinguishing

(a) an I_1 – an interpretation which *gives one of the values 'true' or 'false'* to statements about interphenomena,

(b) an I_2 – an interpretation which *gives a third truth-value* to statements about interphenomena,

(c) an I_3 – an interpretation which *denies sense* to statements about interphenomena,

it is clear that the particle, wave and pilot-wave interpretations are I_1, Reichenbach's interpretation is an I_2, and the Bohr–Heisenberg interpretation an I_3. I_1 corresponds to what Reichenbach calls 'exhaustive', and I_2 plus I_3 to what he calls 'restrictive' interpretations.

Does Reichenbach's argument that any exhaustive interpretation must lead to the assertion of causal anomalies implicitly take assumption C for granted? It seems that it does not. For though, by definition, an exhaustive interpretation provides a description of, i.e., true-or-false statements about, the interphenomena, it is not assumed that for *any* classical property, the statement that the interphenomena have that property is either true or false. An I_1 involves the assumption:

C^1: each entity possesses properties out of *some* of the classical categories

but not the stronger assumption that each entity possesses properties out of *each* of the classical categories. For example, the particle interpretation assumes that the entities have determinate position and momentum, but not that they have (say) determinate frequency. An exhaustive interpretation characterises the interphenomena as entities of some particular kind, and ascribes to them properties out of the classical categories defined for entities of that kind, but not, of course, properties from classical categories, not defined for entities of that kind.

So I do not think that Feyerabend has shown that Reichenbach takes for granted an (illegitimate) classical assumption.

Objection (iv): Reichenbach's logic does not avoid the causal anomalies

The objections to Reichenbach's argument for *a* change of logic have been found wanting. But it by no means follows that *the* change of logic which Reichenbach proposes is acceptable. The system has come in for criticism (Hempel [1945], Levi [1959]) on the score of the obscurity of its third truth-value; and certainly Reichenbach's discussion of this ([1944], p. 42 and pp. 145–8) is very confusing. But there is a clearer, and more immediately damaging, criticism to be made.

A necessary condition of acceptability would be that the changed logic should avoid the causal anomalies, and that it should do this without sacrificing any laws of quantum mechanics; for the motivation for a change of logic was, precisely, to get rid of anomalies without tampering with physics. Reichenbach claims ([1944] pp. 166 and 159–60 respectively) that his system fulfils both these conditions.

However, it is not hard to show that the second condition is *not* met. What is required is that anomalous statements, which would come out true if classical logic were used, come out indeterminate with Reichenbach's logic, and that quantum mechanical laws should continue to take 'true'. But since Reichenbach proceeds on the assumption that a quantum mechanical statement containing non-commuting operators should have the value 'indeterminate', those laws of quantum mechanics which contain such operators must also take that value. Indeed, there is actually an argument used by Reichenbach himself which shows this to be so in the case of the principle of conservation of energy:

> The principle requiring that the sum of kinetic and potential energy be constant connects simultaneous values of momentum and position. If one of the two is measured, a statement about the other entity must be indeterminate, and therefore a statement about the sum of the two values will also be indeterminate. It follows that the principle of conservation of energy is eliminated, by the restrictive interpretation, from the domain of true statements, without being transformed into a false statement; it is an indeterminate statement.
>
> ([1944], p. 166.)

Reichenbach takes this argument to show that one of the causal anomalies (the anomaly arising in connection with potential barriers) is eliminated by the adoption of a 3-valued logic. And so, in a way, it is; but not in the way Reichenbach wishes. Reichenbach clearly intends that the causal anomalies be avoided by quantum-mechanical and classical *laws* taking classical truth-values, and statements about interphenomena, which if true would be inconsistent with these, taking the value 'indeterminate'. But in this example the anomaly is avoided by a *law's* taking the value 'indeterminate'.

So Feyerabend's criticism ([1958], p. 54), that Reichenbach's logic does not avoid, in the required way, the difficulties which it was designed to avoid, seems to be justified.

Gardner ([1972], §6), who argues that Reichenbach's proposal does not cope adequately with the paradoxes which motivated it, argues, further, that Reichenbach's modification of his theory to cope with another paradox, Schrödinger's cat paradox, also fails. And Hempel points out ([1945]) that Reichenbach's claim that his logic avoids the necessity, which Bohr's proposal entails, of expressing certain laws in the meta-language, is dubious; for Reichenbach's object language statement of these laws is inadequate.

So it is, I think, pretty certain that the change of logic Reichenbach suggests will not do what is required.

4. Will a different change of logic avoid the anomalies?

It remains to ask whether any of the other systems proposed for quantum mechanics is more acceptable. The available alternatives include: a 3-valued system, the 'logic of complementarity', and a non-truth-functional system, the 'logic of subjectivity' proposed by Destouches-Février; van Fraassen's interpretation of free logic, proposed by Lambert for the formalisation of quantum mechanics; and the non-truth-functional system of Birkhoff and von Neumann.

I begin by investigating the system proposed by Birkhoff and von Neumann (hereafter B v N).

These writers themselves claim for their 'quantum logic' only 'heuristic' and 'quasi-physical' advantages. Indeed, they take for granted at the outset that quantum theory requires novel logical notions, and apparently suppose that their immediately following observations, that quantum theory entails certain limits on predictability and measurability, support this view. (One might have been excused for thinking that complete predictability and measurability were typical theses of classical *physics* rather than of classical logic.)

The procedure adopted is, in effect, to read off their 'quantum logic' from the mathematics of quantum theory. The propositional operations – conjunction, disjunction, negation – are correlated with lattice-theoretical operations – intersection, span, ortho-complementation (respectively) – and the structure of the resulting propositional calculus derived from the mathematical structure. Given certain assumptions about this structure, and given the correlation of propositional operations and lattice-theoretical operations, the resulting logic is a weakened propositional calculus in which the distributive laws:

(1) $(A$ v $B)$ & $(A$ v $C) \vdash A$ v $(B$ & $C)$
(2) $(A$ v $B)$ & $C \vdash (A$ & $C)$ v $(B$ & $C)$

fail. LEM and double negation hold. It is claimed by Popper (in [1968]) that B v N collapses into classical logic, because Birkhoff and von Neumann refer to '*the* complement' of an element, and if a lattice is uniquely complemented, it must be distributive and so, Boolean, thus yielding a classical logic. This criticism fails, since Birkhoff and von Neumann correlate the negation of a proposition with the ortho-complement of the element associated with that proposition, and an element may have more than one orthocomplement. And since 'even in more general complemented lattices a definite complement can be singled out . . . provided an orthogonality condition is defined'. (Gericke [1966], p. 112) Birkhoff and von Neumann are not necessarily out of order in referring to '*the* complement' of an element.

Although its authors only claim the modest virtue of convenience for $B \vee N$, other writers claim that adoption of this system would be sufficient to avoid all the 'anomalies' of quantum theory. Thus, Finkelstein:

> All the anomalies of quantum mechanics, all the things that make it so hard to understand, complementarity, interference, etc., are instances of non-distributivity.
>
> ([1969], p. 208.)

And Putnam:

> The only laws of classical logic that are given up in quantum logic are distributive laws . . . and every single anomaly vanishes once we give these up.
>
> ([1969], p. 226.)

Neither Finkelstein nor Putnam offers any general proof of this claim. Putnam does, however, give arguments to show that the distributive laws are necessary to the derivation of

(1) the action-at-a-distance anomaly (which, he argues, involves the inference '$(A_1 \vee A_2) \& C \vdash (A_1 \& C) \vee (A_2 \& C)$' which is fallacious in $B \vee N$) (pp. 222–3.)

and

(2) the potential-energy-barrier anomaly (which, he argues, involves the inference '$(E = e) \& (S_1 \vee S_2 \vee \ldots) \vdash (E = e \& S_1) \vee (E = e \& S_2) \vee \ldots$', again fallacious in $B \vee N$.)

These arguments are unfortunately inconclusive, since though it is true that the distributive laws are used in Putnam's derivation of the paradoxes, it doesn't follow that the paradoxes cannot be derived without them.

Gardner claims ([1971], pp. 523–4) that Putnam can be shown to be mistaken in the claim that the causal anomalies are avoided; this, on the very curious grounds that distributivity does not fail in the two-slit case. This is an odd argument, for if one drops a principle of inference, one cannot subsequently use it in some cases but not others. Nor can the explanation be that Gardner has in mind Putnam's claim that classical logic holds at the macrocosmic though not at the micro-cosmic level, since his suggestion is that the classical distributive laws hold, at least in some instances, at the *micro* level.

So far then, it is unclear whether or not dropping the distributive law is sufficient to avoid the anomalies; Putnam hasn't shown that it is, but Gardner hasn't shown, *contra* Putnam, that it isn't. Perhaps some light might be shed on this problem by comparing *B* v *N* with Destouches-Février's proposed system.

Destouches-Février shares the assumption of Birkhoff and von Neumann that the logic for quantum mechanics is to be derived from its mathematics by associating logical with lattice-theoretical opera-tions, but differs from them both in challenging an assumption they make about the mathematical structure, and in proposing an alternative interpretation of the sentential connectives in terms of this structure.

In [1951] two non-standard logics for quantum mechanics are proposed. The first, called the 'logic of complementarity' is a 3-valued system whose third truth-value, 'absolute falsity' is to be taken by propositions which assert that simultaneous values have been dis-covered for position and momentum, which, according to the comple-mentarity principle, can never be true. (Some formal properties of this system are discussed in Törnebohm [1957].) The second, on which I shall concentrate, is called the 'logic of subjectivity', and is a non-truth-functional system said to differ from the Heyting and Johansson calculi, and also from *B* v *N*. This system is said to be needed if one rejects an 'objectivist' view of quantum mechanics, i.e. if one refuses to suppose that in a case where it is theoretically impossible to measure a certain value except within certain limits of precision, the entity in question really has some particular value within these limits, though one is forever unable to find out what that value *is*. A 'subjectivist' theory is thus one which claims that there is no more to be said than that the entity has a value within a certain set of values.

Now, Birkhoff and von Neumann, in describing the mathematical structure from which they derive their logic, assume that the 'modu-larity condition'

$L5$ If $a \subset c$, then $a \cup (b \cap c) = (a \cup b) \cap c$

is satisfied; but they concede that this assumption might be questioned, asking, in their concluding section, 'what simple and plausible motiva-tion is there for condition $L5$?' Adoption of the modularity condition gives *B* v *N* a weakened version of the distributive law. Subsequently, the modularity assumption seems to have come to be considered rather doubtful. (See Mackey [1963], p. 74, Birkhoff [1967], p. 285, Piron [1964].)

So it is interesting that just this assumption is denied by Destouches-Février in the construction of the 'Logic of Subjectivity'. (See Theorem 8, p. 205.) It is dropped, also, by Dishkant in his 'minimal logic' for quantum mechanics. Unfortunately no results are available on the relation of Dishkant's to Destouches-Février's logic. Destouches-Février argues (p. 203) that the acceptability of L_5 depends upon the assumption of 'a finite number of dimensions', for which there is no general justification. The assumption underlying L_5 is said by Birkhoff and von Neumann themselves to be 'an assumption limiting the length of chains of elements (assumption of finite dimensions)'. In consequence, DF is to differ from $B \vee N$ at least in that even the weak distributive law will fail.

In the absence of anything like a complete formulation of Destouches-Février's proposed system, it is very hard to adjudicate between this and $B \vee N$. (cf. McKinsey and Suppes [1954].) But one is, I think, entitled to feel less than convinced by Putnam and Finkelstein's claim, unsupported by any general argument, that $B \vee N$ can be counted on to avoid all the anomalies. The question arises, for instance, whether the weakened distributive law, which results from the acceptance of the modularity condition, may not be implicated in the derivation of the anomalies? (If it were, this might account for Gardner's claim that the distributive law doesn't fail in the two slit case.) And if it were, Destouches-Février's or Dishkant's proposal, in view of their rejection of the modularity condition, might seem more likely to avoid the anomalies.

5. Objection (v): quantum logics are not really 'logics'

An objection which has sometimes been raised, is that the non-standard structures proposed are not really *logics* at all. The very fact that the motivation for their adoption is empirical is sometimes thought to be sufficient to show this. Jauch, for instance, writes:

> The calculus introduced here has an entirely different meaning from the analogous calculus used in formal logic. Our calculus is the formulation of a set of *empirical* relations which are obtained by

making measurements . . . The calculus of formal logic, on the other
hand, is obtained by making an analysis of the meaning of propositions.

([1968], p. 77.)

I argued at length in ch. 2 that there can be reasons, reasons which I
might have called 'empirical' had I not also argued against the factual/
logical distinction, for a change of logic. So I do not accept the argument that a change made for empirical reasons cannot be a change of
logic. I confess, however, that the question, whether alternative logics
are really 'logics' seems to me to lose much of its interest once it is
admitted that logic, like other theories, is revisable.[3]

It seems sometimes to be thought that the manner in which such
systems as Birkhoff and von Neumann's and Destouches-Février's are
devised, by 'reading off' allegedly logical principles from the mathematics of quantum mechanics, prevents them from being properly
speaking 'logics'. I don't think that the manner of their construction,
of itself, at all shows them not to be logics. After all, classical logic,
which presumably is logic if anything is, could be 'read off' a Boolean
algebra. But it does raise a related question, viz, whether the interpretations given to the connectives, via their identification with certain
lattice-theoretical operations, is sufficiently like that of the connectives
of classical logic; and *this* question, of course, bears on the issue,
whether quantum logics are *rivals* of classical logic. This question is,
as usual, peculiarly hard to answer. Putnam claims that Birkhoff and
von Neumann's is the only possible interpretation of the connectives:

if we seek to preserve the 'approximate' operational meaning that
the logical connectives *always* had, then we have to change our logic;
if we insist on the old logic, then *no* operational meaning at all can be
found for the logical connectives, that will work in all cases . . .

([1969], p. 240.)

But this seems doubtful in view of the fact that Destouches-Février's
logic differs from Birkhoff and von Neumann's in containing not one,
but two, disjunctions: 'v', strong disjunction, and 'V', weak disjunction. The former is correlated with *union*, the latter with 'l'addition

[3] Interest in the question, whether set-theory is part of logic, is apt to wane
when the other difficulties in the logicist programme are recognised. The
demarcation question seemed vital only while there was still hope for the
justificationist programme.

des multiplicités associées', i.e, apparently, *span*. (The distributive laws hold for strong but not for weak disjunction.) Although Destouches-Février's discussion of the motivation for the two disjunctions is formidably obscure, the very possibility of the two interpretations to some extent threatens Putnam's claim.

I return to the question, whether quantum logics are really logics. Neither the reasons offered in favour of quantum 'logics', nor the manner of their derivation from quantum mathematics, seems to me to show that they cannot be, strictly, logical. But there is another consideration – which so far as I know is ignored in the literature – which bears on this issue. That is, that some proponents of quantum logic apparently favour *local* reform. They incline to think, that is, that a non-classical logic should be used for quantum mechanical reasoning, but that classical logic can be retained for arguments at the macro level. And in ch. 2 I argued, on quite general grounds, that if a proposed reform is local, that might be taken as evidence that the reform is not strictly one of logic, if logic is supposed to be indifferent to subject matter. However, the tendency to favour local reform should perhaps not be taken too seriously. Some writers, such as Birkhoff and von Neumann, simply confine their attention to quantum mechanical reasoning, and it is this which conveys the impression that they feel the need only for local reform. Putnam, by contrast, does consider the question, whether classical logic can be retained outside quantum mechanics; but he could be interpreted as saying that classical logic, though strictly incorrect, can be used for macro-level reasoning, since it won't lead to any non-eligible errors. And *this* view would be consistent with global reform. Destouches-Février, I think, is the only writer considered whose apparent *penchant* for local reform cannot be explained away; she draws from her investigations into quantum logic the conclusion that there *is* no logic which works for any subject matter whatever. This, however, hardly follows: since all the principles of the weakest logic would presumably hold in any area of discourse. Piron apparently takes this point, since he contrasts Birkhoff and von Neumann's object with his own, commenting:

notre but [est] de développer un formalisme général valable dans les deux cas [la théorie classique et la théorie quantique]

([1964], p. 439.)

Whether the proposed change is really one of logic depends (at least in part) on whether it is proposed as global or local; it does not depend in any straightforward way upon the formal characteristics of the system proposed. It would be possible, for instance, to accept Destouches-Février's proposal as a change of logic, provided it were accepted globally.

6. Conclusions

No simple answer to the question whether problems in quantum mechanics give, or gave, good reason for a change of logic is forthcoming. But at least the following conclusions may be drawn:

(1) It is not in principle impossible that developments in physics should give rise to a need for a change of logic,

(2) nor would such a change necessarily be methodologically vicious.

(3) However, it has not been conclusively established that quantum theory does, or, that when Reichenbach wrote, it did, give rise to such a need.

(4) To establish such a need it would be necessary (i) either to prove that one of the non-standard logics already proposed is adequate to avoid all the anomalies, without being so weak that it also disposes of quantum mechanical laws, or to devise some other system adequate in those respects. Reichenbach's 3-valued logic is definitely not adequate. It would also be necessary (ii) to provide some argument to show, given some reasonably precise account of the notions of simplicity, generality, etc. that the proposed change of logic was preferable, on these scores, to any change in physics which would also avoid the anomalies. Future research in this area might fruitfully address itself to these questions; for the present, this can be no more than a programme.

Appendix of formal systems

For convenience, many valued systems are characterised semantically. For further details consult Ackermann [1967], Rosser and Turquette [1952] or Hackstaff [1966].

[1] 2-valued ('classical') logic

Characterised by the matrices:

~	A
f	t*
t	f

A \ B	A & B	
	t	f
t	t	f
f	f	f

A \ B	A v B	
	t	f
t	t	t
f	t	f

A \ B	A ⊃ B	
	t	f
t	t	f
f	t	t

A \ B	A ≡ B	
	t	f
t	t	f
f	f	t

[2] Łukasiewicz's 3-valued logic

Characterised by the matrices:

~	A
f	t*
i	i
t	f

A \ B	A & B		
	t	i	f
t	t	i	f
i	i	i	f
f	f	f	f

A \ B	A v B		
	t	i	f
t	t	t	t
i	t	i	i
f	t	i	f

A \ B ($A \supset B$)	t	i	f
t	t	i	f
i	t	t	i
f	t	t	t

A \ B ($A \equiv B$)	t	i	f
t	t	i	f
i	i	t	i
f	f	i	t

'i' is to be read 'indeterminate' or 'possible' and is intended to be taken by future-contingent sentences.

Subsequently extended to 4, 5, . . . n-valued systems, and an infinitely many-valued system, on the following principle:

Let the truth-values be represented by real numbers in the interval from 0–1, and base the truth-tables on the rules:

$$\begin{aligned}
|\sim A| &= 1 - |A| \\
|A \lor B| &= \max [|A|, |B|] \\
|A \& B| &= \min [|A|, |B|] \\
|A \supset B| &= \begin{cases} 1 & \text{if } |A| \le |B| \\ 1 - |A| + |B| & \text{if } |A| > |B| \end{cases}
\end{aligned}$$

See Łukasiewicz [1930]

[3] *Bochvar's 3-valued logic*

Characterised by the matrices:

$\sim$	A
f	t*
i	i
t	f

A \ B ($A \& B$)	t	i	f
t	t	i	f
i	i	i	i
f	f	i	f

A \ B ($A \lor B$)	t	i	f
t	t	i	t
i	i	i	i
f	t	i	f

A \ B ($A \supset B$)	t	i	f
t	t	i	f
i	i	i	i
f	t	i	t

A \ B ($A \equiv B$)	t	i	f
t	t	i	f
i	i	i	i
f	f	i	t

for the *internal* connectives.

'*i*' is to be read 'paradoxical' or 'meaningless' and is intended to be taken by sentences such as 'This sentence is false'.

An 'assertion' operator, *a*, is characterised:

$$
\begin{array}{c|c}
a & A \\
\hline
t & t \\
f & i \\
f & f \\
\end{array}
$$

and *external* connectives are defined:

$$
\begin{array}{lll}
\neg A & \text{for} & \sim aA \\
A \,\&\, B & \text{for} & aA \,\&\, aB \\
A \vee B & \text{for} & aA \vee aB \\
A \supset B & \text{for} & aA \supset aB \\
A \equiv B & \text{for} & aA \equiv aB \\
\end{array}
$$

yielding the matrices:

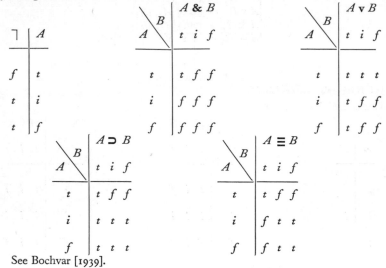

See Bochvar [1939].

[4] *Smiley's 3-valued logic*

The matrices for the *primary* connectives are as for Bochvar's *internal* connectives.

The matrix for the operator '*t*' ('it is true that') is as for Bochvar's 'assertion' operator, '*a*'.

The definitions of the *secondary* connectives are as Bochvar's for the external connectives.

'*i*' is to be read 'undefined' or 'truth-valueless' and is intended to be taken by certain sentences containing non-denoting singular terms, functions undefined for certain arguments, etc.

See Smiley [1960].

[5] *Kleene's 3-valued logic*

Characterised by the matrices:

$\sim$	A
f	t^*
u	u
t	f

A \ B — $A \mathbin{\&} B$	t	u	f
t	t	u	f
u	u	u	f
f	f	f	f

A \ B — $A \vee B$	t	u	f
t	t	t	t
u	t	u	u
f	t	u	f

A \ B — $A \supset B$	t	u	f
t	t	u	f
u	t	u	u
f	t	t	t

A \ B — $A \equiv B$	t	u	f
t	t	u	f
u	u	u	u
f	f	u	t

for the *strong* connectives.

Matrices for the *weak* connectives are as for Bochvar's *internal* (Smiley's *primary*) connectives.

'u' is to be read 'not known whether true or false' or 'indeterminable whether true or false' and is intended to be taken by undecidable sentences.

See Kleene [1952].

[6] *Woodruff's 3-valued logic*

Matrices for negation, conjunction, disjunction, implication, equivalence are as for Kleene's strong connectives. The table for '*T*' ('it is true that') is as for Smiley's '*t*'.

Plus the definitions:

FA for $T \sim A$
$*A$ for $\sim FA$
$+A$ for $(TA \vee FA)$
$(A \to B)$ for $(TA \supset TB)$ (cf. Bochvar's, Smiley's '$A \supset B$')
$(A \Rightarrow B)$ for $(+A \to B)$ ('presupposes')

'u' is to be read 'undefined' or 'lacks truth-value', and is intended to be taken by certain sentences containing denotationless singular terms.

See Woodruff [1970].

[7] *Reichenbach's 3-valued logic*

Matrices for diametrical negation ('$-$'), conjunction, disjunction, standard implication ('$\supset$'), standard equivalence ('$\equiv$'), as for Łukasiewicz's '$\sim$', '&', 'v', '$\supset$', and '$\equiv$'.

R_3 has in addition two new forms of negation:

cyclical negation	
$\sim$	A
i	t^*
f	i
t	f

complete negation	
$\bar{A}$	A
i	t
t	i
t	f

two new forms of implication:

alternative implication

$A \rightarrow B$			
$A \backslash\ ^B$	t	i	f
t	t	f	f
i	t	t	t
f	t	t	t

quasi implication

$A \ni B$			
$A \backslash\ ^B$	t	i	f
t	t	i	f
i	i	i	i
f	i	i	i

and a new form of equivalence:

alternative equivalence

$A \equiv B$			
$A \backslash\ ^B$	t	i	f
t	t	f	f
i	f	t	f
f	f	f	t

'i' is to be read 'indeterminate' and is intended to be taken by sentences about entities which, in certain conditions, it is impossible to measure.

See Reichenbach [1944].

[8] *Destouches-Février's 3-valued logic*

Characterised by the matrices:

negation 1			negation 2	
N	A		$\sim$	A
f	t^*		f	t
t	f		t	f
a	a		t	a

conjunction 1

$A \backslash^B$	t	f	a
t	t	f	a
f	f	f	a
a	a	a	a

conjunction 2

$A \backslash^B$	t	f	a
t	a	a	a
f	a	a	a
a	a	a	a

(Conjunction₂ is to apply to 'complementary' (*incomposables*) propositions.)

exclusive logical sum $A \vee B$

$A \backslash^B$	t	f	a
t	a	t	t
f	t	a	f
a	t	f	a

logical sum $A + B$

$A \backslash^B$	t	f	a
t	F	t	t
f	t	a	f
a	t	f	a

inclusive disjunction 1 $A \vee B$

$A \backslash^B$	t	f	a
t	t	t	t
f	t	f	f
a	t	f	a

inclusive disjunction 2 $A \vee B$

$A \backslash^B$	t	f	a
t	a	t	t
f	t	a	f
a	t	f	a

(Inclusive disjunction$_2$ is to apply to 'complementary' (*incomposables*) propositions.)

implication $A \to B$				logical identity $A \equiv B$				equivalence $A \simeq B$		
A \ B	t	f	a	A \ B	t	f	a	A \ B	t	f	a
t	t	f	f	t	t	f	f	t	t	f	f
f	t	t	f	f	f	t	f	f	f	t	t
a	t	t	t	a	f	f	t	a	f	t	t

'*a*' is to be read 'absolutely false' and is intended to be taken by complementary pairs of propositions, i.e. propositions asserting the value of a measurement of position or momentum such that, if one is true, it follows that it is theoretically impossible that the other should be verified or falsified. '*a*' is distinguished from 'identically false' or 'contradictory'.

'*F*' is to be read 'either false or absolutely false'.

See Destouches-Février [1951].

[9] *Post's many-valued system*

Characterised as follows:

$\sim$	A
2	1
3	2
4	3
.	.
.	.
.	.
$m-1$	$m-2$
m	$m-1$
1	m

A \ B	$A \vee B$					
	1	2	3 ...	$m-2$	$m-1$	m
1	1	1	1	1	1	1
2	1	2	2	2	2	2
3	1	2	3	3	3	3
.						
.						
.						
$m-2$	1	2	3	$m-2$	$m-2$	$m-2$
$m-1$	1	2	3	$m-2$	$m-1$	$m-1$
m	1	2	3	$m-2$	$m-1$	m

where $1, \ldots, m$ are the m 'truth-values'. P_m^μ designates the first μ of the m values of Pm.

We have the definitions:

$$A \,\&\, B \quad \text{for} \quad \sim (\sim A \text{ v} \sim B)$$
$$A \supset B \quad \text{for} \quad \sim A \text{ v } B$$
$$A \equiv B \quad \text{for} \quad (A \supset B) \,\&\, (B \supset A)$$

See Post [1921].

[10] *Łukasiewicz's 4-valued modal logic*

Characterised by the matrices:

$\sim$	A
0	1
3	2
2	3
1	0

$A \backslash B$	1	2	3	0
1	1	2	3	0
2	1	1	3	3
3	1	2	1	2
0	1	1	1	1

(table header: $A \supset B$)

possibly$_1$

M	A
1	1
1	2
3	3
3	0

possibly$_2$

W	A
1	1
2	2
1	3
2	0

The system is the product of L_C with itself; thus, the values of $Ł_4^m$ correspond to ordered pairs of values of L_C:

$$1 = \langle t, t \rangle$$
$$2 = \langle t, f \rangle$$
$$3 = \langle f, t \rangle$$
$$0 = \langle f, f \rangle$$

and the connectives are specified to be such that (ϕ an arbitrary connective, x, y arbitrary values):

$\sim\ <x, y> \ =\ <\sim x,\ \sim y>$ and

$<x_1, y_1>\ \phi\ <x_2, y_2>\ =\ <x_1\ \phi\ x_2, y_1\ \phi\ y_2>$

See Łukasiewicz [1957].

Systems without finite characteristic matrix:

[11] *Heyting's Intuitionist calculus*

Given by the following axiom set:

I $p \to (p \wedge p)$
II $(p \wedge q) \to (q \wedge p)$
III $(p \to q) \to ((p \wedge r) \to (q \wedge r))$
IV $((p \to q) \wedge (q \to r)) \to (p \to r)$
V $q \to (p \to q)$
VI $(p \wedge (p \to q)) \to q$
VII $p \to (p \vee q)$
VIII $(p \vee q) \to (q \vee p)$
IX $((p \to r) \wedge (q \to r)) \to ((p \vee q) \to r)$
X $\rceil p \to (p \to q)$
XI $((p \to q) \wedge (p \to \rceil q)) \to \rceil p$

Rules: substitution and detachment.

[12] *Johansson's Intuitionist calculus*

Results from [11] by dropping axiom X.
See Johansson [1936].

[13] *Birkhoff and von Neumann's calculus*

The system is not axiomatised by its authors, and the fact that it lacks any connective analogous to '⊃' makes it difficult to provide a conventional axiomatisation. It can be described in terms of the conditions (beyond the usual transivity reflexivity etc.) which its deducibility relation must satisfy:

1. $A \vdash A \vee B$
2. $B \vdash A \vee B$
3. If $A \vdash C$ and $B \vdash C$, then $A \vee B \vdash C$
4. $A \& B \vdash A$
5. $A \& B \vdash B$
6. $A, B \vdash A \& B$
7. $\vdash A \vee \sim A$
8. $A \vdash \sim \sim A$
9. $\sim \sim A \vdash A$
10. If $A \vdash B$ then $\sim B \vdash \sim A$
11. If $C \vdash A$ then $A \& (B \vee C) \vdash (A \& B) \vee C$

(11) corresponds to the modularity condition. Notice that (3) does not allow parametric premisses, the admission of which would make the undesired distributive laws provable.

See Birkhoff and von Neumann [1936].[1]

[14] *Destouches-Février's calculus*

The system is not axiomatised by its author, but it would evidently *not* include principle 11 of *B* v *N*, and differs from that system also in having two forms of disjunction.

See Destouches-Février [1951].

[1] I have benefited from a discussion of the axiomatisation of this system with Dr T. J. Smiley.

Bibliography

Ackermann, R. [1967] *Introduction to Many-Valued Logics*, Routledge & Kegan Paul, 1967

Alston, W. [1964] *Philosophy of Language*, Prentice-Hall, 1964

Aristotle [DI] *De Interpretatione*; page references to *Aristotle's Categories and de Interpretatione*, trans. Ackrill, J. L., O.U.P., 1963

Austin, J. L. [1950] 'Truth', *Proceedings of the Aristotelian Society*, Supplement (XXIV), 1950; and in *Philosophical Papers*, ed. Warnock, G. J. and Urmson, J. O., Clarendon, 1961, and *Truth*, ed. Pitcher, G., Prentice-Hall, 1964

Ayer, A. J. [1956] *The Problem of Knowledge*, Macmillan, 1956

Balmer, J. J. [1885] 'Notiz über die Spectrallinien des Wasserstoffs', *Annalen der Physik und Chemie* (25), 1885; and in *A Source Book in Physics*, ed. Magie, W. F., Harvard U.P., 1963; page references to *A Source Book in Physics*

Belnap, N. D. [1960] Review of Hintikka [1959], *Journal of Symbolic Logic* (25), 1960

  [1961] 'Tonk, plonk and plink', *Analysis* (22), 1961; and in *Philosophical Logic*, ed. Strawson, P. F., O.U.P., 1967

Benjamin, A. C. [1939] 'Science and vagueness', *Philosophy of Science* (VI), 1939

Bennett, J. [1959] 'Analytic/Synthetic', *Proceedings of the Aristotelian Society* (LIX), 1958–9

Birkhoff, G. and von Neumann, J. [1936] 'The logic of quantum mechanics', *Annals of Mathematics* (37), 1936

Birkhoff, G. [1967] *Lattice Theory*, American Mathematical Society, 3rd edition, 1967

Black, M. [1937] 'Vagueness', *Philosophy of Science* (IV), 1937; and in *Language and Philosophy*, Cornell U.P., 1949

  [1963] 'Reasoning with loose concepts', *Dialogue* (2), 1963; and in *Margins of Precision*, Cornell U.P., 1970

  [1965] 'The justification of rules of inference', in *The Foundations of Statements and Decisions*, ed. Ajdukiewicz, K., Polish Scientific Publishers, 1965; and in *Margins of Precision*, Cornell U.P., 1970

Bochvar, D. A. [1939] 'On a three-valued logical calculus and its application to the analysis of contradictories', *Matématičéskij sbornik* (4), 1939

Brouwer, L. E. J. [1952] 'Historical background, principles and methods of intuitionism', *South African Journal of Science* (49), 1952

Bunge, M. [1963] *The Myth of Simplicity*, Prentice-Hall, 1963

Burks, A. W. [1946] 'Empiricism and vagueness', *Journal of Philosophy* (XLIII), 1946

Cahn, S. [1967] *Fate, Logic and Time*, Yale U.P., 1967

Campbell, C. A. [1958] 'Contradiction: "Law" or "Convention"?', *Analysis* (18), 1957–8

Campbell, K. [1965] 'Family resemblance predicates', *American Philosophical Quarterly* (2), 1965

Cargile, J. [1969] 'The Sorites paradox', *British Journal for the Philosophy of Science* (20), 1969

Carnap, R. [1928] *Der logische Aufbau der Welt* (1928); trans. George, R. A., *The Logical Structure of the World*, Routledge & Kegan Paul, 1967
[1937] *The Logical Syntax of Language*, Harcourt, Brace, 1937; 2nd imp. Routledge & Kegan Paul, 1949
[1950] *Logical Foundations of Probability*, Chicago U.P., 1950

Cartwright, R. [1954] 'Ontology and the theory of meaning', *Philosophy of Science* (1), 1954

Chomsky, N. and Scheffler, I. [1959] See Scheffler, I. and Chomsky, N. [1959]

Cleave, J. P. [1970] 'The notion of validity in logical systems with inexact predicates', *British Journal for the Philosophy of Science* (21), 1970

Cohen, L. J. [1962] *The Diversity of Meaning*, Methuen, 1962

Cohen, M. and Nagell, E. [1934] *Introduction to Logic and Scientific Method*, Routledge & Kegan Paul, 1934; page references to Part One, *Introduction to Logic*, Routledge & Kegan Paul, 1963

Darwin, C. [1859] *The Origin of Species*, John Murray, 1859; and Penguin, 1968

Descartes, R. [1641] *Meditations on First Philosophy*, in *Philosophical Works of Descartes*, vol. 1, trans. Haldane, E. S. and Ross, G. R. T., C.U.P., 1911

Destouches-Février, P. [1937] 'Les relations d'incertitude de Heisenberg et la logique', *Comptes rendus de l'Académie des Sciences* (204), 1937
[1951] *La structure des théories physiques*, Presses Universitaires de France, 1951

Dishkant, H. [1972] 'Semantics of the minimal logic of quantum mechanics', *Studia Logica* (XXX), 1972

Duhem, P. [1904] *La théorie physique: son objet, sa structure* (1904); page references to *The Aim and Structure of Physical Theory*, translation of 2nd edition, 1914, by Weiner, P. P., Atheneum, 1962

Dummett, M. A. E. [1959] 'Truth', *Proceedings of the Aristotelian Society* (LIX), 1958–9; and in *Truth*, ed. Pitcher, G., Prentice-Hall, 1964; page references to *Truth*
[1959a] 'Wittgenstein's philosophy of mathematics', *Philosophical Review* (68), 1959
[1970] 'Wang's paradox', unpublished paper

Ewing, A. C. [1940] 'The linguistic theory of *a priori* propositions', *Proceedings of the Aristotelian Society* (XL), 1939–40

Farber, M. [1942] 'Logical systems and the principles of logic', *Philosophy of Science* (9), 1942

Février, P. Destouches- [1937], [1951] See Destouches-Février [1937], [1951]

Feyerabend, P. K. [1958] 'Reichenbach's interpretation of quantum mechanics', *Philosophical Studies* (XX), 1958
[1962] 'Explanation, deduction and empiricism', in *Minnesota Studies in the Philosophy of Science*, vol. III, ed. Frege, H. and Maxwell, G., Minnesota U.P., 1962
[1963] 'How to be a good Empiricist', in *The Delaware Seminar in the Philosophy of Science*, vol. II, Interscience, 1963, and in *Philosophy of Science*, ed. Nidditch, P. H., O.U.P., 1968

[1970] 'Against method', in *Minnesota Studies in the Philosophy of Science*, vol. IV, ed. Radner, M. and Winokur, S., Minnesota U.P., 1970

Findlay, J. N. [1933] *Meinong's Theory of Objects*, O.U.P., 1933

Finkelstein, D. [1969] 'Matter, space and logic', in *Boston Studies in the Philosophy of Science*, vol. V, ed. Cohen, R. S., and Wartofsky, M. W., Reidel, 1969

Fitting, M. C. [1969] *Intuitionistic Logic, Model Theory and Forcing*, North-Holland, 1969

van Fraassen, B. C. [1966] 'Singular terms, truth-value gaps, and free logic', *Journal of Philosophy* (LXIII), 1966

[1968] 'Presupposition, implication and self-reference', *Journal of Philosophy* (LXV), 1968

[1969] 'Presuppositions, supervaluations and free logic', in *The Logical Way of Doing Things*, ed. Lambert, K., Yale U.P., 1969

[1970] 'Rejoinder', in *The Paradox of the Liar*, ed. Martin, B. L., Yale U.P., 1970

Frege, G. [1884] *Die Grundlagen der Arithmetik*, Koebner, 1884; translated by Austin, J. L., *The Foundations of Arithmetic*, Blackwell, 1950

[1892] 'Sinn und Bedeutung', *Zeitschrift für Philosophie und philosophische Kritik* (100), 1892; 'On sense and reference', in *Philosophical Writings of Gottlob Frege*, ed. Geach, P. T. and Black, M., Blackwell, 1960; page references to *Philosophical Writings*

[1903] *Grundgesetze der Arithmetik*, Band II, Verlag Hermann Pole, 1903; page references to appendix in *Philosophical Writings of Gottlob Frege*, ed. Geach, P. T. and Black, M., Blackwell, 1960

Fremlin, C. [1938] 'Must we always think in propositions?', *Analysis* (V), 1937–8

Gardner, M. R. [1971] 'Is quantum logic really logic?', *Philosophy of Science* (38), 1971

[1972] 'Two deviant logics for quantum theory', *British Journal for the Philosophy of Science* (23), 1972

Gasking, D. [1960] 'Clusters', *Australasian Journal of Philosophy* (38), 1960

Gericke, H. [1966] *Lattice Theory*, Harrap, 1966

Gilmore, P. C. [1953] 'The effect of Griss' criticism of the intuitionistic logic on deductive theories formalised within the intuitionistic logic', *Koninklijke Nederlandsche Akademie van Wetenschappen*, proceedings of the section of sciences (56), 1953

Gochet, P. [1972] *Esquisse d'une théorie nominaliste de la proposition*, Librairie Armand Colin, 1972

Goddard, L. [1966] 'Predicates, relations and categories', *Australasian Journal of Philosophy* (44), 1966

Grant, E. [1971] *Physical Science in the Middle Ages*, Wiley, 1971

Grice, H. P. and Strawson, P. F. [1956] 'In defense of a dogma', *Philosophical Review* (LXV), 1956

Griss, G. F. C. [1944] 'Negationless intuitionistic mathematics', *Indagationes Mathematicae* (6), 1944

Haack, R. J. and S. [1970] 'Token sentences, translation and truth-value', *Mind* (79), 1970

Haack, S. [1972] 'The justification of deduction', unpublished paper
[1974] 'On a theological argument for fatalism', *Philosophical Quarterly*, 1974
Hacking, I. M. [1971] 'What is logic?', unpublished paper
Hackstaff, L. [1966] *Systems of Formal Logic*, Reidel, 1966
Hailperin, T. [1953] 'Quantification theory and empty individual domain', *Journal of Symbolic Logic* (18), 1953
Hailperin, T. and Leblanc, H. [1959] 'Nondesignating singular terms', *Philosophical Review* (68), 1959
Halldén, S. [1949] *The Logic of Nonsense*, Uppsala Universitets Årsskrift, 1949
Hempel, C. [1945] Review of Reichenbach [1944], *Journal of Symbolic Logic* (10), 1945
Heyting, A. [1959] 'Some remarks on Intuitionism', in *Constructivity in Mathematics*, ed. Heyting, A., North-Holland, 1959
[1961] 'Remarques sur le constructivisme', *Logique et analyse* (4), 1960–1
[1966] *Intuitionism*, North-Holland, 1966
Hintikka, K. J. J. [1959] 'Existential presuppositions and existential commitments', *Journal of Philosophy* (56), 1959
Jaskowśki, S. [1934] 'On the rules of supposition in formal logic', *Studia Logica* (1), 1934
Jauch, J. M. [1968] *Foundations of Quantum Mechanics*, Addison Wesley, 1968
Jeffrey, R. [1967] *Formal Logic, its Scope and Limits*, McGraw-Hill, 1967
Johansson, I. [1936] 'Der Minimalkalkül, ein reduzierter intuitionistische Formalismus', *Compositio Mathematica* (4), 1936
De Jongh, J. J. [1949] 'Restricted forms of intuitionistic mathematics', *Proceedings of the Xth International Congress of Philosophy*, Amsterdam, 1949
Kant, I. [1800] *Logik* (1800); page references to *Kant's Introduction to Logic*, trans. Abbott, T. K., Longmans, Green, 1885
Keenan, E. [1971] 'Two kinds of presupposition in natural languages', in *Studies in Linguistic Semantics*, ed. Fillmore and Langendoen, Holt, Rinehart & Winston, 1971
Kleene, S. C. [1945] 'On the interpretation of Intuitionistic number theory', *Journal of Symbolic Logic* (10), 1945
[1952] *Introduction to Metamathematics*, North-Holland, 1952
Kneale, W. and M. [1962] *The Development of Logic*, O.U.P., 1962
Kohl, M. [1969] 'Bertrand Russell on vagueness', *Australasian Journal of Philosophy* (47), 1969
Kolmogorov, A. N. [1925] 'On the principle of excluded middle', (1925), in *From Frege to Gödel*, ed. Heijenoort, J., Harvard U.P., 1967
Körner, S. [1960] *The Philosophy of Mathematics*, Hutchinson University Library, 1960
[1966] *Experience and Theory*, Routledge & Kegan Paul, 1966
Lambert, K. [1969] 'Logical truth and microphysics', in *The Logical Way of Doing Things*, ed. Lambert, K., Yale U.P., 1969
Land, J. P. N. [1876] 'Brentano's logical innovations', *Mind* (1), 1876
Leblanc, H. and Hailperin, T. [1959] See Hailperin, T. and Leblanc, H. [1959]
Lejewski, C. [1955] 'Logic and existence', *British Journal for the Philosophy of Science* (5), 1955; and in *Logic and Philosophy*, ed. Iseminger, G., Appleton-Century Crofts, 1968; page references to *Logic and Philosophy*

Lemmon, E. J. [1959] 'Is there only one correct system of modal logic?', *Proceedings of the Aristotelian Society*, Supplement (XXXIII), 1959
[1966] 'Sentences, statements and propositions', in *British Analytical Philosophy*, ed. Williams, B. A. O. and Montefiore, A., Routledge & Kegan Paul, 1966
Leonard, H. [1956] 'The logic of existence', *Philosophical Studies* (VII), 1956
Levi, I. [1959] 'Putnam's third truth-value', *Philosophical Studies* (6), 1959
Lewis, C. I. [1932] 'Alternative systems of logic', *Monist* (42), 1932
Lewy, C. [1946] 'How are the calculuses of logic and mathematics applicable to reality?', *Proceedings of the Aristotelian Society*, Supplement (XX), 1946
Linsky, L. [1967] *Referring*, Routledge & Kegan Paul, 1967
Łukasiewicz, J. [1920] 'On 3-valued logic' (1920) in McCall, S., *Polish Logic*, O.U.P., 1967
[1930] 'Many-valued systems of propositional logic' (1930) in McCall, S., *Polish Logic*, O.U.P., 1967
[1957] *Aristotle's Syllogistic*, O.U.P., 1957
MacColl, H. [1906] *Symbolic Logic and Its Applications*, Longmans, Green, 1906
Mackey, G. [1963] *Mathematical Foundations of Quantum Mechanics*, Benjamin, 1963
Marcus, R. Barcan [1962] 'Interpreting quantification', *Inquiry* (5), 1962
[1963] 'Modalities and intensional languages', in *Boston Studies in the Philosophy of Science*, ed. Wartofsky, M. R., Reidel, 1963
McCall, S. [1970] 'A non-classical theory of truth, with an application to Intuitionism', *American Philosophical Quarterly* (7), 1970
McKinsey, J. C. C. and Suppes, P. [1954] Review of Destouches-Février [1951] *Journal of Symbolic Logic* (19), 1954
Meinong, A. [1904] *Untersuchungen zur Gegenstandstheorie und Psychologie*, Leipzig, 1904; translated in *Realism and the Background of Phenomenology*, ed. Chisholm, R., Free Press, 1960; reprinted in *Logic and Philosophy*, ed. Iseminger, G., Appleton-Century Crofts, 1968; page references to *Logic and Philosophy*
[1915] *Über Möglichkeit und Wahrscheinlichkeit*, Barth, 1915
Mellor, D. H. [1965] 'Experimental error and deducibility', *Philosophy of Science* (32), 1965
Mostowski, A. [1951] 'On the rules of proof in the pure functional calculus of first order', *Journal of Symbolic Logic* (16), 1951
[1960] *Thirty Years of Foundational Studies*, Barnes and Nook, 1960; Blackwell 1966
Nagel, E. and Cohen, M. [1934] See Cohen, M. and Nagel, E. [1934]
Nelson, D. [1959] 'Negation and separation of concepts', in *Constructivity in Mathematics*, ed. Heyting, A., North-Holland, 1959
Nerlich, G. [1965] 'Presupposition and entailment', *American Philosophical Quarterly* (2), 1965
von Neumann, J. and Birkhoff, G. [1936] See Birkhoff, G. and von Neumann, J. [1936]
Odegard, D. [1965] 'Excluding the middle from loose concepts', *Theoria* (31), 1965
Pap, A. [1949] *Elements of Analytic Philosophy*, Macmillan, 1949

Parsons, C. [1971] 'Ontology and mathematics', *Philosophical Review* (80), 1971

Peirce, C. S. [1877] 'The fixation of belief', *Popular Science Monthly*, 1877; and in *Readings on Logic*, ed. Copi, I. M., and Gould, J. A., Macmillan, 1971; page references to *Readings on Logic*
[1902] 'Minute Logic' in Peirce, C. S. [CP]
[CP] *Collected Papers*, ed. Hartshorne, C. and Weiss, P., Harvard U.P., 1934

Pepper, S. [1961] *World Hypotheses*, California U.P., 1961

Péter, R. [1959] 'Rekursitivität und Konstructivität', in *Constructivity in Mathematics*, ed. Heyting, A., North-Holland, 1959

Pike, N. [1965] 'Divine omniscience and voluntary action', *Philosophical Review* (74), 1965

Piron, C. [1964] 'Axiomatique quantique', *Helvetica Physica Acta* (37), 1964

Poincaré, H. [1952] *Science and Hypothesis*, Dover, 1952

Popper, K. R. [1959] *The Logic of Scientific Discovery*, Hutchinson, 1959
[1968] 'Birkhoff and von Neumann's interpretation of quantum mechanics', *Nature* (219), 1968
[1970] 'A realist view of physics, logic and history', in *Physics, Logic and History*, ed. Yourgrau, W. and Breck, D. A., Plenum, 1970
[1972] 'Two faces of commonsense', in *Objective Knowledge*, O.U.P., 1972

Post, E. [1921] 'Introduction to the general theory of elementary propositions', *American Journal of Mathematics* (43), 1921; and in *From Frege to Gödel*, ed. Heijenoort, J., Harvard U.P., 1967

Prior, A. N. [1953] 'Three-valued logic and future contingents', *Philosophical Quarterly* (3), 1953
[1954] 'Many-valued and modal systems: an intuitive approach', *Philosophical Review* (64), 1955
[1957] *Time and Modality*, O.U.P., 1957
[1960] 'The runabout inference ticket', *Analysis* (21), 1960; and in *Philosophical Logic*, ed. Strawson, P. F., O.U.P., 1967
[1964] 'Conjunction and contonktion revisited', *Analysis* (24), 1963–4

Putnam, H. [1957] 'Three valued logic', *Philosophical Studies* (8), 1957
[1962] 'The analytic and the synthetic', in *Minnesota Studies in the Philosophy of Science*, vol. III, ed. Feigl, H. and Maxwell, G., Minnesota U.P., 1962
[1969] 'Is logic empirical?', in *Boston Studies in the Philosophy of Science*, vol. V., ed. Cohen, R. S. and Wartofsky, M. R., Reidel, 1969

Quine, W. V. O. [1936] 'Truth by convention', in *Philosophical Essays for A. N. Whitehead*, ed. Lee, O. H., Longmans, Green, 1936; and in *Readings in Philosophical Analysis*, ed. Feigl, H. and Sellars, W., Appleton-Century Crofts, 1949
[1947] 'The problem of interpreting modal logic', *Journal of Symbolic Logic* (12), 1947; and in *Contemporary Readings in Logical Theory*, ed. Copi, I. M. and Gould, J. A., Macmillan, 1967
[1950] *Methods of Logic*, Holt, 1950
[1951] 'Two dogmas of empiricism', *Philosophical Review* (LX), 1951; and in *From A Logical Point of View*, Harper Torchbooks, 1953; page references to *From A Logical Point of View*
[1953] 'The problem of meaning in linguistics', in *From A Logical Point of View*, Harper Torchbooks, 1953

[1953a] 'Three grades of modal involvement', *Proceedings of the XIth International Congress of Philosophy*, vol. 14, North-Holland, 1953; and in *The Ways of Paradox*, Random House, 1966

[1954] 'Quantification and the empty domain', *Journal of Symbolic Logic* (19), 1954

[1959] 'Meaning and translation', in *On Translation*, ed. Brower, R. A., Harvard U.P., 1959; and in *The Structure of Language*, ed. Fodor, J. A. and Katz, J. J., Prentice-Hall, 1964

[1960] *Word and Object*, Wiley, 1960

[1960a] 'Carnap and logical truth', *Synthèse* (18), 1960; and in *The Philosophy of Rudolf Carnap*, ed. Schilpp, P. A., Open Court, 1963; and in *The Ways of Paradox*, Random House, 1966; page references to *The Philosophy of Rudolf Carnap*

[1960b] 'Variables explained away', *Proceedings of the American Philosophical Society* (104), 1960; and in *Selected Logic Papers*, Random House, 1966

[1962] 'Reply to Professor Marcus', (1962), in *Boston Studies in the Philosophy of Science*, ed. Wartofsky, M. R., Reidel, 1963; and in *Ways of Paradox*, Random House, 1966; page references to *Ways of Paradox*

[1968] 'Ontological relativity', *Journal of Philosophy* (65), 1968; and in *Ontological Relativity*, Columbia U.P., 1969

[1969] 'Epistemology naturalised', in *Ontological Relativity*, Columbia U.P., 1969

[1970] *Philosophy of Logic*, Prentice-Hall, 1970

[1970a] 'On the reasons for the indeterminacy of translation', *Journal of Philosophy* (67), 1970

[1970b] 'Grades of theoreticity', in *Experience and Theory*, ed. Foster, L. and Swanson, J. W., Duckworth, 1970

Quine, W. V. O. and Ullian, J. S. [1970] *The Web of Belief*, Random House, 1970

Reichenbach, H. [1935] *Wahrscheinlichkeit*, Leiden, 1935; *The Theory of Probability*, California U.P., 1949

[1944] *Philosophic Foundations of Quantum Mechanics*, California U.P., 1944

[1948] 'The principle of anomaly', *Dialectica* (2), 1948

Rescher, N. [1969] *Many-valued Logic*, McGraw-Hill, 1969

Rose, G. F. [1953] 'Propositional calculus and realisability', *Transactions of the American Mathematical Society* (75), 1953

Rosser, J. B. and Turquette, A. R. [1952] *Many-valued Logics*, North-Holland, 1952

Routley, R. [1966] 'On a significance theory', *Australasian Journal of Philosophy* (44), 1966

[1969] 'The need for nonsense', *Australasian Journal of Philosophy* (47), 1969

Russell, B. [1905] 'On denoting', *Mind* (14), 1905

[1905a] Review of Meinong [1904], *Mind* (14), 1905

[1906] Review of MacColl [1906], *Mind* (15), 1906

[1910] 'Knowledge by acquaintance and knowledge by description' (1910), in *Mysticism and Logic*, Doubleday, 1957

[1923] 'Vagueness', *Australasian Journal of Philosophy and Psychology* (1), 1923

Ryle, G. [1954] 'Formal and informal logic', in *Dilemmas*, C.U.P., 1954
Scheffler, I. and Chomsky, N. [1959] 'What is said to be', *Proceedings of the Aristotelian Society* (LIX), 1958–9
Scheurer, P. B. [1972] 'Logique fermionique et logique bosonique', *Rassegna Internazionale di Logica* (III), 1972
Schneider, H. [1961] 'A syntactical characterisation of the predicate calculus with identity and validity in all individual domains', *Portugalia Mathematica* (20), 1961
Schock, R. [1968] *Logics without existence assumptions*, Almqvist & Wiksell, 1968
Scott, D. [1967] 'Existence and description in formal logic', in *Bertrand Russell, Philosopher of the Century*, ed. Schoenman, R., Allen & Unwin, 1967
[1973] 'Does many-valued logic make sense?', paper read to *British Society for the Philosophy of Science*, 1973
Shapere, D. [1966] 'Meaning and scientific change', in *Mind and Cosmos*, ed. Colodny, R., Pittsburgh, 1966
Smiley, T. J. [1959] 'Entailment and deducibility', *Proceedings of the Aristotelian Society* (LIX), 1959
[1960] 'Sense without denotation', *Analysis* (20), 1960
Stevenson, J. T. [1961] 'Roundabout the runabout inference ticket', *Analysis* (21), 1961
Strawson, P. F. [1950] 'On referring', *Mind* (59), 1950
[1952] *Introduction to Logical Theory*, Methuen, 1952
[1954] 'Reply to Mr. Sellars', *Philosophical Review* (63), 1954
Strawson, P. F. and Grice, H. P. [1956] See Grice, H. P. and Strawson, P. F. [1956]
Strawson, P. F. [1959] *Individuals*, Methuen, 1959
[1964] 'Identifying reference and truth-values', *Theoria* (30), 1964
Suppes, P. and McKinsey, J. C. C. [1954] See McKinsey, J. C. C. and Suppes, P., [1954]
Swinburne, R. G. [1969] 'Vagueness, inexactness and imprecision', *British Journal for the Philosophy of Science* (19), 1969
Tarski, A. [1931] 'The concept of truth in formalised languages' (1931) in *Logic, Semantics and Metamathematics*, trans. Woodger, J. H., O.U.P., 1956
Taylor, R. [1962] 'Fatalism', *Philosophical Review* (71), 1962
Törnebohm [1957] 'Two logics for quantum mechanics', *Theoria* (23), 1957
Turquette, A. R. and Rosser, J. B. [1952] See Rosser, J. B. and Turquette, A. R. [1952]
Ullian, J. S. and Quine, W. V. O. [1970] See Quine, W. V. O., and Ullian, J. S. [1970]
Vasiliev, N. A. [1910] 'On particular propositions, the triangle of opposition, and the law of excluded fourths', *Včěnié Zapiski Kazan' skogo Universteté* (47), 1910
[1911] *Imaginary Logic*, Kazan, 1911
Waismann, F. [1945] 'Verifiability', *Proceedings of the Aristotelian Society*, Supplement (XIX), 1945
[1946] 'Are there alternative logics?', *Proceedings of the Aristotelian Society* (XLVI), 1945–6

Wallace[1971] 'Convention *T* and substitutional quantification', *Noûs* (v), 1971
White, Morton G. [1956] *Towards Reunion in Philosophy*, Harvard U.P., 1956
Wittgenstein, L. [1953] *Philosophical Investigations*, Blackwell, 1953
Woodruff, P. [1970] 'Logic and truth-value gaps', in *Philosophical Problems in Logic*, ed. Lambert, K., Reidel, 1970
Zinoviev, A. A. [1963] *Philosophical Problems of Many-Valued Logic*, Reidel, 1963

Index

Ackerman R., 2
absolutist view of logic, see logic
Alston, W., 110–12 passim, 120
'alternative' logics, see logic
analysis, paradox of, 104
analytic/synthetic distinction, 32–5
Ångström, A. J., 123n
anomalies, causal, 150, 156–60,
  162–4
Anscombe, G. E. M., 66n
Aristotle, xi, 25, 27, 40, 48, 58–9,
  73 81, 82 90 passim, 115n
assertibility-condition theory of
  meaning, 103–8 passim
assertion, 129; see also statements
Austin, J. L., 56
Ayer, A. J., 79–81

Balmer, J. J., 122, 123n
Barcan Marcus, R., 143–4
Belnap, N. D., 13, 137
Benjamin, A. C., 121–2
Bennett, J., 36
Birkhoff, G. (and von Neumann, J.),
  2, 3, 13, 20, 22, 148, 149, 156,
  161–7 passim
Bivalence, principle of, 41, 65–70,
  74–5, 77–81, 83–7, 91, 109, 112,
  114, 137; see also Excluded Middle,
  law of
Black, M., 33, 109, 113, 120
Bocheński, I. M., 74
Bochvar, D. A., 2, 6, 22, 60, 61, 65
Boethius, 77
Bohr, N., 150, 154, 160
borderline cases, 109, 113, 116; see
  also vagueness
Borel, E., 93
Brouwer, L. E. J., 3, 41, 92–4 passim,
  100; see also Intuitionism
Bunge, M., 62

Buridan, J., 154
Burks, A., 121

Cahn, S., 74, 81n
Campbell, C. A., 11
Campbell, K., 111
Cargile, J., 113
Carnap, R., 11, 33, 120, 125
Cartwright, R., 146
Cat paradox, Schrödinger's, see
  Schrödinger's cat paradox
Chomoky, N. (and Scheffler, I.), 146
Church's thesis, 100
Cleave, J. P., 118
Cohen, J. L., 130–1
Cohen, M. (and Nagel, E.), 49
Connectives, meaning of, 8–26, 32,
  95–7, 103, 119, 161–2
constructivism, 91–3, 98–103
Contradiction, law of, 35–6, 109
contraries, 54, 75, 115; see also
  denial, negation
correspondence theory of truth, see
  truth

Darwin, C., 154
Davidson, D., 107
deducibility, 10. 86–7, 97, 115; see
  also validity
denial, 74–5; see also contraries,
  negation
deontic logic, 2, 51
Descartes, R., 154
Descriptions, theory of, 130–5
Destouches-Février, P., 2, 148–9,
  156, 161, 164–7 passim
Dewey, J., 26n
Dewey principle, 17
Diodorus Cronus, 73
Dishkant, H., 149, 164
Distributive laws, 161–4

domain: empty, 126, 129-31, 135-7, 142; indenumerable, 145-6
Dugundji, J., 88
Duhem, P., 31, 33-4, 123-4, 154
Duhem theses, 17
Dummett, M. A. E.: as global reformer, 3; on strict finitism, 99; on Intuitionist theory of meaning, 103-8; on vagueness 113-5

epistemic logics, 2
Evolution, theory of, 154
Ewing, A., 25
Excluded Middle, law of, 8, 25, 66-8, 81, 83-7, 91-2, 93-5, 101, 109, 114; see also Bivalence, principle of
existential assumptions, 126-47 passim; see also domain, empty, and singular terms, non-denoting
existential generalisation, rule of, 136-7
experimental error, 64, 122-4, 155, 166; see also Scott, D.
extended logics, see logic

falsification, 33, 37; see also Duhem, P., and Popper, K. R.
Farber, M., 3
fatalism, 40, 74-7, 79-81
Février, P. Destouches, see Destouches-Février, P.
Feyerabend, P. K.: on hypothetico-deductivism, 124; meaning-variance thesis, 11; methodological pluralism, 43; on quantum logics, 37, 153-5, 156, 157-9
Finkelstein, D., 148
form, logical, 45-6, 53, 55; see also misleading-form thesis, topic-neutrality
van Fraassen, B. C., 2, 6, 14, 43, 48, 58-9, 67, 85-7, 114, 115n, 141, 142, 156, 161
free logic, 135-7
Frege, G.: on formalisation, aim of, 119; on logical laws, self-evidence of, 29; on logicism, 33, 91; on

sense and reference, 60, 137-41; on singular terms, non-denoting, 48, 56, 127-9, 133
Fremlin, C., 11
Future contingents, 73-90

Gardner, M., 148, 160, 164
Gasking, D., 111
Gentzen, G., 10
geometry, 26-7, 39, 46
Gilmore, P. C., 100
global reform of logic, see logic
Gochet, P., 51, 83
Goddard, L., 55, 117
Gödel numbering, 100
Gödel's theorem, 93
Grant, E., 154
Grice, H. P. (and Strawson, P. F.), 15
Griss, G. F. C., 95n, 99

Haack, R. J. (and Haack, S.), 51
Haack, S., 33, 77; (and Haack, R. J.), 51
Hacking, I. M., 36
Hackstaff, L., 5
Hailperin, T., 136; (and Leblanc, H.), 137
Halldén, S., 55, 117
Heisenberg, W., 150, 154
Hempel, C., 159, 160
Heyting, A., 10, 41, 56, 94-103 passim; see also Intuitionism
Hintikka, K. J., 136-7

imperative logic, 51, 118
indeterminacy of translation, 14-21, 33
interference experiments, 150-3; see also anomalies, causal, and quantum mechanics
Intuitionism, 91-108; view of logic and mathematics, 29, 41, 56, 91-3; Intuitionist logic, 1-3 passim, 5, 8-10 passim, 14, 19, 21-2, 38, 57, 95-7, 101-2; see also Brouwer, L. E. J., Heyting, A., Johansson, I.

Jaśkowski, S., 136
Jauch, J. M., 164
Jeffrey, R., 49, 117
Johansson, I., 95 101–2; *see also*
 Intuitionism
de Jough, J. J., 100

Kant, I., 26–8
Keenan, E., 48
Kleene, S. C., 59–61, 67, 100–1
Kneale, W. and M., 48, 74, 82–3, 90
Kohl, M., 120
Kolmogorov, A. N., 102
Körner, S., 112, 114
Kronecker, L., 93

Lambert, K., 43, 58–9, 67, 131, 141,
 148–9, 156–7
Land, J. P. N., 137
Lebesgue, H. L., 93
Leblanc, H. (and Hailperin, T.), 137
Leibniz' Law, 138–9, 144
Lejewski, C., 143
Lemmon, E. J., 44, 83
Leonard, H., 136
Le Roy, E., 31
Leśniewski, S., 143
Levi, I., 159
Lewis, C. I., 13, 22–3
Lewy, C., 49, 52, 117
Linsky, L., 133
local reform of logic, *see* logic
logic: absolutist view of, 26–30;
 'alternative' logics, 1–24; Deviant
 logic, definitions, 4, 5 *passim*;
 extended logics, 4–5, 43–6, 95–7;
 local versus global reform of, 3,
 42–6, 166–7; pragmatist view of,
 15, 25–6, 30–40; psychologism in,
 29n, 91; realist view of, 3;
 revisability of, 15, 24–46; rival
 logics, 2, 5–6, 8–14, 25, 40, 43–6,
 95–7, 165; supplementary logics,
 4–5, 43–6, 95–7; deontic logic,
 free logic, imperative logic,
 Intuitionism, many-valued logic,
 minimal logic, modal logic
logically proper names, 132

logical subjects, 132
logicism, 29, 33, 91; *see also* Frege,
 G., Russell, B.
Löwenheim-Skolem theorem, *see*
 Skolem-Löwenheim theorem
Łukasiewicz, J., xi, 3–4, 7, 40, 43,
 73–4 ,84–90 *passim*; Ł₃, 61, 65–7,
 85; Łₘ₄, 87–90

McCall, S., 56, 67
MacColl, H., xi, 54–5, 109
Mackey, G., 164
McKinsey, J. C. C. (and Suppes, P.),
 164
Many-valued logic, 1–3, 8, 57, 64;
 see also truth-values, intermediate
Marcus, R. Barcan, 143–4
mathematics, 41, 91–3; *see also*
 logicism, set theory
maximising agreement, principle of,
 18–21
meaning: indeterminacy of, 14–21;
 Intuitionist view of, 103–8;
 sameness of, 32; of connectives,
 see connectives, meaning of
meaninglessness, 55, 117
Meinong, A., 133–5
Mellor, H., 111, 124
Menger, K., 94, 98
metalanguages, 70–1, 115
Miller, D., 64n
minimal logic: Johansson's, 2, 10,
 101–2; Dishkant's, 164
misleading form thesis, 47, 53–5,
 127, 131–5
modal logic, 1–2, 4, 38, 44, 143–4;
 modal fallacies, 78–80; modal
 interpretation of Ł₃, 87–8; modal
 interpretation of Łₘ₄, 88–90
Mostowski, A., 101, 136

Nagel, E. (and Cohen, M.), 49
negation, 75, 95–6, 135, 139–40; *see*
 also contraries, denial
Nerlich, G., 128n
von Neumann, J. (and Birkhoff, G.),
 2–3, 13, 20, 22, 148–9, 156, 161–7
 passim

Neurath, O., 37
no-item thesis, 47–53, 117–18,
  126–31; *see also* truth-bearers
notation, xiv
notational variance, 7, 21–2

objectual interpretation of the
  quantifiers, 143–4
Odegard, D., 115
Omniscience, God's, 77
ostensive definition, 121–2

Pap, A., 109
Paradoxes, *see* analysis, paradox of,
  Russell's paradox, Schrödinger's
  cat paradox, strict implication,
  paradoxes of, set theory
Parsons, C., 97
Peirce, C. S., xi, 27, 109–10, 119n
Pepper, S., 30
Péter, R., 101
physics, Einsteinian versus
  Newtonian, 25–7, 39
Pike, N., 77
Piron, C., 148
Poincaré, H., 39, 93, 156
Popper, K. R.: falsificationism, 33;
  methodological objections to
  change of logic, 37–8; on
  quantum mechanics, 153–5, 161;
  on verisimilitude, 63–4
Post, E., xi, 5, 61, 62–3
pragmatist view of logic, *see* logic
presupposition, 52, 137–41; *see also*
  Frege, G., van Fraassen, B. C.,
  Strawson, P. F.
Prior, A. N.: on future contingents,
  74; interpretation of 4-valued
  logic, 61; on Ł₃, 87–8; misleading-
  form thesis, 48–54; on 'statement',
  69; on 'tonk', 12–14
propositions, 48–9, 82–3, 117; *see
  also* statements, truth-bearers
Putnam, H.: on connectives,
  meanings of, 8, 11–13, 22–3;
  pragmatist view of logic, 3, 26;
  on quantum mechanics 40, 156;
  on truth in Deviant logics, 69–71

quantifiers, interpretation of, *see*
  objectual interpretation of the
  quantifiers, substitutional
  interpretation of the quantifiers,
  Intuitionism
quantum mechanics, 37–8, 40,
  148–67
Quine, W.V.O.: on analytic/syn-
  thetic distinction, 32–3; on
  connectives, meanings of, 8 11,
  14–26 *passim*, 64; on constructivism, 93; on disjunction, truth
  table for, 85; criterion of
  ontological commitment, 146; on
  domain, empty, 112; 129–31, 136,
  on existential quantifier, interpretation of, 143–7; on quantum
  mechanics, 155–7; on logic, scope
  of, 36, revisibility of, 25, 30–1; on
  set theory, relations to logic of,
  29; simplicity, definition of, 39;
  on singular terms, eliminability of,
  121; on truth in Deviant logics, 65

realisability, 100–1
realist view of logic, *see* logic
reductio ad absurdum, 100
redundancy theory of truth, *see*
  truth
reference failure, 128–9; *see also*
  singular terms, non-denoting
Reichenbach, H.: on quantum
  mechanics, 2, 5, 36, 40–3, 148–60;
  on truth and probability, 56
Rescher, N., xi, 3, 26, 66
rival logics, *see* logic
revisability of logic, *see* logic
Rose, G. F., 101
Ross, D., 74
Rosser, J. B., xii, 53
Routley, R., 67, 117
Russell, B.: Descriptions, theory of,
  131–5; on Frege on non-denoting
  terms, 128; on impredicative
  definitions, 93; logicism, 91;
  misleading form thesis, 48, 53–5;
  Russell's paradox, 29; on
  vagueness, 112–3, 116–17, 120–1

Ryle, G., 45

Scheffler, I. (and Chomsky, N.),
146
Schrödinger's cat paradox, 160
science, Popper's definition of, 38,
153
Scheurer, P. B., 148
Schock, R., 136–7, 142
Scott, D., 64, 124, 128
self-evidence, 29–30
sense and reference, theory of,
137–41
set theory, 29, 81, 92–3
Shapere, D., 11
simplicity, 26, 37, 39, 41, 130–1,
141–2, 147, 155–7
singular terms, elimination of,
120–1, 146; non-denoting, 40,
126–7
Skolem–Löwenheim theorem, 146
Słupecki, T., 4
Smiley, T. J., 10, 22, 60, 140–1
Sorites paradox, 113–14, 116
statements, 48–9, 51, 69, 117, 128;
see also propositions, truth-
bearers
Stevenson, J. T., 13
Strawson, P. F.: on analytic/
synthetic distinction, 15; on
connectives, meaning of, 14; on
Descriptions, theory of, 55; on
existential quantifier, reading of,
143; on formalisation, aim of, 119;
no-item thesis, 48–9; on
statements, logical relations
between, 51, as truth-bearers, 82;
on singular terms, non-denoting,
128–9, 133, 140; truth-value gap
thesis, 48, 52
strict finitism, 99, 108
strict implication, paradoxes of, 10
substitutional interpretation of
quantifiers, 143–7
supervaluations, 6, 58, 67
Suppes, P. (and McInsey, J. C. C.),
164

supplementary logics, *see* logic
Swinburne, R., 122–3

Tarski, A., 65, 68–71, 119, 121,
144–5; *see also* truth
Taylor, R., 66, 73
tense, 54–5, 69–70, 82–3, 143
'tonk', 12–13
topic-neutrality, 45; *see also* form,
logical
truth: correspondence theory of,
104–5; Deviance and theory of,
47–71; partial, 56, 62–4;
redundancy theory of, 104;
Tarski's material adequacy
condition for theories of, 65, 67;
see also Tarski, A., and
substitutional quantification,
144–5
truth-bearers, 51, 81–3; *see also*
no-item thesis, propositions,
statements
truth-condition theory of meaning,
104–8
truth-value gaps, 47–60 *passim*
truth-values, intermediate, 47–8,
55–64
Turquette, A. R., xii, 53
twin prime problem, 56, 93

Ullian, J. S. (and Quine, W. V. O.),
39, 156

vagueness, 109–25; *see also*
borderline cases
validity, 117–18; *see also* deducibility
values, designated, 66, 85
Vasiliev, N. A., xi

Waismann, F., 62, 112–14
Wallace, J., 145, 146n
Weyl, H., 93
White, Morton G., 26n, 32
Wittgenstein, L, 111
Woodruff, P. 140–1

Zinoviev, A. A., xi